ADVANCED

Paul Dummett

John Hughes

Helen Stephenson

Contents

Listening	Reading	Critical thinking	Speaking	Writing
a conversation about important lessons in life a talk by a sociologist about defining who you are	an article about the lessons we learn from the past an article about the language of Shakespeare	developing an argument	your favourite saying personality types call my bluff	a covering letter writing skill: fixed expressions
a speech about the livelihood of Kazakh nomads an interview with a woman firefighter	an article about the Moken people of Myanmar an article about rock climbing in Yosemite	using contrasts	work as a way of life health and safety measures your comfort zone	taking notes writing skill: abbreviations
a discussion about an unusual building in Utah an interview with an architect about small homes	an article about two model towns an article about the architect Zaha Hadid	fact or opinion	your ideal home town planning how spaces affect you	an opinion essay writing skill: linking devices
an extract from a radio programme about an innovative transport system an interview about the inspiration for inventions	an article about origami engineering an article about a social entrepreneur	finding counter arguments	what you can't live without origami ideas being on the spot	describing how things work writing skill: punctuation
an extract from a talk by a travel writer an extract from a radio programme about an extraordinary journey into the Himalayas	an article about the graphic novel an extract from *In Patagonia*	analysing descriptive language	a good read speech bubbles describing impressions	a book review writing skill: descriptive words
a conversation between two friends about health and exercise an interview with an ultrarunner about sports injuries	an article about different exercise regimes an article about beauty	identifying aims	exercise trends describing an injury does beauty sell?	a formal report writing skill: linking adverbs and adverbial phrases

Listening	Reading	Critical thinking	Speaking	Writing
an extract from a radio programme about how history views Genghis Khan a radio interview about an archaeological find	an article about Herodotus and the story of the Persian invasion of Greece a story about hidden treasure	fact or conjecture	stories from history social history historical irony	describing a past event writing skill: sequencing events
a talk by a journalist about digital technology an interview about social media marketing	a photographer's blog about sinkholes an article about a day at a hacker's conference	identifying personal opinions	blogging using social media IT security	an online news report writing skill: cautious language
an interview with a busker a talk by a neuroscientist about music therapy	an interview with a musician about music and culture a review of a documentary about Bob Marley	identifying text types	themes of songs mood music a charity concert	a description writing skill: parallel structures
an extract from a radio programme about ethnic communities an interview with a sociologist about citizenship education	an article about ant society an article about the Hadza of Tanzania	reading between the lines	civic duties social animals a conservation project	a discursive essay writing skill: critical thinking in writing
a short talk by a photographer about photographing people an interview with a psychologist about understanding emotions	an article about irrational thinking an article about the new generation of robots	understanding style	modern life mind games technology ethics	an email message writing skill: avoiding misunderstandings
three people describe landscapes they like an extract from a radio programme about the Japanese poet Basho	an article about William Allard's American West an article about a camera obscura	identifying aims	special places events in nature explaining a technique	a speculative letter writing skill: persuasive language

Life around the world

Unit 1 Arctic wisdom

Learn how generations pass on their accumulated wisdom in Iqaluit, Canada.

Unit 12 Canada oil sands

Find out about the impact of the excavation of the oil sands in Canada.

Canada

Unit 4 Ethical Ocean

Learn how David Damberger became a social entrepreneur and what his business does.

UK

USA

Spain

Unit 2 Climbing Yosemite

Find out how Jimmy Chin made a career out of mountaineer photography.

Jamaica

Unit 5 On the road: Andrew McCarthy

Learn how a travel experience changed the life of travel writer Andrew McCarthy.

Brazil

Unit 10 Initiation with ants

Find out about an unusual ceremony in the Amazonian jungle in Brazil.

Unit 9 A biopic

Learn about the inspiration behind the making of the biopic *Marley*.

Unit 3 Denmark bridge

Find out about the challenges behind the construction of the Oresund Bridge, which links Denmark and Sweden.

Unit 8 Talking dictionaries

Learn about a project which is helping to preserve dying languages.

mark

Russia

Japan

Palestine

China

Unit 11 Self-teaching robots

Discover how robots are helping themselves to progress.

Unit 6 Palestinian free running

Discover the liberating influence of free running on teenagers in Gaza.

Unit 7 Collecting the past

Find out how China's cultural heritage is being preserved by shopping.

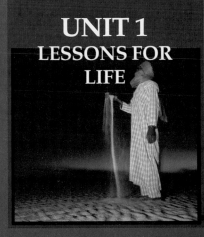

UNIT 1
LESSONS FOR LIFE

UNIT 2
MORE THAN A JOB

UNIT 3
FOUR WALLS

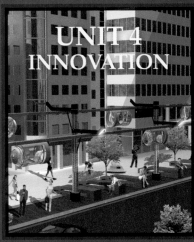

UNIT 4
INNOVATION

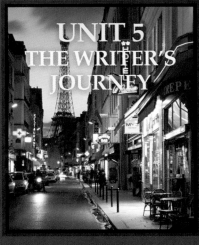

UNIT 5
THE WRITER'S JOURNEY

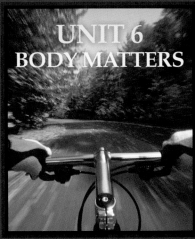

UNIT 6
BODY MATTERS

UNIT 7
STORIES FROM HISTORY

UNIT 8
DIGITAL MEDIA

UNIT 9
THE MUSIC IN US

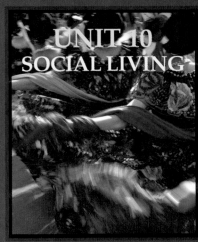

UNIT 10
SOCIAL LIVING

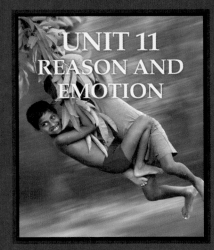

UNIT 11
REASON AND EMOTION

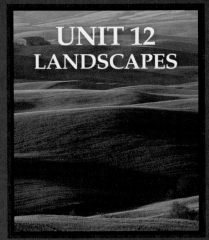

UNIT 12
LANDSCAPES

Unit 1 Lessons for life

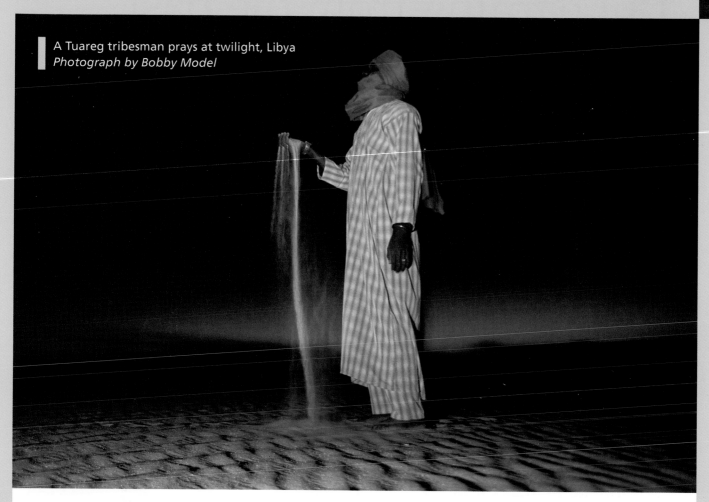

A Tuareg tribesman prays at twilight, Libya
Photograph by Bobby Model

FEATURES

1 Work in pairs. Look at the photo and the Tuareg proverbs. What do these tell you about the Tuareg outlook on life?

" Better to walk without knowing where than to sit doing nothing.

In life, it is always possible to reach agreement in the end. "

2 🎧 **1.1** Listen to two people talking about important lessons they have learned in life. Answer the questions.

1 What lesson have they tried to follow?
2 What experience illustrated the importance of the lesson?
3 Which lesson is similar to one of the Tuareg proverbs?

3 🎧 **1.1** Complete the phrases the speakers use to describe life lessons. Then listen and check.

1 The most _____ lesson anyone has ever taught me …
2 That's become a sort of _____ principle for me …
3 It's _____ me in very good _____ .
4 Here's a good rule of _____ .
5 But it's a lot easier _____ than _____ .
6 I always make a _____ of not reacting too quickly to things I disagree with.

4 Think of an occasion when you learned an important lesson. Describe what happened to your partner. What did you do about it? What principle do you now try to follow?

1a Learning from the past

Reading

1 Work in pairs. Read the quotation. Do you think this is good advice? Is it easy to act on? Discuss with your partner.

> "Learn from the mistakes of others. You can't live long enough to make them all yourself."
> *Eleanor Roosevelt, Diplomat*

2 Read the article. Match the people with the types of lesson they taught (a–c). There is one extra type of lesson.

1 Confucius
2 Nelson Mandela

a a lesson that is difficult to act on
b a lesson that has been misinterpreted
c a lesson that has been forgotten

3 Read the article again. According to the text, are the sentences true (T) or false (F)?

1 Sometimes people don't want to understand the lessons of the past.
2 A lot of Chinese people feel that their society has turned its back on the past.
3 China's rapid development has begun to slow down.
4 Nelson Mandela wanted the two sides in South Africa to stop fighting.
5 Mandela was not opposed to violence in principle.
6 The writer suggests that most people are too selfish.

4 Find expressions in the article for these definitions.

1 show the right direction (paragraph 1)
2 summarises an idea or approach (paragraph 3)
3 work hard towards a goal (paragraph 5)
4 copy someone's behaviour (paragraph 5)
5 paying attention to danger (paragraph 5)

> ► **WORDBUILDING suffix -ness**
>
> We can add *-ness* to the end of an adjective to make nouns describing human qualities.
> *kindness, thoughtfulness, unselfishness*
>
> For further information and practice, see Workbook page 11.

LEARNING FROM THE PAST

Why do we never seem to learn the lessons of the past? The actions of others could point the way for us in the future. But either we forget these lessons or we deliberately choose to misinterpret them, or knowing them, we simply fail to act on them.

Because of the economic boom in China, its government has become worried in recent years about selfish motives overtaking society. Many Chinese have been saying for some time that the traditional values of harmony, respect and hard work have been lost. So a few years ago the government focused attention again on the teachings of Confucius, the ancient philosopher.

> 'Consideration for others is the basis of a good life, a good society.'

Prior to the 1990s, Confucianism had not been fashionable, but now, in a country which is currently developing at a dizzying speed, it offers a sense of stability and order. The Confucian saying that nowadays sums up the government's philosophy is 'harmonious society'.

Sometimes it is difficult to learn from the past because the standards of the 'teacher' are so high. This is certainly the case with Nelson Mandela, who preached the message of reconciliation to two sides in South Africa who hated each other deeply. Mandela had always been ideologically committed to peace, and while he was living in prison, he became determined that reconciliation was the only way to unite his divided country:

> 'If you want to make peace with your enemy, you have to work with your enemy.'

All those who strive for peace know that in the long term they will have to begin this dialogue. Yet few are able to follow the example set by Mandela, because it requires such a high degree of unselfishness. It seems that heeding this warning – not to be selfish – is perhaps the hardest lesson of all for people to learn.

> **dizzying** (adj) /ˈdɪziɪŋ/ very fast and confusing
> **reconciliation** (n) /ˌrek(ə)nsɪlɪˈeɪʃ(ə)n/ making peace and re-establishing relations

Language focus time phrases

5 Look at the article. Identify the verb that accompanies these time phrases and name the tense used in each case.

1 in recent years	5 currently
2 for some time	6 nowadays
3 a few years ago	7 while
4 prior to the 1990s	8 in the long term

> **► TIME PHRASES**
>
> Certain time phrases are commonly (but not always) used with certain tenses.
>
> **Present simple**
> *often, never, every week, generally*
>
> **Present continuous**
> *now, at the moment, this week*
>
> **Past simple**
> *three days ago, last week, at the time*
>
> **Past continuous**
> *while, at the time*
>
> **Present perfect simple**
> *already, just, recently, so far, over the last two years, how long, for, since, ever, never*
>
> **Present perfect continuous**
> *how long, for, since*
>
> **Past perfect simple and continuous**
> *already, before that, up to then*
>
> ***will, going to* and present continuous for future**
> *next week, in three days' time, soon, on Friday*
>
> For further information and practice, see page 157.

6 Work in pairs. Look at the language focus box. Choose the correct time phrase to complete the sentences. Then compare answers with your partner. Sometimes there is more than one answer.

> | | | | |
> |---|---|---|---|
> | at the moment | at the time | before that | ever |
> | for some time | in the coming years | nowadays | often |
> | over the last 25 years | 50 years ago | | |

a Military service was compulsory in the UK
 ¹_____ . But ²_____ young people don't
 have to go to the army. I think this will change
 ³_____ because there is a feeling that young people
 need the discipline that military service gives you.
b ⁴_____ people have definitely become more greedy.
 I've been arguing ⁵_____ that it is not acceptable
 for the president of a bank to earn 150 times what a
 cashier earns.
c People ⁶_____ complain that young people don't
 show respect to their elders anymore. I'm having the same
 debate with my daughter ⁷_____ . She says you
 can't just demand someone's respect; you have to earn it.
d When I was 40 I decided to stop working so hard.
 ⁸_____ , I was working 60 hours a week and
 I was exhausted. It was the best decision that I have
 ⁹_____ made. ¹⁰_____ I had had no time
 to spend with my family or just to enjoy life.

7 Complete the sentences by writing facts about yourself. Then exchange this information with your partner.

1 Currently I …
2 A few years ago, I …
3 I … for several years.
4 Sooner or later I …
5 Generally I …

> *Currently I'm looking for a new job.*

8 Work with a new partner. Tell your new partner two interesting facts you learned about your first partner.

Speaking

9 Match the two parts of these English sayings. Use the time phrases to help you, where necessary.

1 The only easy day was …
2 You always …
3 It will all be OK …
4 No one has ever …
5 Don't sweat …

a … become poor by giving.
b … yesterday.
c … have a choice.
d … the small stuff.
e … in the end.

10 Work in groups. Discuss your favourite sayings. Follow these steps:

- Think of a saying from your country or from English that you like or has helped you in life.
- Write the saying on a piece of paper.
- Put all the sayings in a pile in the middle.
- Take turns to take a paper and read the saying.
- Together discuss the meaning and guess whose favourite saying it is. Ask the person why they chose it.

TALK ABOUT ► **YOUR FAVOURITE SAYING** ► PERSONALITY TYPES ► CALL MY BLUFF ► PRESENTING YOURSELF
WRITE ► **A COVERING LETTER**

11

1b Who do you think you are?

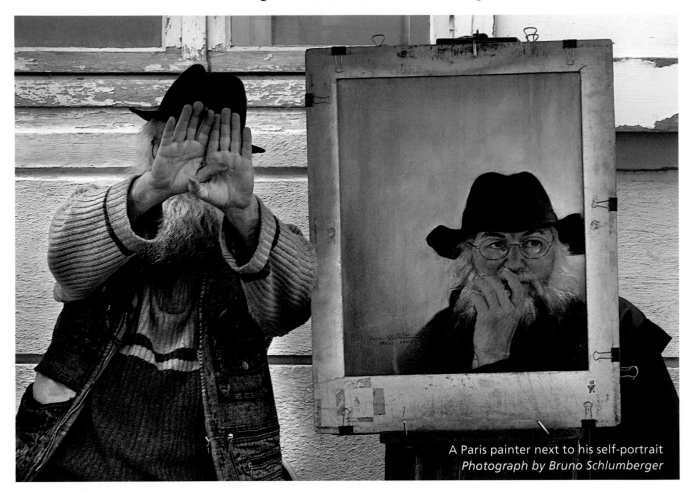

A Paris painter next to his self-portrait
Photograph by Bruno Schlumberger

Listening

1 Work in pairs. Look carefully at the photo and caption. Discuss the questions.

1 Did the painter want his photo taken? Explain why / why not.
2 What image of himself is the painter projecting through his self-portrait?

2 Which of the following factors are most important in defining who you are? Discuss with your partner.

a your friends
b your interests/hobbies
c your work
d your cultural background
e your outlook on life
f your beliefs and values
g your life experiences

3 🔊 **1.2** Listen to a talk by a sociologist describing how we define ourselves. Tick (✓) the factors in Exercise 2 the sociologist mentions. Which is the most important, according to her?

4 🔊 **1.2** Listen again and choose the correct option (a–c) to complete the sentences.

1 Anne's friends feel … about her commitment to animal rights.
   a surprised   b angry   c defensive
2 Children are defined by their … qualities.
   a individual   b adult   c shared
3 Teenagers like to define themselves by what … .
   a they like   b their friends like   c they don't like
4 For John, the important thing about his job is that it is … .
   a comfortable   b secure   c independent
5 Sarah studies Bonobo … .
   a eating habits   b society   c work tasks
6 Jack finds it difficult to commit to … .
   a relationships   b new environments   c his work

Idioms irreversible word pairs

5 Look at these three irreversible word pairs from the talk. Choose the correct option.

1 What defines them *foremost and first / first and foremost* is the fact that …
2 He picks up work *as and when / when and as* he can.
3 He has been doing *pieces and bits / bits and pieces* of carpentry and building work.

6 Work in pairs. Look at the irreversible word pairs in bold in the sentences (1–4) and match them one with these definitions.

| all one's efforts | basic | control of crime | in general |
| nowadays | objections | small things | a state of calm |

1 The builders still have a few **odds and ends** to finish off, but **by and large** they've done a great job.
2 After three days of unrest, **law and order** has been restored and there is **peace and quiet** on the streets again.
3 Sorry, no **ifs and buts**. We've decided to sell the company. You can't be sentimental **in this day and age**.
4 It's a **rough and ready** film, made on a small budget, but the actors put their **heart and soul** into their performances.

7 Pronunciation linking in idiomatic phrases

a 🔊 **1.3** Listen to the word pairs in Exercise 6. Note a) how the words are linked and b) the pronunciation of *and*.

1 odds_and_ends

b Work in pairs. Practise reading the sentences in Exercise 6.

Language focus the perfect aspect

8 Look at the sentences from the talk (1–4) and match them with the times they describe (a–d).

1 Sarah **has visited** Central Africa many times to study Bonobo apes.
2 Frank **has been collecting** coins since he was a boy.
3 Jack **will have been** just about everywhere by the time he's 60.
4 Anne **had never even owned** a pet before she joined the Animal Defence League.

a look back from now at something that started in the past and is still continuing
b look back from a point in the future to a completed action
c look back from a point in the past to an earlier event
d look back from now to a completed action at an indefinite time in the past

> ▶ THE PERFECT ASPECT
>
> 'Aspect' describes not the time of an event but the speaker's perspective. In the perfect aspect the important thing is the time the speaker is looking back from.
>
> **Present perfect simple**
> *He hasn't committed to another relationship since they split up.*
>
> **Present perfect continuous**
> *He has been moving from place to place, doing various jobs.*
>
> **Past perfect simple**
> *He had run his own business before he joined Microsoft.*
>
> **Past perfect continuous**
> *She had been waiting a long time for such an opportunity.*
>
> **Future perfect simple**
> *Three years from now, he will have left school.*
>
> For further information and practice, see page 157.

9 Work in pairs. Look at the language focus box. Then explain the difference in meaning between these pairs of sentences.

1 a I've travelled a lot in my time.
   b I travelled a lot in my 20s.
2 a I've been wondering whether to join the Red Cross.
   b I am wondering whether to join the Red Cross.
3 a By this time next year I will have retired from teaching.
   b This time next year I will retire from teaching.
4 a When I left school, I had decided to become an actor.
   b When I left school, I decided to become an actor.

10 🔊 **1.4** Choose the most appropriate option to complete these sentences. Then listen and check.

1 Oscar's a dreamer. Each evening he *has been spending / spends* hours reading astronomy magazines, hoping to become an astronaut one day.
2 Kate's a worrier. When I first met her, she *had just left / just left* her job and *has been wondering / was wondering* what to do with her life.
3 Ben's a free spirit. I imagine he *will have settled / will settle* down one day. But he *will have done / will do* a lot more than the rest of us by then.
4 I like to think of myself as a doer. I *have written / wrote* eight books so far and now I *have been working / am working* on my ninth.
5 Harry's a joker. For a long time *he'd been joking / he was joking* about joining the army, so his friends were shocked to hear he actually had.

Speaking

11 Work in groups. Look at the expressions to describe types of people. Discuss their meaning.

a chatterbox	a control freak	a doer
a dreamer	a drifter	a fighter
a free spirit	a go-getter	a joker
a planner	an outgoing type	a worrier

12 Choose expressions that describe you, a friend or a member of your family. Give examples of behaviour that support this.

> *People often describe me as a chatterbox because I can't stop talking!*

1c Immortal words

Reading

1 Work in pairs. Discuss the questions.

1 Who are the great writers in your country's history? Do you know any famous quotations from their work?
2 Is Shakespeare well known in your country?
3 What Shakespeare plays do you know the names of? What do you know about them?
4 Do you know any famous quotations from Shakespeare plays?

2 Read the article about the language of Shakespeare. According to the author, why are Shakespeare's plays still so popular today?

3 Read the article again and answer the questions.

1 What adjective describes what England was like in Shakespeare's time? (para 1)
2 What new element did Shakespeare bring to play writing, according to Bloom? (para 2)
3 What two words describe how Shakespeare conveyed his observations about life? (para 2)
4 What expression tells you that Shakespeare created new words and expressions? (para 3)
5 What has happened to the phrase 'the be all and end all' over time? (para 4)
6 What two qualities have helped Shakespeare's words to survive? (para 5)

4 Look at the phrases in the article taken from Michael Macrone's book (listed after paragraph 3). Match the phrases with the definitions (a–h).

a past its best
b show your feelings
c anything is possible
d unimportant
e the result is obvious
f something sad to see
g in one single action
h arriving back at the starting point

Critical thinking developing an argument

5 The writer uses the views of other commentators to develop his argument about Shakespeare's enduring popularity. What reasons, if any, do these commentators give for Shakespeare's popularity?

a scholars
b Harold Bloom
c Michael Macrone
d Ben Jonson

6 Work in pairs. Find evidence for what the author thinks about each of the commentators in Exercise 5.

7 What is the author's own conclusion and which commentator does he agree with most?

Word focus *life*

8 Look at the article again. Find two expressions with *life* that mean the following.

1 realistic
2 to animate or make alive

9 Work in pairs. Look at the expressions in bold with *life* and discuss what they mean.

1 I sold my old Citroen 2CV car last year for £300. Now I've just read that they have become really collectable. **Story of my life!**
2 He was **larger than life** and would always light up a room with his presence.
3 Work stress is just **a fact of life** these days – you have to learn to deal with it.
4 It was a very interesting conference. There were people there from **all walks of life** – writers, students, business people.
5 My daughter was worried about going to university, but actually she's **having the time of her life**.
6 Thanks for driving me to the station – it was a real **life-saver**. I'd have missed my train otherwise.

10 Work in groups. Think of a personal example for two of the phrases in Exercise 9.

> Not doing well in exams has been the story of my life!

Speaking

11 Work in two groups of three. You are going to play a game called *Call my bluff*. Each group looks at a set of words coined by Shakespeare and follows the steps below.

Group A: Turn to page 153. Look at the words and definitions.

Group B: Turn to page 154. Look at the words and definitions.

- For each word, rewrite the true definition in your own words, then write two more false definitions. For each definition, write an example sentence.
- Group A reads the three definitions and example sentences of the first word to Group B. Group B has to guess which is the true definition.
- Now it is Group B's turn to read the three definitions of their first word and for Group A to guess which is the true definition.
- Repeat until all the words have been read and guessed.

The 16th-century dramatist Ben Jonson generously called his rival Shakespeare a writer 'not of an age, but for all time'. And so it has proved to be, for Shakespeare's plays are still the most translated and most performed of any playwright's in the world. But if you ask people what accounts for Shakespeare's enduring popularity, you will get a number of different answers. Some will say that he was a great storyteller, others that the magic lies in the beauty of his poetry. Some scholars point out that he was born in a very vibrant period in England's history, a time both of great national confidence and of cultural activity, particularly in the theatre. As a consequence, they claim, he was able to produce an extraordinary volume of work.

This last explanation seems rather unsatisfactory. A more interesting answer is put forward, albeit a little over-enthusiastically, by Harold Bloom in his book *Shakespeare: The Invention of the Human*. Bloom argues that Shakespeare gave us something in his writing that the world had not seen in literature before – characters with a strong personality. These lifelike characters give us a real insight into the human condition: Iago, the trusted advisor of Othello, whose jealousy of others leads him to betray his honest master; Rosalind, the heroine in *As You Like It*, who remains true to her friends and family in spite of the danger to herself. Through the mouths of such characters, we learn truths about life that we can all identify with. These truths are made more moving and more memorable by the way in which they are phrased – both succinctly and poetically.

> 'But love is blind, and lovers cannot see.'
> **The Merchant of Venice**
>
> 'There is nothing either good or bad, but thinking makes it so.' **Hamlet**
>
> 'Talking isn't doing. It is a kind of good deed to say well; and yet words are not deeds.'
> **Henry VIII**

Shakespeare has been dead almost 400 years, but the words and sayings attributed to him still colour the English language today. His plays also expanded on the audience's vocabulary. So whether you are 'fashionable' or 'sanctimonious,' thank Shakespeare, who probably coined the terms. In fact, it is amazing just how great Shakespeare's influence on everyday language has been. Take, for example, these phrases from Michael Macrone's light-hearted book *Brush Up Your Shakespeare*:

foregone conclusion	seen better days
full circle	a sorry sight
at one fell swoop	neither here nor there
wear my heart upon my sleeve	the world is (my) oyster

Macrone is more interested in *what* Shakespearean language has survived than the reasons for its popularity. According to his research, some of these sayings have strayed slightly from their original meaning once taken out of the context of the plays in which they first appeared. For example, the phrase 'the be all and end all' is used today to mean 'the most important thing', but in Shakespeare's *Macbeth*, it means 'the end of the matter'.

Regardless of such technicalities, it is still remarkable that so many of Shakespeare's words have survived the large shifts in language between the time that they were written and the present day. The beauty of those words is certainly one reason for this, but as his fellow playwright Ben Jonson suggested, it is the humanity and enduring relevance of their message that brings them to life and keeps them current.

> **albeit** (conj) /ɔːlˈbiːɪt/ even if it is/was
> **insight** (n) /ˈɪnsaɪt/ new understanding
> **stray** (v) /streɪ/ wander

Immortal words

1d Tell me about yourself

Real life presenting yourself

1 Work in pairs. Read the definition of *brand* below and answer the questions.

1 What brands can you think of?
2 Which are your favourite brands and why?

> **brand** (n) /brænd/ *1* a particular name of a product or a manufacturer; *2* a particular set of characteristics to identify a product or manufacturer

2 What do you think a 'personal brand' is? Discuss with your partner. Then read the text below and compare your ideas.

> Just as a company promotes a consumer brand to customers through advertising, so an individual can promote themselves through their CV, their profile on a social networking site, their own website, and at interview. This is known as 'personal branding'. Successful personal branding involves recognising your particular characteristics and skills, and then shouting about these. Here are five tips for creating your personal brand:
>
> 1 Identify your most important qualities. They don't have to be spectacular (sociable, a good explainer, etc.).
> 2 Be yourself. Don't pretend to be something you are not.
> 3 Show passion. We are all passionate about something (computer games, knitting, etc.).
> 4 List your achievements. You may not be so interested in your past, but others are.
> 5 A brand is an image, so present yourself as you would like to see yourself.

3 🔊 **1.5** Listen to an extract from an interview for a job with a housing charity. The candidate, Katy, presents herself to the interviewer. How well does she follow the guidelines in Exercise 2?

4 Speaking skill keeping going

🔊 **1.5** Katy paused at one point to think about what she was going to say next. Listen again and say which phrases in the box she used to deal with this pause.

> ▶ **KEEPING GOING**
>
> Sorry, let me just look at my notes ... Ah, yes ...
> Excuse me, I'll just take a sip of water ...
>
> Sorry, I lost the thread ...
> Sorry, I'll begin that again ...
>
> Now, where was I? Ah, yes ...
> So, as I was saying ...

5 What other strategies do you use to keep talking when you feel nervous or under pressure? Discuss with your partner.

6 Pronunciation content words

a 🔊 **1.6** Look at the first three sentences of Katy's introduction. Think about what the content words are, i.e. the words that carry the meaning. Then listen and underline the content words she stresses and slows down for.

'OK, so I'm Katy. I'm 24 years old and I'm a very active person. I don't just mean that I play a lot of sports – although I do run and go to the gym several times a week. What I mean is that ... I'm a person who likes to get involved in things.'

b Work in pairs. Practise reading the sentences with the same stress and rhythm.

7 Work in pairs. Read the description of the charity and prepare to present yourself as a potential employee. Roleplay the interview. Use the notes in Exercise 2 and the phrases in the box to help you keep going.

> *Oxtail Housing*
>
> Passionate about communities | Diversity at work champion
>
> We own and manage over 12,000 properties, providing accommodation and care services to vulnerable people: the elderly, disabled and young.
>
> We have a wide range of career opportunities in all aspects of housing management and maintenance, marketing, business management and care services roles. Interested? Give us a call.

TALK ABOUT ▶ YOUR FAVOURITE SAYING ▶ PERSONALITY TYPES ▶ CALL MY BLUFF ▶ PRESENTING YOURSELF
WRITE ▶ A COVERING LETTER

1e A letter of application

Writing a covering letter

1 Work in pairs. Read the letter of application. Find and underline the following key elements of a covering letter. Compare your answers.

1 the job applied for
2 where and when it was advertised
3 the candidate's current situation
4 why the writer is a good candidate
5 where and when the candidate can be contacted
6 thanks for their time

2 Look at the statements about a covering letter. Using the letter as a model, are the statements true (T) or false (F)?

1 Keep it short. The letter should basically just refer the reader to your CV.
2 Show interest in the reader and knowledge of the organisation you are writing to.
3 Just mention your general suitability for the job. The letter should not respond to specific requirements the company has listed.
4 The letter should give a personal touch to your application.

3 **Writing skill fixed expressions**

The writer follows the conventions of letter writing by using certain fixed expressions. Find words and expressions in the letter with the following meanings.

a I am looking for
b I am sending
c a good person to consider for the job
d I am free to come
e the things you say you need
f I am writing to apply for the post advertised
g please feel free to
h I was interested in the job

4 Write a covering letter to Oxtail Housing, the company described on page 16.

Dear Mr Fairburn

In response to your advertisement in last Tuesday's *Guardian* newspaper for a Trainee accounts manager, please find enclosed my CV. The job attracted me because it emphasised that your company had great opportunities for people who were keen to learn. I also know that your company is a world leader in the creation of innovative products.

As a recent graduate from university, I am well aware that I still have much to learn and it is exactly this kind of challenging environment that I am seeking. You will also see from my CV that I am someone who believes in getting results. My two proudest achievements are raising over £15,000 for a local charity and finishing the London Marathon.

Regarding the other requirements you mention, I think I am a suitable candidate as:

• I have a degree in Economics
• I am flexible about where in the south-east I work
• I have good organisational skills, acquired when I was Treasurer of the Student Social Committee

I am available for interview at any time. Thank you for considering this application and please do not hesitate to contact me at any time by phone or in writing if you have questions about any of the above.

I look forward to hearing from you.

Yours sincerely

Philip Morrissey

Philip Morrissey

---

5 Exchange letters with your partner. Look at their letter as if you were the employer. Use these questions to check your letters.

• Is it well organised? Does it include all the key points?
• Is it grammatically correct and without spelling mistakes?
• Does it use appropriate fixed expressions?
• Do the skills offered match the needs of the organisation?
• Is it interesting and does it have a personal touch?
• Would you call this person for an interview?

1f Arctic wisdom

The phrase 'Respect your elders' is very alive and well in Iqaluit.

Map legend:
- Nunavut
- Kalaallit Nunaat (Greenland)
- Alaska (USA)
- Iqaluit
- Atlantic Ocean
- CANADA
- 0   1000 km   USA

Before you watch

1 Look at the photo and the map. Then choose the options (a or b) that you think best describe this environment as a place to live. Give your reasons.

1 a mild weather conditions
  b harsh weather conditions
2 a calm people
  b stressed people
3 a a traditional way of life
  b a modern way of life
4 a a population that's getting younger
  b an ageing population
5 a a cut-off area
  b an area with good communication links

2 Work in pairs. You are going to watch a film in which Inuit elders talk about their society and their relationship with the younger generation. Think of three things they might say about modern life and the younger generation.

While you watch

3 Watch the video and check your ideas from Exercise 2.

4 Watch the first part of the video (to 02.24) featuring an interview with the Mayor of Iqaluit. Answer the questions.

1 What has happened to the elders in a short time?

2 What is important about the elders?

3 What phrase is alive in Iqaluit?

4 How did the elders' parents live?

5 How were traditions passed down between generations?

5 Watch the second part of the video (02.25 to 03.39) and complete the summary.

In the past, elders were ¹ _____ for the others in the community. Each one was an ² _____ on a particular area, helping the community to ³ _____ : on the weather, on the environment, on different kinds of ⁴ _____ . Inuits were happy with the ⁵ _____ . The woman's mother told her daughter that she would see many ⁶ _____ , but she said, 'Never ⁷ _____ who you are.'

6 Watch the third part of the video (03.40 to end) and answer the questions.

1 What has happened to the Iqaluit population in recent times? Why?

2 Name two things the woman mentions when talking about the key to a happy life.

3 Why does she have a communication problem with the younger generation?

4 What is significant about the number 23?

5 What was the main characteristic of the culture of the Inuit in the past?

6 What does the narrator say is the key to these people's future?

After you watch

7 Roleplay a meeting of generations

Work in groups.

Imagine you come from a small fishing community in a remote area in northern Canada. An oil company wants to build a refinery near your town. It will employ some local people but also bring in a lot of workers from outside. You have a village meeting to decide if you should oppose this idea or not. Divide into two groups. Think about the effects the new oil refinery will have on your community.

Group A: Imagine you are the elders. Think about the following.

• preserving traditions
• the effect of newcomers on community life
• looking after the older generation
• the effect on the environment

Group B: Imagine you are the younger generation. Think about the following.

• preserving traditions
• job opportunities
• opportunities to meet other people
• the effect on the environment

Act out the meeting to discuss your feelings about this proposal.

8 Work in pairs. Are the advice and wisdom of elders highly respected in your society? Is this as it should be? Why ? / Why not?

---

disproportionate (adj) /ˌdɪsprə'pɔːʃ(ə)nət/ unexpected or out of proportion (of a number or amount)
elders (n) /'eldəz/ the elder or senior members of a community
infant mortality (n) /'ɪnf(ə)nt mɔː'tælɪti/ the rate of death among children aged 0–2 years

Iqaluit /ɪ'kæluːɪt/ the capital city of the Canadian territory of Nunavut
pass on (v) /'pɑːs ɒn/ transfer from one person to another
self-esteem (n) /self ɪ'stiːm/ the opinion you have of yourself

UNIT 1 REVIEW

Grammar

1 Read the article. What is a griot? What lesson did the writer take away from his visit to Timbuktu?

2 Work in pairs. Choose the correct tense to complete the article.

3 What stories did you read as a child that told you lessons about life? Describe one to your partner.

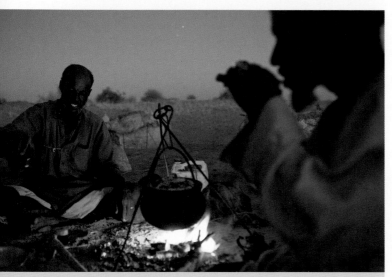

Some years ago I ¹ *visited / have visited* Timbuktu in Mali. Generally, people ² *are thinking / think* of Timbuktu as a desert town somewhere at the end of the world. But it ³ *hasn't always been / hadn't always been* this way. Once upon a time, Timbuktu ⁴ *was / has been* a thriving city and key trading post, a place in Africa with a long history, rich with tales.

In the marketplace you get a sense of this: women in brightly coloured clothes selling produce of all kinds: peanuts, shoes, rice, buckets. But my attention was drawn to a very old man who ⁵ *had sat / was sitting* in a corner. A few others ⁶ *have already gathered / had already gathered* around him, so I joined them. He was a griot, or traditional storyteller.

Griots ⁷ *sing / have sung* about kings and magicians, wars and journeys. This is how Malians ⁸ *learned / have learned* about their history for generations. He poured me a glass of tea and then I ⁹ *listened / have listened* to him tell the story of King Mansa and the golden age of Timbuktu, a story he¹⁰ *was telling / had told* countless times before.

At the end, the griot ¹¹ *quoted / has quoted* an old Mali saying: 'To succeed you need three things – a brazier, time, and friends.' The brazier is to heat water for tea. Time and friends are what you need to share stories. It's a lesson that ¹² *will stay / will have stayed* with me for a long time.

I CAN	
combine time phrases and tenses	☐
use the perfect aspect to look back at events and actions	☐

Vocabulary

4 Complete these idiomatic expressions.

1 Jack is a _____ than life character.
2 There was a great mix at the conference: people from all _____ of life.
3 I loved being at university. I had the _____ of my life there.
4 Learning lessons from the past is easier said than _____ .
5 If you are annoyed with someone, a good rule of _____ is to speak to them, not write.
6 I have one guiding principle in life: don't sweat the _____ stuff.

5 Work in pairs. Put the irreversible word pairs in the correct order.

1 soul / and / heart
2 large / and / by
3 first / and / foremost
4 quiet / and / peace
5 day / and / age

6 Choose two of the word pairs in Exercise 5 and make sentences about life.

I CAN	
describe lessons in life	☐
use irreversible word pairs	☐

Real life

7 Look at the phrases used for keeping going when talking. Complete phrases b–e.

a I'll begin that again.
b _____ I was saying, …
c I'll just take a _____ of water.
d I _____ the thread.
e _____ me just look at my notes.

8 Match the underlined phrases with a phrase from Exercise 7 (a–e) that has a similar meaning.

1 Now <u>where was I</u>? …
2 Sorry, <u>I just need to check my facts</u> …
3 Sorry, <u>I forgot what I was about to say</u> …
4 <u>I'd better rephrase that</u>.
5 Sorry, <u>I just need to have a drink</u>.

9 Work in pairs. Present yourself briefly to each other as if you were answering the question at an interview: 'So tell me a little about yourself.'

I CAN	
present myself as if at an interview	☐
keep going when I feel under pressure	☐

Speaking

10 Work in pairs. Talk about a successful or unsuccessful interview you've had. Why did it work out this way? What did you do right or wrong?

Unit 2 More than a job

A golden eagle flies to the call of a Kazakh hunter, Mongolia.
Photograph by Viacheslav Smilyk

FEATURES

1 🔊 **1.7** Work in pairs. Look at the photo and caption. What do you think this man is doing? Discuss with your partner. Then listen and check your ideas.

2 🔊 **1.7** Listen again and answer the questions.

1 What is the livelihood of the nomads in western Mongolia?
2 How do many former Kazakh nomads make a living now?
3 What is their more traditional way of life?
4 What sort of activity is eagle hunting classed as these days?
5 What task requires great patience?
6 What aspect of eagle hunting is still commercial?

3 Look at the phrases in bold. Discuss the difference between the phrases in each pair.

1 **a way of life** and **a livelihood**
2 **a career** and **a vocation**
3 **a profession** and **a trade**
4 **an occupation** and **a living**
5 **a job** and **a task**

4 Work in groups. Think of examples of each of the following.

a people who depend on animals for their livelihood
b a traditional occupation which is now dying out
c a task that requires great patience

TALK ABOUT ▶ WORK AS A WAY OF LIFE ▶ HEALTH AND SAFETY MEASURES ▶ YOUR COMFORT ZONE ▶ GIVING A TALK
WRITE ▶ NOTES

2a Sea gypsies of Myanmar

Reading

1 Work in pairs. Look at the photo and the title of the article and answer the questions. Then read the article and check your answers.

1 What is meant by 'sea gypsies'?
2 What is these people's livelihood?
3 What particular skills or talents do they possess?

2 Read the article again and answer the questions.

1 Why did the Moken boats not want to stop when they saw the author approaching?
2 What kind of boats are the *kabang*?
3 In what way does the Moken way of life have a low impact on the environment?
4 Why do the Moken move to the land for four months of the year?
5 What is happening to the Moken population?
6 What will be the consequence if they move permanently to the land?

3 Work in groups. Discuss what the advantages and disadvantages of the Moken way of life are.

Sea gypsies of Myanmar

We had been travelling for a few hours when on the horizon we spotted the group of small hand-built boats, called *kabang*. The Moken are wary of strangers, so as we approached, I called out some reassuring words in their language. The family elder, Gatcha, was at first reluctant to stop. Outsiders have been harassing the Moken throughout their history and his instinct told him to keep his distance. But after hearing that I had been researching the Moken way of life since 1982, in the end he accepted us into his 'home'.

Home for this nomadic sea people are the *kabang*, on which they live, eat and sleep for eight months of the year. In these light craft, they traverse the Mergui Archipelago, 800 islands dotted across the Andaman Sea, off Myanmar, collecting what they need to survive and moving on. They get by only on what they take from the sea and beaches each day – fish, molluscs and sandworms to eat; shells and oysters to trade with Malay and Chinese merchants. They accumulate little and live on land only during the monsoons. But the world is closing in on the Moken way of life.

As divers and beachcombers, they pose no threat to others who share these waters. In spite of this, the authorities are always pressuring them to settle in one place. Ten years ago, 2,500 Moken were still leading a traditional seafaring life, but that population is slowly declining and now stands at around 1,000. If they cease to be sea gypsies, it is feared that their unique understanding of the sea will disappear also. Moken people can dive down 20 metres without breathing equipment and have developed extraordinary underwater vision. They are experts at reading changes in the sea and it is even said they can anticipate a tsunami.

A day spent fishing and gathering was followed by a night of eating and ritual. The following morning Gatcha and his family pushed out to sea to continue their journey. The dry season was nearing its end and soon they would be setting up a temporary camp on land. But just as the rains come and go, I wonder if the Moken will still be living here when I next return.

Vocabulary phrasal verb *get*

4 Look at the phrasal verbs with *get*. Match the phrasal verbs (1–6) with the correct meanings (a–f).

1 The Moken **get by** on what they take from the sea each day.
2 They are very content with their simple way of life; **getting ahead** in life is a western concept.
3 There is often work to **get through** in the day, but it doesn't seem like work to them.
4 While other divers prepare their equipment carefully, the Moken just seem to **get on with** it.
5 It seems some people would like the Moken to **get down to** leading a more conventional life.
6 What the author seems to be **getting at** is that it is important that the Moken way of life survives.

a complete
b imply
c survive
d continue with the job
e apply oneself to
f become more prosperous

5 Work in pairs. Make three sentences about your own experiences using phrasal verbs with *get*.

Language focus the continuous aspect

6 Work in pairs. Match the extracts (1–6) from the article with the descriptions of the continuous form (a–f).

1 We had been travelling for a few hours …
2 Outsiders have been harassing the Moken …
3 … the world is closing in on the Moken way of life.
4 … the authorities are always pressuring them …
5 Ten years ago, 2,500 Moken were still leading a traditional seafaring life.
6 I wonder if the Moken will still be living here …

a a present trend
b a continuous action in the past that was interrupted
c an action continuing from a point in the past to now
d an action in progress at a specific point in the past
e (+ *always*) a repetitive action to express annoyance
f an action in progress at a point in the future

7 Look at these pairs of sentences using the continuous and simple aspects. With your partner, explain the difference in meaning in each case.

1 a I'm living on a houseboat.
  b I live on a houseboat.
2 a We were eating when they arrived.
  b We ate when they arrived.
3 a She's been writing a travel book.
  b She's written a travel book.
4 a They had been travelling for days.
  b They had travelled 300 kilometres.
5 a I will be making my supper at eight o'clock.
  b I will make my supper at eight o'clock.

▶ **THE CONTINUOUS ASPECT**

Verbs in the continuous aspect describe incomplete actions that are in progress at a specific time.

Present continuous
The number of sea gypsies is declining.

Past continuous
Ten years ago, 2,500 Moken were leading this way of life.

Present perfect continuous
Outsiders have been exploiting the Moken for years.

Past perfect continuous
I had been researching their way of life for many years before this.

Future continuous
I hope they will still be living here in ten years' time.

For further information and practice, see page 158.

8 Look at the language focus box. Choose the correct form (simple or continuous) to complete the text.

Moken children [1] *are learning / learn* to swim before they can walk. Because of this, the Moken [2] *have been developing / have developed* extraordinary swimming skills. They can hold their breath for twice as long as you or me. Moreover, as one Swedish researcher [3] *was discovering / discovered*, they can shrink their pupils to see more clearly underwater. Sadly, these skills [4] *are being lost / are lost* as more and more Moken settle on the land.

The Moken are experts at reading the ways of the sea. When a tsunami hit the region, some Moken [5] *had already been moving / had already moved* to higher ground. Several minutes before the wave [6] *was arriving / arrived*, they saw that the sea [7] *was receding / receded* and recognised this as a sign of an imminent wave.

Why don't the Moken exploit their skills and knowledge to make more money? What [8] *have they been waiting / have they waited* for? The fact is, they [9] *are not wishing / do not wish* to live complicated lives or accumulate possessions. Left in peace, in 100 years' time, they [10] *will still be leading / will still lead* their simple life.

Speaking

9 Work in groups. Look at these jobs and decide which are a way of life (i.e. more than a job) for the people who do them. What factors make the jobs a way of life?

banker   coal miner   farmer   firefighter
fisherman/woman   lorry driver
physiotherapist   teacher

10 Think of another job that is a way of life. Describe the job and your reasons for adding this to the list.

Smokejumpers

Listening

1 Work in pairs. Look at the photo and answer the questions about fire.

1 What kind of fire is shown in the photo? How do these fires start? How can they be stopped?
2 What is the difference between a *fireman* and a *firefighter*?
3 What qualities are needed to be a firefighter? Make a list.

2 💿 **1.8** Read the sentences. Then listen to an interview with smokejumper Kerry Franklin. Are the sentences true (T) or false (F)?

1 Smokejumpers are used in places that are difficult to reach.
2 Smokejumpers get their name from their ability to run through forest fires.
3 Their job is to evaluate a fire, but not to combat it.
4 It's difficult for most male smokejumpers to accept women doing this job.

3 💿 **1.8** Listen again and choose the correct option (a–c).

1 It's important for a smokejumper to be the right weight so that they can:
   a land properly.   b carry equipment.
   c wear a protective suit.
2 According to Kerry, a smokejumper's personal safety is:
   a a priority.   b unimportant.
   c not the first consideration.
3 Smokejumpers arrive at the scene of the fire:
   a first.   b if other fire crews have failed.
   c to help other crews.
4 They try to contain the fire by:
   a hosing it with water.
   b clearing an area in front of it.
   c changing its direction.
5 After their training, men and women smokejumpers treat each other:
   a a little suspiciously.   b as equals.
   c as doing different jobs.

4 Look at this statement of Kerry's. What does it tell you about her attitude to her job? What does she mean by *you either make the grade or you don't*?

"Fire doesn't distinguish between men and women, nor do the trainers at smokejumping school for that matter – you either make the grade or you don't."

> ▶ **WORDBUILDING phrases with *do***
>
> There are many expressions with *do* in English.
> *do your best, do someone a favour, do your duty*
>
> For further information and practice, see Workbook page 19.

Language focus present and perfect participles

5 Rewrite the sentences, replacing the participles in bold with a conjunction + pronoun + verb. Choose the correct conjunction from the box.

> after   and in order to do this   because (x3)
> with the result that

1 **Weighing** around 70–80 kilos, women firefighters are well suited to this kind of work.
   Because they weigh around 70–80 kilos, women firefighters are well suited to this kind of work.
2 If you're too heavy, you descend too fast and hit the ground hard, **risking** serious injury.
3 **Not having** a fire engine or a fire hydrant nearby, you can't fight the fire in the conventional way.
4 **Having located** a firebreak, we do our best to make sure it's going to be effective.
5 We get anything that could burn easily out of the way, **using** controlled burning, if necessary.
6 **Having faced** the same challenges in training, we have a natural respect for each other.

▶ **PRESENT AND PERFECT PARTICIPLES**

Present participle
Landing near the fire, they quickly assessed the situation.
Not thinking of his own safety, he rushed into the house.

Perfect participle
Having fought forest fires for 15 years, she is now an expert.
Not having ever *been* near a forest fire, I can't imagine the heat.

Notes
1 The main clause describes the most important event and the participial clause a secondary event.
2 The subject of a participial clause is the same as the subject of the main clause
3 We use a perfect participle only to emphasise one thing which happened before another.

For further information and practice, see page 159.

6 Look at the language focus box. Rewrite the sentences with a participial clause.

1 Because I had failed the course twice, I decided not to try again.
2 I burnt my hand while I was trying to put the fire out.
3 As I work in forestry, I know the dangers of forest fires very well.
4 He remained calm and got everyone out of the building.
5 When I look back on it, I can see that it was a mistake to leave him in charge.
6 I called the fire brigade because I thought it was the best thing to do.
7 After the smokejumpers have landed, they search for the equipment that has been dropped.
8 The smokejumpers work closely together and keep in radio contact.

7 Work in pairs. Look at the second note in the language focus box. In which sentences (1–4) has the speaker not followed this rule?

1 Having called the fire brigade, we quickly got out of the house.
2 Having finished my main course, the waiter offered to bring me dessert.
3 While waiting for the taxi, a dog came and sat down next to me.
4 Speaking to her, I realised that we had a lot in common.

8 Work in groups. Complete these sentences in a natural way. Then compare your sentences and vote on the best for each item.

1 Having studied English for ten years, …
2 Walking around the centre of our town, …
3 Opening the fridge, …
4 Not wanting to make a fuss, …

Idioms health and safety

9 Work in pairs. What do you think the idiom in bold used by Kerry, the smokejumper, means?

"We're very aware of safety, but at the same time in this kind of job you can't **wrap** people **in cotton wool**."

10 🔊 1.9 Use the words to complete the idioms used in this health and safety talk. Then listen and check. Discuss with your partner what you think each idiom means.

book	corners	danger	nature	net
precaution	side			

The aim of today's session is to raise awareness of health and safety issues and to ensure they become second ¹_____ to you all, so that everyone who works here learns to always be on the safe ²_____ . As I'm sure you'll appreciate, food preparation on this scale is fraught with ³_____ . There's no safety ⁴_____ here – mistakes can seriously endanger people's health. So we take every ⁵_____ to ensure that there's no risk to health. Everything has to be done by the ⁶_____ – there's no room for improvisation or for cutting ⁷_____ .

11 Think of a job where awareness of health and safety is very important. Discuss with your partner what the dangers are in this job and what safety measures can be taken.

Speaking

12 Work in groups. Consider these health and safety issues. Use them to make a list of health and safety rules for a company which supplies office furniture to other companies.

- smoking in delivery vans
- minimum number of breaks for delivery drivers and workers
- minimum number of people to lift and move any piece of furniture
- installation of furniture that involves electrical equipment
- collecting old furniture when delivering new furniture

2c Daring, defiant and free

Reading

1 What professional sports can you think of that are particularly dangerous? What motivates people to do this kind of thing?

2 Look at the photo and answer the questions. Then read the article and check your answers.

1 How do you think this man is able to do this?
2 How was the picture taken?

3 Read the article again and complete the sentences.

1 Honnold had nearly reached the top of the rock face when he _____ .
2 The only equipment needed in this type of climbing is _____ .
3 Climbing for 2 hours 45 minutes had left Honnold feeling _____ .
4 When he first visited Yosemite, Jimmy Chin was _____ by it.
5 When on an expedition with other climbers, the most important thing for Chin is _____ .
6 Chin wants his photographs to tell _____ .

4 Find words and expressions in the article with the following meanings.

1 two verbs that mean to hold tightly onto something (para 1)
2 an expression that means to be very focused (para 2)
3 an adverb meaning perfectly (para 2)
4 a verb meaning to hesitate between two courses of action (para 3)
5 a verb that means to recover your strength (para 4)
6 a verb that means hanging loosely (para 8)

Critical thinking using contrasts

5 The author uses images to describe the extraordinary things these climbers do and simple facts to describe their ordinary backgrounds. Find five images that describe the following.

1 how flat the rock is (3 images, paras 1 and 2)
2 how Honnold escaped being unable to move (para 4)
3 Jimmy Chin's athleticism (para 8)

6 Now find other factual information which contrasts with the descriptions in Exercise 5.

1 two statements about Honnold's and Chin's ordinary backgrounds (paras 4 and 6)
2 two quotations which show that they think their achievements are ordinary (paras 4 and 7)

7 Work in pairs. Compare your answers from Exercises 5 and 6 with your partner. What is the impact of these contrasts? Which of the sentences made the strongest impression on you? Why?

Word focus *foot*

8 Work in pairs. Find two words in the article built from the root word *foot*. Discuss with your partner what they mean.

9 Look at these other expressions with *foot* and discuss what each one means.

1 It's difficult to get a job with a newspaper. If you can **get your foot in the door** by getting one article published, you stand a better chance.
2 It's an expensive repair and I don't see why I have to **foot the bill** for something that is clearly the garage's fault.
3 When she told them at the interview that the money wasn't important to her, she really **shot herself in the foot**.
4 You **put your foot in it** when you asked Jim about his job – he was made redundant two weeks ago.
5 She's **followed in her mother's footsteps** and become a dentist.
6 You've got to **put your foot down**. If your children think you don't mean what you say, they'll carry on misbehaving.

10 Make two questions using two of the expressions with *foot*. Then ask and answer the questions with your partner.

Speaking

11 Work in pairs. Climbers like to live at the limits of their comfort zone. Do the quiz on page 153 to find out what your comfort zone is.

12 Work in groups. Which of the following motivates people, including yourself, most to stay in their comfort zone and why?

- fear of failure
- general dislike of being in the spotlight
- fear that success will bring more challenges and responsibilities
- fear of physical discomfort
- fear for your personal safety
- fear of confrontation

DARING, DEFIANT
AND
FREE

On a bright Saturday morning in September, a young man is clinging to the face of Half Dome, a sheer 2,130-foot wall of granite in the heart of Yosemite Valley. He's alone, so high off the ground that perhaps only the eagles take notice. Hanging on by his fingertips to an edge of rock as thin as a coin, shoes resting on mere ripples in the rock, professional climber Alex Honnold is attempting something no one has ever tried before: to climb the Northwest Face route on Half Dome without a rope. In many ways it's another day at the office for Honnold, but less than a hundred feet from the summit, something potentially disastrous occurs – he loses the smallest measure of confidence.

For two hours and 45 minutes, Honnold has been in the zone, flawlessly performing one precise athletic move after another, and not once has he hesitated. In the sport of free soloing, which means climbing with only a chalk bag and rock shoes – no rope, no gear, nothing to keep you stuck to the stone but your own belief and ability – doubt is dangerous. If Honnold merely believes his fingertips can't hold, he will fall to his death. Now, with mental fatigue and the glass-slick slab in front of him, he's paralysed, out of his comfort zone.

'My foot will never stay on that,' Honnold says to himself, staring at a greasy bump on the rock face. He hadn't felt that way two days before, when he'd raced up the same route with a rope. Now, clinging to the granite, Honnold vacillates, delicately chalking one hand, then the other, carefully adjusting his feet on invisibly small footholds. Then abruptly he's in motion again, stepping up, smearing his shoe on the slick stone. It sticks. He moves his hand to another hold and within minutes he's at the top.

'I rallied because there was nothing else I could do,' Honnold tells me later, releasing a boyish laugh. 'I stepped up and trusted that foothold and was freed of the prison where I'd stood silently for five minutes.' Word of his three-hour free solo of Half Dome flashes around the world. Climbers are stunned and bloggers buzz. On this warm fall day in 2008, the shy 23-year-old from the suburbs has just set a new record in climbing's big league.

This is the magic of Yosemite: it forges heroes. One such is Jimmy Chin. He is no less accomplished a mountaineer; in fact in some ways his achievements are greater, for as well as climbing, Chin takes photographs as he does it.

Chin had a traditional upbringing from his Chinese-American parents in the flat countryside of southern Minnesota. Rock climbing has been his passion since Glacier National Park first 'blew his mind' as a boy on a family vacation. Photography came later, when an outdoor clothing company bought one of the photos he had taken on an expedition. Encouraged, he bought his own camera and hasn't looked back.

He thanks his parents, who taught him Chinese calligraphy, for his sense of composition. 'When I started shooting photos I didn't really think too much about it.' Combining this with his mountaineering skills, he has become the ultimate practitioner of what has been called 'participatory photography.' Chin is able to carry a camera where few dare to go, at the same time remaining a solid and reliable member of the climbing team, which is always his priority.

'Photographing an expedition is like building a film – it's storytelling.' His favourite photo moment was on an expedition to China's Chang Tang Plateau with Galen Rowell. Climbing a nearby mountain, Chin's team had to chop a hole through a snow cornice just below the summit. 'I put my head through the hole,' says Chin, 'looked down and saw Galen climbing toward me.' Dangling like a spider, there was only one thing on his mind. 'I should have found a more secure footing, but I knew the moment would be lost, so hanging on by one arm I squeezed out three shots.'

---

chalk (n) /tʃɔːk/ soft white stone (formed from limestone)
cornice (n) /ˈkɔːnɪs/ a horizontal projection (usually at the top edge of a building)
ripple (n) /ˈrɪp(ə)l/ a very small wave on the surface (usually of water)
slab (n) /slæb/ a large thick flat piece of stone

2d In my experience

Real life giving a talk

1 Work in pairs. Think about when you started a job, university or a training course. Answer the questions.

1 Before you started the job or course, how did you find out what it was going to be like?
2 What induction or orientation did the employer or organisation offer when you started?

2 🔊 **1.10** Listen to a speech from an orientation day and answer the questions. Discuss your answers with your partner.

1 Who is the orientation day for?
2 Who is the speaker?
3 What does he advise his audience to do?
4 What did he do when he was in their situation and how did it help him?

3 Speaking skill keeping people's attention

🔊 **1.10** The speaker used certain techniques to keep people's attention: stressing the main message; telling stories from personal experience; and using rhetorical questions. Listen again and tick (✓) the phrases in the box that he used.

> ### ▶ KEEPING PEOPLE'S ATTENTION
>
> **Stressing the main message**
> I'd just like to say one thing …
> If there's one thing I'd like you to take away from this talk it's …
> So that's really my message to you today.
> That's the key thing.
>
> **Telling stories from personal experience**
> Just the other day I was …
> I remember when I first …
> I'll just give you an example of something that happened to me.
>
> **Using rhetorical questions**
> So, why should that be important? Well, …
> How many of you actually …?
> So what does that tell us?

4 Work in groups. What other techniques can you think of for keeping your audience's attention? Are these techniques appropriate for all kinds of talk and audience? Why? / Why not?

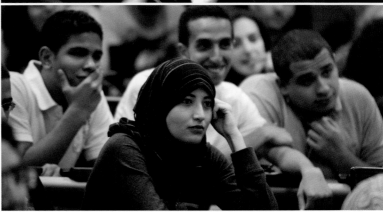

5 Pronunciation checking specific words

a 🔊 **1.11** Work in pairs. When preparing to give a talk, you should always check the pronunciation of difficult words (those words where the relationship between spelling and pronunciation is not always obvious). Think about the pronunciation of the underlined words in the opening part of the talk. Then listen and check.

'Hello, everyone. I hope you're enjoying your first day. I <u>imagine</u> you're feeling pretty <u>overwhelmed</u> by <u>everything</u> you've had to take in, and I don't want to keep you long. I've been <u>brought</u> back as someone who's been <u>through</u> the system and come out the other side, and so the university asked me to <u>talk</u> to you as one of you and to give a <u>student's</u> side of the story.'

b Work in groups. Practise saying the extract yourselves.

6 Prepare to give a short informal talk to people who are new to your university, company or organisation. Decide on your main message and build your talk around this. Use the language in the box and these points to help you.

- KISS – keep it short and simple
- make the aim of your talk clear
- introduce what you're going to say; then say it; then at the end, remind the audience of what you've said
- talk to your audience directly – use 'you'
- use rhetorical questions
- begin and end powerfully
- in a long talk, include one or two activities to involve your audience and to change the pace

TALK ABOUT ▶ WORK AS A WAY OF LIFE ▶ HEALTH AND SAFETY MEASURES ▶ YOUR COMFORT ZONE ▶ **GIVING A TALK**
WRITE ▶ NOTES

2e Your first day

Writing taking notes

1 🎧 **1.12** Look at the notes taken by a student at a university orientation day for overseas students. Then listen to an extract from the talk and complete the information marked ??? in points 1 and 2 that the student was not sure about.

Talk by principal to new students _____ or ???

1 Course reg Mon 10 a.m. – (3 p.m.) in main uni hall
  – compulsory.

2 Overseas students i.e. all except UK and EU,
  _____ (room number ???)
  must take docs to (Admissions office) – incl.
  education certificates, student visas + bank
  account details – by end of next week.

3 Uni has 'buddy' system (a 2nd year student)
  to help OS sts know where things are and what
  to do.

4 Most courses approx. 9-12 contact hrs p.w.; plan
  study time carefully. Lots of places to work,
  e.g. faculty library, main library, IT centre.

5 If worried about study or sthg else, see
  student counsellor. NB each group has native
  speaker counsellor.

6 Extra academic writing skills tuition available
  for 1st year students – details in student
  booklet (times, level, etc.)

---

2 Work in pairs. What other information did the speaker give that isn't in notes 1 and 2? Discuss with your partner.

3 🎧 **1.12** Listen again and check your answers. Why do you think this information wasn't included?

4 Writing skill abbreviations

a Work in pairs. How many different abbreviations can you find in the notes? What does each one mean?

b Compare your answers in Exercises 4a with another pair. Which abbreviations have the following meanings?

a including   d that is to say
b roughly   e please note
c for example   f and so on

c The use of abbreviations is acceptable in semi-formal writing and when writing in note form. It is not considered good style in more formal contexts. In which of the following could abbreviations be used?

1 an academic essay
2 the footnotes to an academic essay
3 a letter of complaint to a hospital
4 an internal memo to a colleague

d Look at this memo and rewrite it in note form. Then compare notes with your partner.

Please note that the meeting with Ellis & Company will be tomorrow, Tuesday 12th May at three o'clock. Please can you send me any information you have about them, including financial details, names of directors and so on.

5 🎧 **1.13** Listen to a talk from a university tutor about reading for your university course. Take notes on the talk. Remember to include only the relevant points and to use abbreviations where necessary.

6 Exchange notes with your partner. Use these questions to check your notes.

- Have they included the same relevant points?
- Have they left out unnecessary information?
- Have they used abbreviations correctly?

Climbing Yosemite

You have to be able to control
the fear.

Before you watch

1 Look at the photo taken by the photographer Jimmy Chin. How was he able to get this photograph?

2 How would you describe this kind of activity/job? Choose from these adjectives.

cerebral	difficult	methodical	monotonous
rewarding	scary	slow	thrilling

While you watch

3 Watch the first part of the video (to 01.04). Say which of the adjectives in Exercise 2 Jimmy Chin used to describe his work. Did his use of any of these adjectives surprise you?

4 Read these sentences about Jimmy Chin's career. Then watch the second part of the video (01.05 to end). Are the sentences true (T) or false (F)?

1 Jimmy Chin's parents hoped he would follow a professional career.
2 Chin realised straightaway that climbing was something he wanted to do permanently.
3 Chin felt very at home in Yosemite.
4 Chin's real ambition was to be a photographer.

5 Watch the second part of the video again (01.05 to end) and complete the notes about Jimmy Chin's career. Use one word in each space.

1 In college Chin was part of the _____ team.
2 After college he went to the Bay area to find a job in the _____ realm.
3 Not finding a job, he decided to take a _____ off and _____ and ski full time.
4 Seven years later Chin was still living in the back of his _____ and doing odd jobs, shovelling _____ and waiting tables.
5 He spent most of his time in Yosemite, where he found his _____ .
6 Here he lived the _____ life.
7 After some time in Yosemite, Chin decided he would like to visit the greater _____ of the world.
8 He took a photo, which a friend sold for $_____ , and could help him _____ what he was doing.

6 Work in pairs. Look at the phrases that Jimmy Chin used. Discuss with your partner what he was referring to and what he meant in each case.

1 'I couldn't get myself excited about it.'
2 'I've got to get it out of my system.'
3 'I've got to do it for me.'
4 'I was just doing odds and ends for jobs.'
5 'I was going to throw myself at climbing and skiing.'

After you watch

7 Roleplay an interview with an adventure photographer

Work in pairs.

Student A: Imagine you are a journalist from a photography magazine. You are going to interview an adventure photographer. Look at the points below and prepare a list of questions to ask the photographer.

Student B: Imagine you are an adventure photographer: someone who combines an extreme sport with photography, e.g. climbing, scuba diving, exploring, etc. Look at the points below and think about what you are going to say to the journalist.

- how you became involved with this activity
- where you do this activity
- what the activity typically involves doing and what the dangers are
- why you are passionate about it

Act out the interview, then change roles and act out the interview again.

8 Work in pairs. Think about your own life and interests. Then ask and answer the questions.

1 Did your parents have an ambition for you that you couldn't get excited about?
2 Is there something that you would still like to get out of your system?
3 If you could take a year off, what would you do?
4 Is there something – a job or hobby or adventure – that you would like to do 'for you'? What is it and why do you feel this?
5 What odd jobs have you done in your life? Which was the best? What was the worst?

---

awesome (adj) /ˈɔːs(ə)m/ amazing, incredible
cerebral (adj) /ˈserɪbr(ə)l/ involving a lot of thought and concentration
cringe (v) /krɪn(d)ʒ/ shrink back in fear or embarrassment
free-soloing (n) /friː ˈsəʊləʊɪŋ/ climbing without any ropes
realm (n) /relm/ a particular sphere or world
shovel (v) /ˈʃʌv(ə)l/ move earth or snow with a spade
wait tables (v) /weɪt ˈteɪbls/ work as a waiter

UNIT 2 REVIEW

Grammar

1 Complete the article about an unusual job. Put the verbs into the correct tense or participle form.

What would be your dream job? Tommy Lynch ¹_____ (believe) that he has found his. A few years ago he ² _____ (work) as a waiter in a restaurant, but now he ³_____ (travel) around the world ⁴_____ (test) water slides at various holiday resorts from Turkey to Mexico. ⁵_____ (work) for the holiday operator *First Choice*, Lynch's job is to find the best water parks to put into the company's holiday brochure. Lynch ⁶_____ (do) this for the last eighteen months and ⁷_____ (test) over fifty water slides and pools.

⁸_____ (create) their own selection of 'Splash Resorts', the company realised they needed someone to control the quality. A spokesperson for the company said, '⁹_____ (understand) how important swimming pools are to families, we knew that to offer the best we would have to appoint a full-time tester. Tommy ¹⁰_____ (take) his job very seriously and ¹¹_____ (succeed) in finding some of the world's best pools.'

¹²_____ (beat) hundreds of other applicants to get the job, Tommy says, 'I ¹³_____ (have) the time of my life. It's not all fun, though. I ¹⁴_____ (have) a lot of paperwork, but I hope I ¹⁵_____ (still / do) this in five years' time!'

2 Answer the questions.

1 What does Tommy's job involve?
2 Why was this job created?
3 What are the less enjoyable parts of the job?

3 Work in pairs. What would be your dream job? Why? Discuss with your partner.

I CAN	
describe actions that are/were in progress (continuous aspect)	☐
use present and perfect participles to connect ideas	☐

Vocabulary

4 Complete the questions about work with the correct words.

1 What do you consider a reasonable monthly salary to get _____ on?
2 In the area you want to work in, is it difficult to get your foot _____ the door?
3 How much work correspondence – letters, emails, etc. – do you have to get _____ each day?
4 In your work, have you followed _____ either of your parents' footsteps?
5 Is getting _____ in life and moving up the career ladder important to you?
6 Would you rather do a job that really challenged you or stay _____ the safe side and do something you feel completely in control of?

5 Work in pairs. Ask and answer the questions in Exercise 4.

I CAN	
talk about jobs and careers	☐
use phrasal verbs with *get*	☐
use health and safety idioms	☐

Real life

6 Complete the extract from an orientation talk using these phrases (a–d).

a I remember when I first started
b So that's really my message to you today
c So what does that tell us
d That's the key thing

'So always check at the end of each call that the customer feels they have got an answer to the question they asked. ¹_____ . I know it sounds obvious but ²_____ , I was so conscious of trying to sell the customer some extra product or service that I would fail to deal properly with their question. Last month our call centre had a 97% customer satisfaction rating. ³_____ ? That our operators are giving customers the right answers to their questions. We would like to keep it that way. ⁴_____ : always try to put yourself in the customer's shoes.'

7 Work in pairs. Give a short talk to some new students about to start an English language course. What key point would you like to make? What advice from your own experience can you give?

I CAN	
give a talk about a certain subject	☐
keep people's attention when giving a talk	☐

Speaking

8 Work in pairs. Which person in Unit 2 do you admire the most for the work that they do? Why?

Unit 3 Four walls

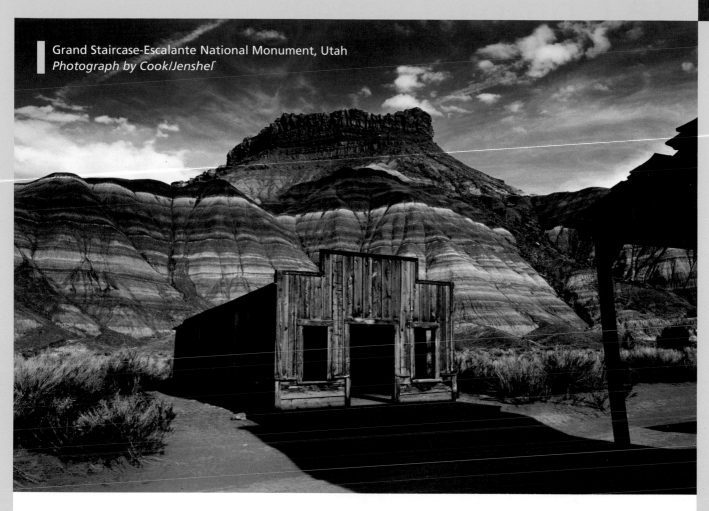

Grand Staircase-Escalante National Monument, Utah
Photograph by Cook/Jenshel

FEATURES

1 🔊 **1.14** Work in pairs. Look at the photo and caption and answer the questions. Then listen to two people discussing the photo and compare your answers.

1 What type of building is this? What does it remind you of?
2 What do you think it is used for these days?

2 🔊 **1.14** Read the sentences below. Then listen again and replace the words in bold with the ones the speaker uses.

1 A(n) **ordinary**, **timber**, Old-West-style shop – nothing fancy about it.
2 It **fits** in very naturally with its surroundings.
3 What's interesting too is the **fake** front on the building.
4 They were usually bigger and more **elaborate** … disguising a more **simple** structure behind it.

3 Put these words describing buildings into four categories: material, period/style, impression and type.

> 1960s   brick   characterless   colonial   concrete
> cottage   elegant   futuristic   glass   imposing   modern
> office block   plain   shack   steel   striking   tower
> traditional   warehouse   wooden

4 Work in groups. Think of a building that you know. Describe it to your group, saying what you like or dislike about it. It could be the building you are in now.

TALK ABOUT ▶ YOUR IDEAL HOME ▶ TOWN PLANNING ▶ HOW SPACES AFFECT YOU ▶ MAKING RECOMMENDATIONS
WRITE ▶ AN OPINION ESSAY

33

3a Compact spaces

Listening

1 Work in pairs. Ask and answer the questions.

1 How many different rooms are there in your home?
2 Do any of the rooms have more than one function?
3 If you had more space, what would you use it for?

2 🔊 **1.15** Look at the photos. Then listen to an interview with an architect who specialises in compact designs. Answer the questions.

1 Where are these two homes?
2 Why is he inspired by them?

3 🔊 **1.15** Read the sentences. Then listen to the interview again and choose the best option to complete the sentences.

1 Jonas Wilfstrand is a specialist in *small holiday homes / the efficient use of space*.
2 An increasing number of people *would like to own / are curious about* smaller homes.
3 Dolgan homes consist of *one room / a communal space and a bedroom*.
4 The Dolgan need to move house easily because of *the weather / their animals*.
5 In Gary Chang's apartment you can *move / fold away* the walls.
6 The interviewer *dislikes / has mixed feelings about* Chang's apartment.

4 Do either of the homes the architect describes appeal to you? Why? / Why not?

Language focus intensifying adverbs

5 Look at the sentences from the interview (1–8). For each sentence, identify the intensifying adverb, the word it intensifies and what type of word (adjective, verb or adverb) this is.

↙ *intensifying adverb*

1 We're <u>changing</u> focus (completely) today and looking at small homes.
   The word it intensifies = changing (verb)
2 I'm very pleased to welcome Swedish architect Jonas Wilfstrand.
3 I must say some of them are absolutely stunning.
4 People are either incredibly short of space or they simply can't afford a bigger house.
5 When it's time to find new feeding grounds, the Dolgan move house, quite literally.
6 I was impressed by the fact that they're just so simple.
7 As you probably know, Hong Kong is a really overcrowded city.
8 He entirely rethought the way we arrange living space.

6 Look at the words *stunning* and *short* in Exercise 5. Which of these adjectives can vary in intensity (gradable)? Which has a meaning that is already intense (ungradable)?

7 Work in pairs. Look at these adjectives. Which are gradable? Which are ungradable?

| brilliant | difficult | filthy | freezing | huge |
| innovative | perfect | plain | simple | strong |

▶ INTENSIFYING ADVERBS

extremely, incredibly, very (+ gradable adjective)
They are extremely basic.

absolutely, utterly (+ ungradable adjective or ungradable verb)
The designs are absolutely wonderful.
I utterly detest that building.

really (+ gradable/ungradable adjective or gradable/ungradable verb)
I would really like to go.

completely, entirely, totally (+ ungradable adjective or verb)
It was completely empty.
I accept the blame entirely.

quite (+ ungradable adverb or adjective)
They quite literally built it by hand.
I am quite sure it's the best thing to do.

so (+ gradable or ungradable adjective)
We're so happy in our new house.

Notes
1 *Utterly* is usually used with ungradable adjectives with a negative meaning.
2 *So* is like *very, really*, etc. but is used in conversation.

For further information and practice, see page 159.

8 Look at the language focus box. Then choose the correct adverb to complete the sentences.

1 Our house is *so / utterly* cold at the moment. The heating broke down last week.
2 It's *completely / extremely* sad that so many people live in just a single room.
3 For ages nothing seemed to be happening on the site and then *absolutely / quite* suddenly the house went up.
4 I agree with you *extremely / completely* about the colour of the walls.
5 The price of houses in London is *utterly / incredibly* ridiculous.
6 It's an *entirely / absolutely* beautiful apartment.
7 I *really / completely* want to live in a penthouse apartment in the centre.
8 The design of the house is *very / totally* clever.

9 **Pronunciation stress in intensifying adverbs**

a 🔊 **1.16** Listen to the sentences with intensifiers and underline the syllables which are stressed.

1 You're absolutely right.
2 That's really kind of you.
3 I'd be very grateful.
4 It's completely out of the question.
5 Yes, I'm quite certain.
6 That's so typical.

b Work in pairs. Make two-line conversations using the expressions in Exercise 9a. Then act out your conversations using the correct stress.

Vocabulary adverb and adjective collocations

10 Look at this example of an adverb + adjective collocation from the interview. What does *distinctly* mean here: *very* or *a little*?

It looks **distinctly** cramped.

11 Look at these other adverb + adjective collocations. In all cases but two the adverb has the meaning of *very* or *absolutely*. Find the two collocations where this is NOT the case.

deadly serious
desperately unlucky
hopelessly wrong
mildly amused
painfully slow
patently obvious
perfectly reasonable
simply unacceptable
vaguely familiar
wildly optimistic

12 Work in pairs. Think of examples that fit the descriptions (1–5). Then discuss your situations with another pair.

1 a process which is painfully slow
2 a prediction that seems wildly optimistic
3 a statement that is patently obvious
4 a result in a sporting competition where someone was desperately unlucky
5 an employee's demand which is perfectly reasonable

Speaking

13 Work in pairs. The architect in the interview had designed a timber and glass vacation house with built-in sauna. Look at these rooms and features in a home. Discuss what each one is. Which are the most desirable features in a home in your country?

conservatory   courtyard   games room
garage/workshop   gym   home cinema
roof garden   sauna   veranda
walk-in wardrobe

14 Work in groups. Describe what your ideal home would be and what rooms and features it would contain.

3b Old new towns

Vocabulary towns

1 Work in pairs. Match words from A with the nouns from B to make collocations. Then match the collocations with the definitions (1–8).

A

dormitory	historic
housing	leafy
market	sleepy
sprawling	vibrant

B

city	estate
metropolis	
neighbourhood	suburb
town	village

1 famous for its old buildings
2 attracts shoppers from the countryside around it
3 a concentration of affordable residential homes
4 a large lively city
5 lots of commuters live here
6 nothing much happens here
7 a rich green residential area outside the centre
8 an urban area that keeps growing outwards

2 Describe the place where you live now or a place you have lived in. Use the collocations in Exercise 1.

Reading

3 Look at the photos. Where do you think these towns are? What makes you say this? Read the article and check your answers.

4 Read the article again and answer the questions.

1 What do Poundbury and Thames Town have in common?
2 For what reasons was each town built?
3 Are they successful?

5 Work in pairs. Find examples of the following in the article.

1 two things that characterised town planning in Britain in the 1960s
2 two types of building found in Poundbury
3 two buildings found in Thames Town
4 two examples of good town planning ideas in Poundbury

OLD NEW TOWNS

Where would you look for inspiration if you were planning a new town? If you are Prince Charles or the Shanghai Planning Commission, the past would seem to be the answer; or to be more precise, the English past. The town of Poundbury in the south of England, designed by Prince Charles, is an answer to what he calls the 'heartless urban planning' of the 1960s. It was here that he could offer an alternative to 'ugly' high-rise apartment blocks, large housing estates and zonal planning – where industry, shops and homes are all separated into different areas of a city.

Poundbury's buildings imitate the quaint cottages and grander houses of 18th-century Dorset. All are built with local stone, helping the community take root in familiar surroundings. 'What I was trying to do,' the prince said, 'was remind people that it is pointless to throw away the knowledge and experience of what has gone before.'

If you find such reproductions of the past artificial, then you will certainly not enjoy Thames Town, a new development just outside Shanghai. Rarely do you find nostalgia taken to such extremes. But this is not nostalgia for traditional Chinese living. Thames Town is modelled on the English town of Dorchester, not far from Poundbury, and is part of a plan to create a new suburbia for Shanghai's richer classes. It boasts a pub, a fish and chip shop, and a 19th-century church. Nine such replica towns are planned around Shanghai, each based on a different Western style: Italian, Austrian, etc.

But are these model towns a success? As far as friendly urban planning goes, Poundbury does seem to work. Businesses are placed close to residential buildings, enabling residents to walk to work. A third of the houses are 'affordable housing', giving the town a good social and economic mix. They have small gardens, but there is plenty of communal green space, making it easy to get to know your neighbours.

Unfortunately, the same cannot be said for Thames Town. It is popular with day visitors and Chinese couples wanting to recreate Western-style weddings, but, going there, you get the distinct feeling you are in a museum rather than somewhere lived in.

affordable housing (n) /əˈfɔːdəbəl haʊzɪŋ/ homes for people on low incomes
quaint (adj) /kweɪnt/ attractively old fashioned or unusual
take root (v) /teɪk ruːt/ become settled

> ▶ **WORDBUILDING suffix -able**
>
> We can add -able to the end of a verb to make adjectives describing what can be done.
> *affordable, doable, workable*
>
> For further information and practice, see Workbook page 27.

6 Do you like the idea of recreating old towns? Do you think it is a realistic model for other towns? Why? / Why not? Discuss with your partner.

Language focus emphatic structures

7 Work in pairs. Look at the sentences (1–4) and find similar sentences in the text. Then answer the questions (a–c).

1   He could offer an alternative here to 'ugly' high-rise apartment blocks …
2   I was trying to remind people that it is pointless to throw away the knowledge …
3   You rarely find nostalgia taken to such extremes.
4   As far as friendly urban planning goes, Poundbury seems to work.

a   Which sentence in each pair has more emphasis?
b   What idea in each case is being emphasised?
c   What changes have been made to the sentence to add this emphasis?

> ▶ **EMPHATIC STRUCTURES**
>
> **Cleft sentences**
> *The design of the buildings strikes you.*
> (no emphasis)
> *What strikes you is the design of the buildings.*
> *It's the design of the buildings that strikes you.*
> *The thing that strikes you is the design of the buildings.*
>
> **Negative inversion**
> *Rarely do you see so much thought put into design.*
> *Never before has a country tried to recreate a whole English town.*
>
> **do, does, did**
> *He does genuinely care about ordinary people.*
> *Admittedly, they did employ a British architect to help them.*
>
> Note: Inversion is used mainly in writing and only rarely in speech.
>
> For further information and practice, see page 160.

8 Look at the language focus box. Rewrite these sentences with more emphasis.

1   I love the human scale of Poundbury.
     What I _____ .
2   You seldom need a car to go shopping.
     Seldom _____ .
3   The architects wanted to encourage people to mix, so they included communal green spaces in the design of the town.
     The thing the architects _____ .
4   Children socialise in these public spaces.
     It's in these _____ .
5   It isn't surprising that Poundbury has cost a lot of money to build.
     What _____ .
6   The developers didn't once opt for cheaper materials like concrete when they were building Poundbury.
     Not once _____ .
7   When asked, the developers admitted that they expected Thames Town to be more popular.
     When asked, the developers _____ .
8   They think, however, that the Italian and Austrian towns will be popular.
     They _____ .

9 Work in pairs. Three of the sentences use an emphatic structure when the context does not really justify it. Which three sentences are they?

1   I've travelled a lot, but never have I been to England.
2   It's in big cities that we really need to address the problems of bad town planning.
3   What's normal is that I get up at 7.30 a.m. Then I have my breakfast.
4   It's in the canteen that we usually eat our lunch, but sometimes we go out.
5   How can she possibly argue that? Never have I heard such nonsense!
6   It's a wonderful town. What's unusual is that there aren't more towns like this.

Speaking

10 Work in groups. Look at the following choices in town planning and discuss the advantages and disadvantages of each choice for society and the environment.

1   Mixing residential, commercial and industrial areas OR keeping them separate.
2   Mixing expensive and affordable housing OR keeping them separate.
3   Allowing cars in the town centre OR banning them.
4   Having dense residential areas OR creating space around each home.

3c The paper architect

Reading

1 Work in pairs. Why do you think this woman is called 'The paper architect'? Discuss.

2 Read the article about architect Zaha Hadid and choose the statement that best summarises her aim.

   a   to create unusual buildings
   b   to be a successful woman architect
   c   to create buildings people like to be in

3 Read the article again and answer the questions.

   1   Why was Hadid called the paper architect?
   2   Why do many women architects in Britain not stay in the profession?
   3   What did her tutor mean when he called her 'a planet in her own orbit'?
   4   What characterises the buildings designed by Hadid's contemporaries?
   5   What kind of buildings does Hadid like to work on?
   6   Why did Hadid try to create a feeling of space in the Evelyn Grace Academy?
   7   How do visitors to the MAXXI Rome feel when they are inside the museum?
   8   What does Hadid say her designs are influenced by?

Critical thinking fact or opinion

4 Work in pairs. Find evidence in the article to support the following statements. Compare answers with your partner.

   1   There are not many women architects in Britain compared to men.
   2   Hadid's style is in the same spirit as some of her contemporaries.
   3   She has an interest in designing public buildings.
   4   People are captivated by the spaces she creates within buildings.
   5   She is interested in giving people the experience of a journey within her buildings.
   6   Architecture would be more human if there were more architects like Hadid.

5 Mark each statement in Exercise 4 according to whether it is a fact (F) or the author's opinion (O).

6 Use the facts to write a short summary of what you now know about Zaha Hadid and her work.

Word focus *wall*

7 Find these expressions with *wall* in the article and choose the correct meaning.

   1   **bang your head against a brick wall**
       a fail to persuade others after trying repeatedly
       b fail to achieve your own personal goals
   2   **off the wall**
       a strange or eccentric
       b unstable and dangerous

8 Work in pairs. What do these other expressions with *wall* mean? Discuss with your partner.

   1   Can you ask Jimmy to stop practising on his drums? The noise is **driving me up the wall**.
   2   The banks are closed now, but you can get some money from **the hole in the wall**.
   3   Over 300 architecture firms **went to the wall** last year because of the slowdown in construction.
   4   **The writing is on the wall** for St Jude's Academy. Unless their results improve, they will be closed down.
   5   I wish I could have been **a fly on the wall** when Jen had her meeting with the boss.
   6   The first chapter was easy to write, but I**'ve hit a wall** now.

9 Think of examples of the following. Discuss your examples with your partner.

   1   something that drives you up the wall
   2   a situation where you would have liked to be a fly on the wall
   3   a company that has recently gone to the wall

Speaking

10 Some of the public spaces mentioned in the article can have bad associations for people, for example, schools and hospitals. Look at these places which people in a survey said they didn't like being in. How do you feel in each of them? Why?

   1   a dentist's surgery
   2   a lift
   3   an airport departure lounge
   4   a classroom or lecture hall
   5   a large open plan office

11 Work in groups of three or four. Choose one of the public spaces in Exercise 10 and discuss how its design could be improved to make people feel more comfortable. Think about the following:

   •   shape and size of the space
   •   lighting
   •   arrangement of furniture
   •   other additions (music, plants, etc.)

THE PAPER ARCHITECT

For a long time, Zaha Hadid was known as 'the paper architect', someone whose grand designs never left the page to become real buildings. But in recent years her buildings have sprouted up like mushrooms all over the world: the Guangzhou Opera House in China, a car factory in Germany, a contemporary art museum in Rome, a transport museum in Scotland, and the Aquatics Centre for the 2012 Olympics in London.

Hadid is now one of the most sought-after architects of our age. She is also one of the few women to have made it in a profession still dominated by men. In Britain, where Hadid lives (she was born in Iraq in 1950), less than 15% of practising architects are women. A lot more than that enter the profession, but either because of difficulty in getting recognised or because of the deep conservatism surrounding most British architecture, over half of them leave. But being 'a woman in a man's world' seems to have given Hadid extra strength. At times she felt she was banging her head against a wall trying to get her designs accepted, but she persevered. Famous for her fierce independence, one of her former tutors called her 'a planet in her own orbit'.

Pinning down her individual style is difficult. Certainly she has been influenced by the modern trend in architecture that likes to play with the traditional shape of buildings and fragment them, creating unpredictable angles and surfaces. Working in this way, she and her fellow architects have produced various rather off the wall spaceship-like structures that seem to defy the normal laws of engineering, but which have intrigued and excited the public.

So the visual impact of her designs from the outside is clearly important to her, but Hadid maintains that the key consideration when she creates an architectural design is people's well-being. In other words, how they will feel inside the spaces she creates. This has drawn her increasingly to become interested in public projects, such as housing, schools and hospitals. Recently she won the RIBA Stirling Prize for her design of a school complex in Brixton, south London.

Shaped as a zig-zag, the steel and glass structure of Evelyn Grace Academy takes up only 1.4 hectares compared to eight hectares for a typical secondary school. To compensate for the lack of internal space, Hadid designed a building with lots of natural light and dramatic angles, so that students view the activity of other students from each different perspective within the structure. The masterstroke is the insertion of a 100m running track right in the middle of the site between buildings to celebrate the school's emphasis on sports.

This idea of offering the viewer multiple perspectives from within the building is a theme that runs through Hadid's work. Her most famous building, MAXXI – a museum for the 21st century – in Rome, is a great example. It is a complex and spectacular structure of interlocking concrete shapes. Inside spaces interconnect 'like winding streets compressed into one single site in the building', so that the visitor is surprised and charmed at each turn. The Rosenthal Center in Cincinatti produces a similar effect. Like an extension of the street it sits on, it draws you in, with walkways directing you this way and that, and windows inviting you to sample the view. 'It's about promenading,' says Hadid, 'being able to pause, to look out, look above, look sideways.'

So what inspires someone like Hadid to produce such radically different buildings? She speaks in complimentary terms about the work of her contemporaries. She also cites the natural landscape and organic geological patterns as an influence. But it is not a question that she seems too concerned with and nor perhaps should we be. Hadid is an artist, sharing with us her vision of what buildings should be like and always, as she does so, trying to keep human interests – our interests as users and viewers – at heart. Perhaps we could do with more architects like her.

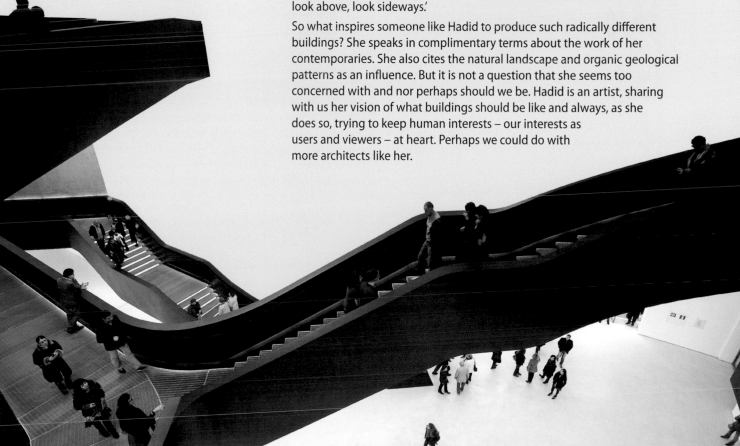

3d A public project

Real life making recommendations

1 Work in pairs. Think about a public work of art in your town or area. Describe it to your partner, saying what you like or dislike about it.

2 Look at the photo and caption and discuss the questions.

1 Do you like this public work of art? Why? / Why not?
2 What benefits do you think the city authorities hoped it would bring (to both the locals and visitors)?

3 🔊 **1.17** Listen to part of a debate about a proposal for a public work of art in a city. Answer the questions.

1 What piece of art is being proposed?
2 Is the speaker in favour of or against it?
3 What are the main arguments he puts forward to support his view?

4 Speaking skill making a case

a 🔊 **1.17** Listen again and complete the sentences in the box.

> ▶ MAKING A CASE
>
> I have to say, ¹ _____ .
> It has ² _____ to recommend it.
> First of all, it seems ³ _____ .
> What I mean is ⁴ _____ .
> I think everyone should ⁵ _____ .
> Also, the fact that ⁶ _____ will give it popular appeal.
> It's a clever touch, I think.
> Thirdly, and I don't think we should underestimate this, ⁷ _____ .
> I think this is important, given
> ⁸ _____ .
> And the idea that ⁹ _____ also really appeals to me.

b Look at the phrases in the box that the speaker used to make his argument.

1 Which phrases are always positive (P)?
2 Which phrases give extra emphasis (E) to the point the speaker makes?

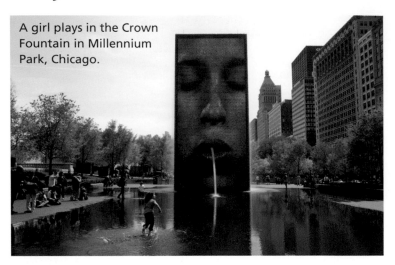

A girl plays in the Crown Fountain in Millennium Park, Chicago.

5 Pronunciation linking

a 🔊 **1.18** Work in pairs. Which words are linked in these phrases? How do words that end in a vowel link to ones that begin with a vowel? Listen and check.

1 'What I mean is it's not too intellectual …'
   What_I mean_is_it's not too_intellectual …
   /w/
2 'The idea that it could be a tourist destination …'
3 'The water and the area in front of the fountain …'

b Practise saying the sentences aloud.

6 Read the guidelines for a proposal for a public work of art in a park in the city centre. What are the city authorities hoping to do with the park and why?

> The city would like to commission a public work of art for its central park, which is used mainly by joggers and office workers on their lunch breaks. The local authority feels it has the potential to attract many more visitors. The successful proposal will add to the park without taking anything away from its natural beauty, and respect environmental considerations. It is also hoped the proposal will make reference to the traditions of our public-spirited city.

7 Work in pairs. You are each going to make a proposal for a public work of art for the city centre park.

Student A: Turn to page 153 and look at the proposal.

Student B: Turn to page 155 and look at the proposal.

Prepare to make the case in favour of your proposal. Look at the guidelines in Exercise 6 and the language in the box in Exercise 4 to help you. Then take turns to present your proposal. Decide which proposal you find most convincing.

3e Old and new

Writing an opinion essay

1 Look at the photo. Do these two buildings complement each other? Why? / Why not?

2 Read the essay question and the essay. Answer the questions.

  1 What is the writer's opinion?
  2 What examples does he give to support this?

3 Look at the essay again and underline examples of the following.

  1 an example where the writer considers other people's arguments
  2 an example where the writer tries to be reasonable when giving his opinion
  3 a sentence in the final paragraph where the writer makes his point more forcefully

4 Look at the four key elements of an opinion essay. Find each element in the essay. What is the correct order?

  a make your conclusion
  b give your opinion and present the arguments supporting it
  c evaluate counter arguments
  d analyse the question and set your terms of reference

5 Writing skill linking devices

a The writer uses linking and adverbial phrases to connect and balance the ideas in his argument. Answer the questions using these words.

admittedly	although	but
even though	however	indeed
so	thus	

  1 Which words link two contrasting ideas?
  2 Which words balance an argument by accepting there is some evidence against it?
  3 Which word reinforces an idea by giving further evidence?
  4 Which words make a conclusion?

Should we allow modern buildings to be built next to older buildings in a historic area of a city?

In order to answer this question, we must first examine whether people really want to preserve the historic feel of an area. Not all historical buildings are attractive. However, there may be other reasons – for example, economic reasons – why they should be preserved. So, let us assume that the historical buildings are both attractive and important to the majority of people. What should we do then if a new building is needed?

In my view, new architectural styles can exist perfectly well alongside an older style. Indeed, there are many examples in my own home town of Tours where radical modern designs have been placed very successfully next to old buildings. As long as the building in question is pleasing and does not dominate its surroundings too much, it often enhances the attractiveness of the area.

Admittedly, there are examples of new buildings which have spoilt the area they are in. But the same can be said of some old buildings too. Yet people still object to new buildings in historical areas. I think this is simply because people are naturally conservative and do not like change.

Although we have to respect people's feelings as fellow users and viewers of the buildings, I believe that it is the duty of the architect and planner to move things forward. If we constantly reproduced what was there before, we would all still be living in caves. Thus, I would argue against building imitations and choose something fresh and different, even though that might be the riskier option.

b Work in pairs. Use linking devices from Exercise 5a to complete this text.

Buildings that imitate previous styles of architecture do not always work. [1] _____ , they can often look cheap and nasty. Yet some local authorities will insist on building in a 'traditional' style, [2] _____ there may be much more attractive modern designs to choose from. [3] _____ , choosing the right modern design is not easy. [4] _____ , the rewards for getting it right are much greater. [5] _____ , we should encourage authorities to be more adventurous in their choices of designs.

6 Write an opinion essay about this question (250–300 words).

Should we create more socially mixed residential areas, where rich people live next to poorer people, instead of in separate communities?

7 Exchange essays with your partner. Use these questions to check your essays.

• Is their opinion clear and are the arguments balanced?
• Have they followed the structure suggested in Exercise 4?
• Have they used linking devices correctly to connect the ideas?

3f Denmark bridge

| Enter the Øresund Bridge

Before you watch

1 Work in pairs. Look at the photo of the bridge and discuss the questions.

1 What kind of bridge is it and what does it connect?
2 What difficulties do you think the architects faced in its construction?
3 What are the alternatives to joining two pieces of land separated by sea?

While you watch

2 Watch the video and answer the questions.

1 What were the obstacles to joining Sweden to Denmark?

2 What solution did the architects come up with?

3 Look at the table. Then watch the first part of the video (to 01.54) and complete the facts.

1	The width of the Øresund Strait:	
2	The weather in this region:	
3	Needs of Copenhagen:	
4	Needs of Malmö:	
5	What the bridge carries:	
6	Height above the sea:	
7	Height of support towers:	

4 Watch the second part of the video (01.55 to end). Then answer the questions.

1 How did the architects know it would be dangerous to build a bridge close to the Danish shoreline?

2 What would the result of building a lower bridge have been?

3 What two adjectives does the project director use to describe the tunnel solution?

4 What was the problem with the part-bridge, part-tunnel solution?

5 How did the architects get around this problem?

5 Complete the summary using one word in each space. Then watch the video again to check.

The Øresund Bridge was built to connect Denmark and Sweden over the Øresund ^{1} _____ in the Baltic Sea. The idea was to merge Malmö and Copenhagen to create one large ^{2} _____ with economic benefits for all.
The two countries signed a(n) ^{3} _____ and a ^{4} _____ was formed to carry out the work. But the project faced a lot of technical difficulties because of ^{5} _____ and sea traffic. A tunnel would have been the ideal solution but it was too ^{6} _____. So in the end they decided to build part-tunnel and part- ^{7} _____. The result is one of the ^{8} _____ cable-stayed bridges in the world.

After you watch

6 Roleplay a debate about local communications

Work in groups.

Imagine you live in a city built around the base of a hill. At the moment people have to drive around the hill to get from the north side, where most of the residential areas are, to the south side, where most of the commercial and industrial activity is. The local population want to connect the two sides more easily. Look at these options and think about the benefits and drawbacks of each.

• building a tunnel of five kilometres through the hill
• building a new six-lane motorway ring road running around the city and the hill
• building a new high-speed railway line around the hill
• something else

Debate which you think is the best solution.

7 Work in groups and discuss the questions.

1 Why are good transport links important in big cities?
2 How do you rate the transport links in your own city? How could they be improved?

---

cable-stayed (adj) /'keɪb(ə)l steɪd/ a way of supporting a deck or road by attaching cables to a tall column
consortium (n) /kən'sɔːtɪəm; *US* kənsɔː(r)ʃəm/ a number of companies which join together to work on a project
converge (v) /kən'vɜːdʒ/ come together
dangle (v) /'dæŋg(ə)l/ hang in the air
lousy (adj) /'laʊzi/ bad or poor quality
pact (n) /pækt/ an agreement
setback (n) /'setbæk/ something which stops or reverses your progress
soar (v) /sɔː/ rise or fly very high
strait (n) /streɪt/ a narrow strip of water between two pieces of land

UNIT 3 REVIEW

Grammar

1 Look at the photo. What do you think this building is for? Read the text and check your answers.

2 Choose the correct options to complete the text.

I ¹*really / so* love the London Olympics Aquatics Centre. It's a great example of architect Zaha Hadid's ability to design large public buildings which work. It's rare for design and function to come together as successfully as this. It's both practical and ²*extremely / absolutely* stunning to look at. I like the way that she has made the roof look like moving water. From the outside, it's been compared to a(n) ³*very / absolutely* large turtle with its flippers outstretched. The 'flippers' are in fact rectangular structures at each side of the building which were put there to accommodate seating for the 15,000 spectators attending the swimming competitions at the Olympics. Hadid ⁴*really / completely* wanted the whole structure to be under one undulating roof, but the organisers were ⁵*quite / incredibly* certain about the question of seating capacity. After the Olympics, most of the seats were removed and the seating capacity reduced to 2,500. Inside the centre, the bare concrete sweeps this way and that in beautiful curves, the diving boards seeming to grow out of the floor. At floor level lies the blue 50-metre pool, 3 metres deep to help the athletes to swim faster. The whole effect is ⁶*utterly / incredibly* dramatic.

3 Rewrite these three sentences from the text to make them more emphatic. Use the words given.

1 … Zaha Hadid's ability to design large public buildings which work. (do)
2 It's rare for design and function to come together as successfully as this. (rarely)
3 I like the way that she has made the roof look like moving water. (what)

4 Work in pairs. What's your favourite sports building or stadium? Why do you like it?

I CAN	
use adverbs to intensify meaning	☐
give emphasis to statements	☐

Vocabulary

5 Complete the definitions of buildings and places.

characterless	housing	leafy	metropolis
shack	sleepy		

1 A wooden _____ is a very basic structure, often with just one room.
2 A _____ suburb is a pleasant, green residential area in a town.
3 A _____ building is one that is plain and has no special features.
4 A vibrant _____ is a very large and lively city, like New York.
5 A _____ estate is an area of densely packed affordable homes.
6 A _____ village is a village where very little happens.

6 Work in pairs. Describe examples of buildings and places in Exercise 5 that you know from your experience.

I CAN	
describe buildings	☐
talk about places	☐

Real life

7 Choose the correct options to complete this extract from a talk supporting the idea of a water park.

I ¹*ought / have* to say, I really like Helen's idea to create a water park. It has lots of things to ²*recommend / suggest* it. First of all, we don't have many water features in the centre of the city. Secondly, it will attract a lot of birds and other wildlife. Thirdly, and I don't think we should ³*overestimate / underestimate* this, it will attract children. And I ⁴*think / say* that's important, because at the moment families don't come downtown much. And that's what ⁵*appealed / called* to me about the idea. Also, the idea of having a café and boats for hire is a clever ⁶*touch / point*, because over time it will help us to recoup some of the cost.

8 Work in groups. Make a short proposal for a new leisure feature in a park in the city centre, e.g. a small zoo, a museum or gallery. Present your ideas to your group using language to support the proposal.

I CAN	
propose an idea	☐
use expressions to make a case	☐

Speaking

9 Work in pairs. Look at the photos of the different buildings in Unit 3. Are there any you would like to live in or visit? Give your reasons.

Unit 4 Innovation

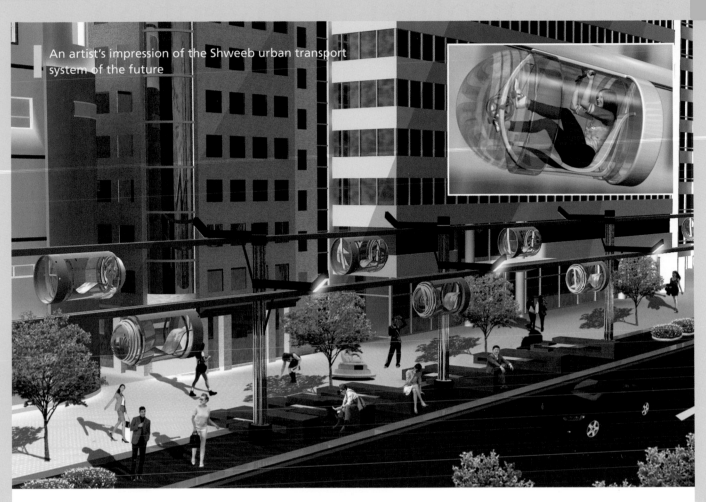

An artist's impression of the Shweeb urban transport system of the future

FEATURES

1 🔊 **1.19** Work in pairs. Look at the picture and caption and discuss how this transport system works and what its advantages are. Then listen to an extract from *Science Today* and check your answers.

2 🔊 **1.19** Complete the summary using one word in each space. Then listen to the radio programme again and check.

The original idea for putting a bicycle on [1] _____ so that it could run more [2] _____ appeared in the 1800s. The idea was updated by a company called Shweeb for an [3] _____ park. [4] _____ have now invested money to develop it into an urban transport system. Drivers sit in pods hanging from a monorail, and [5] _____ while almost lying down. They travel [6] _____ the traffic. It is a solution with many advantages: it is green, convenient, cheap and [7] _____ .

3 Match the two halves of the collocations. Discuss what they mean.

1	have	a	a need
2	make	b	a breakthrough
3	spot	c	(an idea) one stage further
4	take	d	a bright idea
5	fill	e	the wheel
6	reinvent	f	a trend

4 Work in groups. Each describe an innovation or invention from the last 100 years. Which innovation had more impact?

4a The mother of invention

Listening

1 Work in pairs. Look at the saying below.
Discuss what it means and if it is always
true.

"Necessity is the mother of invention."

2 Look at the photo and the caption. What
adjectives would you use to describe
this invention? What other inventions
have you seen that fit that description?

3 🎵 **1.20** Listen to an interview about
what inspires inventions. Choose the
statement that best summarises the
speaker's view.

  a Most inventions are an answer to an
     urgent need.

  b Most inventions are things that we
     didn't imagine we needed until we
     became used to them.

  c Most inventions come from
     companies who want to make a
     commercial profit.

4 🎵 **1.20** Listen to the interview again
and choose the correct option to
complete the sentences.

  1 People in their teens or twenties
     probably can't imagine *doing
     research / following the news* without
     the Internet.

  2 Martha Kay is *a business woman / an
     academic.*

  3 A British parliamentary committee
     said the telephone was *too expensive /
     of little use.*

  4 The presenter uses the telephone as
     an example of a case where a need
     was filled / didn't exist before.

  5 Most innovations make our lives
     richer / easier.

  6 The presenter suggests that women
     in the 1960s liked *going out to shop /
     staying in the house.*

  7 The mobile phone and the computer
     are examples of innovations that
     were *very expensive at first / seen as
     unnecessary.*

  8 *Literary Digest* predicted that the
     motor car would *remain a luxury / go
     out of fashion.*

5 What fact or point of view did you find
most interesting? Why? Discuss with
your partner.

Charles Steinlauf's invention: a four-position
bicycle which also contains a built-in sewing machine

Vocabulary phrasal verb *come*

6 Look at the sentences from the interview (1–3) which use
phrasal verbs with *come*. Choose the correct meaning (a–c).
Then do the same for the other phrasal verbs (4–6).

  1 But how do such inventions **come about**?
     a succeed   b happen   c work

  2 Entrepreneurs often **come up with** ideas that will make
     our lives a little more convenient …
     a think of   b ignore   c search for

  3 What it **comes down to** in the end is wants rather than
     needs.
     a relies on   b emphasises   c is a question of

  4 A researcher **came across** the material for sticking post-it
     notes when looking for a new kind of glue.
     a thought of   b found by chance   c stole

  5 People's early experiments with flying didn't really **come
     off**.
     a succeed   b get noticed
     c get taken seriously

  6 Perrelet was so respected that when other watchmakers
     came up against a problem, they would consult him.
     a solved   b encountered   c analysed

7 Work in pairs. Write three sentences using the phrasal verbs
in Exercise 6. Then read your sentences to your partner
omitting the verb and see if they can guess the missing verb.

Language focus past modals

8 Look at the sentences from the interview (1–4) which use past modal verbs. Match each sentence with the function of the modal verb (a–d).

1 It's difficult to imagine what life **must have been** like before the invention of certain things.
2 In 1878, a British parliamentary committee **had to comment** on the usefulness of the telephone.
3 Perhaps they **should have been** more open-minded.
4 But in 1878 people **didn't need to have** phones.

a to talk about obligation
b to talk about necessity / lack of necessity
c to speculate about the past
d to say what was advisable/inadvisable

▶ **PAST MODALS**

Obligation
They had to patent the product before trying to sell it.

Necessity
They needed to have a way to communicate more quickly.
They didn't need to / have to make the instructions very complicated.
They needn't have made the instructions so complicated.

Speculation
He must have realised it was an important discovery.
He may/might/could have wanted to keep it a secret.
It can't/couldn't have been easy to convince people of the idea.

Advisability
They should have included more safety features.
They ought to have tested it properly first.

Note: *needn't have done* means it wasn't necessary but they did it anyway; with *didn't need to do* we don't know if they did it or not.

For further information and practice, see page 160.

---

9 Look at the language box and complete the sentences using past modals. Sometimes more than one answer is possible.

1 Before cars were invented, it ⎯⎯⎯⎯⎯ (not / be) easy to take your family for a weekend outing.
2 In the 1940s, people ⎯⎯⎯⎯⎯ (not / own) a television, because they could get news and entertainment from their radios.
3 Before satellite navigation in cars, people ⎯⎯⎯⎯⎯ (depend) on a passenger for directions.
4 Some people ⎯⎯⎯⎯⎯ (drive) with the steering wheel in one hand and a map in the other.
5 I ⎯⎯⎯⎯⎯ (buy) this microwave oven. I never use it.
6 Before we all had digital cameras, it ⎯⎯⎯⎯⎯ (be) expensive to keep buying film for your camera.
7 The electric spaghetti fork is a useless invention. The inventor really ⎯⎯⎯⎯⎯ (bother).
8 The inventor of 'cats eyes' in the road ⎯⎯⎯⎯⎯ (be given) a medal. They have saved so many lives.
9 When James Watt invented the steam engine, he ⎯⎯⎯⎯⎯ (realise) that the railway locomotive would follow.
10 Who knows what inventions people like Leonardo da Vinci ⎯⎯⎯⎯⎯ (come) up with if they had had modern technology!

10 Pronunciation weak forms

a 🔊 **1.21** Circle the weak forms (not stressed) in these phrases using past modals. Then listen and check.

1 You should have told me.
2 Did you have to wait?
3 He must have forgotten.
4 You needn't have worried.
5 She may have left already.
6 I didn't need to be there.

b 🔊 **1.22** Work in pairs. Listen to how these phrases are pronounced and underline the stressed words. What is the difference in meaning in each one?

1 a You might have told me.
  b You might have told me.
2 a You shouldn't have waited.
  b Flowers? Oh, you shouldn't have.

11 Work in groups. Use past modals to speculate on the answers to these questions.

How did people:
- wake up in time before there were alarm clocks?
- keep money safe before savings banks existed?
- amuse themselves in the evenings without electricity?
- deal with pains and aches without medicines?
- contact each other in an emergency before the telephone existed?
- light candles before matches were invented?
- find out if bones were broken before x-rays existed?

Speaking

12 Work in pairs. Think of two commonly used inventions: one that you couldn't live without and one that you find unnecessary. Discuss the inventions with your partner and the reasons why you chose them.

TALK ABOUT ▶ WHAT YOU CAN'T LIVE WITHOUT ▶ ORIGAMI IDEAS ▶ BEING ON THE SPOT ▶ MAKING A SHORT PITCH
WRITE ▶ HOW THINGS WORK

47

4b Fold everything

Reading

1 Look at the picture of a horse made using origami, the traditional Japanese art of paper folding. Answer the questions.

    1   Do you do any kind of hand crafts? What are they?
    2   Have you ever tried origami? What did you make?

2 Work in pairs. What are the basic principles of origami? Are these sentences true (T) or false (F)? Read the first paragraph of the article and check your answers.

    1   You need more than one piece of paper.
    2   The paper should be square.
    3   You mustn't use scissors.
    4   Sometimes you need to use glue.

3 Read the rest of the article and find the following.

    1   two things used in space exploration that are folded using origami techniques
    2   two origami-inspired devices that help to save lives
    3   a use of origami that seems like a fantasy
    4   a use of origami that can make machines more powerful

Fold EVERYTHING

Almost certainly you have at one time in your life practised origami, even if it was just making a paper aeroplane. Perhaps it was something more sophisticated like a paper crane. The chances are that as you did it, you reflected on how ingenious this traditional Japanese art is. Animals, boxes, flowers, boats – all can be created from a single square or rectangular sheet of paper simply by folding it – no cutting, no pasting.

But did you ever stop to think how the same techniques might be applied to engineer equipment that could be of real practical use? In fact, origami-inspired creations have already flown in space; in 1995, Japanese engineers launched a satellite with solar panels that folded like a map. And very soon origami engineering may well be seen in a host of other applications.

'It's now mathematically proven that you can pretty much fold anything,' says physicist Robert J. Lang, who quit his engineering job in California eight years ago to fold things full-time. Lang, an origami enthusiast since the age of six, advised a well-known car manufacturer on the best way to fold an airbag into a dashboard. He is currently working on a space telescope lens that, if all goes to plan, should be able to unfold to the size of a football pitch.

At the other end of the scale, researchers are also working on tiny folding devices that could lead to breakthroughs in medicine and computing. These include origami stents that are inserted into arteries and open up to keep the blood flowing. Computers of the future are likely to contain tiny, folded motors or capacitors, which will mean faster processing and better memory storage.

There's no doubt that saving space has become important in our world, as the search for ever smaller electronic components shows. But origami also meets the demand for things which need to be small when transported and large when they arrive, like the everyday umbrella.

Applications for origami engineering go further than many of us might imagine. 'Some day,' says MIT's* Erik Demaine, 'we'll build reconfigurable robots that can fold on their own from one thing into another,' like Transformers. Too much like science fiction to be true? Maybe; though you certainly wouldn't bet against it.

* MIT = Massachusetts Institute of Technology

---

crane (n) /kreɪn/ a large bird with long legs
ingenious (adj) /ɪnˈdʒiːnɪəs/ very clever
stent (n) /stent/ a thin rod used in medicine to support a cavity in the body

4 Work in pairs. Explain the following terms and expressions from the article.

1 How is a paper crane 'more sophisticated' than an aeroplane? (para 1)
2 What is meant by 'applications'? (para 2)
3 What 'plan' is referred to in the phrase 'if all goes to plan'? (para 3)
4 What scale is referred to in the phrase 'At the other end of the scale'? (para 4)
5 What does 'it' mean in the phrase 'you wouldn't bet against it'? (para 6)

> **WORDBUILDING past participles as adjectives**
>
> We often use past participles as adjectives.
> a well-**known** car manufacturer, tiny **folded** motors
> In a few cases, the adjective form is different from the past participle.
> It has been **proved**.   A **proven** method.
>
> For further information and practice, see Workbook page 35.

Idioms partitives

5 Compare these two expressions. Which expression means 'some' or 'a piece of' and which means 'a small piece'?

1 **a sheet** of paper
2 **a scrap** of paper

6 Look at the partitive expressions in bold and say which mean 'some' and which 'a small piece or amount'.

1 I'm really thirsty. I haven't had **a drop** of water all day.
2 It was **a stroke** of luck getting those tickets. They were the last two available.
3 There's not **a shred** of evidence to suggest that there is life on other planets.
4 The latest figures offer **a glimmer** of hope that the recession is coming to an end.
5 She had **a flash** of inspiration. Why not use the principles of origami to make foldable furniture?
6 There was **a hint** of disappointment in his voice, but he took the news very well.

Language focus probability

7 Work in pairs. How many examples of the following can you find in the article? Compare your answers with your partner.

1 phrases that say something is possible
2 phrases that say something is probable
3 phrases that say something is more or less sure

Example:
1 *Perhaps it was … (paragraph 1)*

8 Look at the sentences and say whether they use a verb, an adverb, an adjective or a noun phrase to express probability. Is there any difference in meaning or register between them?

1 He probably won't come with us.
2 It's unlikely that he'll come with us.
3 He may (well) not come with us.
4 The chances are that he won't come with us.

> **PROBABILITY**
>
> **Modal verbs**
> may/could/might; should
> Origami may (well) be the answer.
> The telescope should help us to explore the universe.
>
> **Adverbs**
> perhaps; maybe; probably; almost certainly
> Perhaps one day they will invent foldable robots.
>
> **The adjective (un)likely**
> It's (un)likely that this technology will be used in computers.
> This technology is (un)likely to be used in computers.
>
> **Noun phrases**
> The likelihood is; The chances are; There is a good chance
> The chances are that it will be used in robot design.
>
> Note: should is not used for the probability of something bad happening.
>
> For further information and practice, see page 161.

9 Look at the language box. Then rewrite the sentences in the text using the words given.

The grocery shopping bag of the future [1] *will perhaps be made of steel* (could). The folding steel bag, invented by Dr Zhong You from Oxford University, [2] *will probably inspire other packaging solutions too* (likely to). Flat-pack boxes used by industry these days have to be fastened at the bottom. But with Dr You's origami design [3] *you can make boxes with a fixed base* (possible). [4] *This is likely to save industry a lot of time and money* (should).

Dr You thinks that if this process works for steel, [5] *it will probably work for a range of other materials* (the chances). Origami engineers hope that [6] *one day perhaps it will be possible to build houses from flat-pack materials* (might). In ten years' time, [7] *it's very possible that we will be folding away our kitchen counters or table* (may well). [8] *The likelihood is that we won't have foldable TVs or cars* (unlikely), but who knows?

Speaking

10 Work in pairs. Think of three more ideas for how origami methods could be used to help save space in the modern home. Then present your ideas to another pair.

TALK ABOUT ▶ WHAT YOU CAN'T LIVE WITHOUT ▶ ORIGAMI IDEAS ▶ BEING ON THE SPOT ▶ MAKING A SHORT PITCH
WRITE ▶ HOW THINGS WORK

49

4c The shoe giver

Reading

1 Read the definition of *social entrepreneurship* and say which of the examples (a–c) fit the definition and why. How would you describe the other operations?

> Social entrepreneurship is the art of creating a socially responsible business that aims to generate profit while solving social and environmental problems.

a An organisation which collects food near its sell-by date from supermarkets and distributes it free to homeless people.

b An organisation which sells gardening services to companies. The people it employs are all long-term unemployed people who get training, work experience and a small salary.

c An organisation that collects old clothes that people are throwing out and recycles the material to make new clothes which it sells.

2 Read the article on page 51. In what ways does TOMS fit the definition of social entrepreneurship given in Exercise 1? Why? / Why not?

3 Read the article again. Are the sentences true (T) or false (F)?

1 Mycoskie's early career was characterised by establishing and then selling companies.

2 Mycoskie immediately saw the Argentinian children's shoe problem as another business challenge.

3 The main advantage of the one-for-one scheme is that each child is given one pair of shoes.

4 Podoconiosis is a disease that affects children in developed countries as much as in developing countries.

5 The author suggests that, in business, energy and enthusiasm are as important as knowledge.

6 Any business could profit from making a similar one-for-one offer to its customers.

Critical thinking finding counter arguments

4 The author presents a positive picture of TOMS, but there are suggestions that there are also arguments against the initiative. Find possible criticisms in the text in these areas.

a the price and quality of the product
b buying shoes as a way of giving to charity
c the business model

5 Work in pairs. Compare your answers from Exercise 4. Then write some questions for Blake Mycoskie that would challenge him on these points.

Word focus *give*

6 Work in pairs. Find these expressions with *give* in the article and discuss what they mean.

> give it a break   give it some thought

7 Complete the expressions with *give* using these words. Discuss what each expression means.

> best   break   go   go ahead   thought   time

1 There's no need to tell me your answer now.
   Give it some _____ and then let me know.

2 Don't worry if you don't win: just **give it your**
   _____ .

3 I wasn't actually expecting him to like our business proposal, but he **gave us the** _____ .

4 **Give him a** _____ . He's only been doing the job two months. He can't be expected to know everything.

5 It's difficult to be in a new environment, but **give it some** _____ and you'll feel more at home.

6 The only way to find out if you can mend it yourself is to **give it a** _____ .

8 Match these expressions with a similar expression from Exercise 7.

> a chance   consideration   the green light
> a try   a while   your all

Speaking

9 Work in pairs. You are going to act out an interview between a journalist for an ecology magazine and Blake Mycoskie. Take turns to play the roles of interviewer (the journalist) and interviewee (Blake Mycoskie). Think about the questions that were raised about the shoe-giving initiative in Exercise 5.

Student A: You are the journalist. Focus on the possible problems with the one-for-one shoe giving business and ask questions that test Mycoskie to defend it.

Student B: You are Blake Mycoskie. Defend your business and its philosophy.

Blake Mycoskie is a self-confessed serial entrepreneur. He set up his first business, EZ Laundry, a door-to-door laundry service for students, when he was still at college. Having grown the company to service seven colleges in the south-west of the USA, he sold his share to his business partner and moved on to a media advertising business in Nashville. This again he sold on to Clear Channel, one of the industry's leading companies.

Three more businesses later, still only 29 years old, and feeling a bit 'burned out' from work, Mycoskie decided to give it a break for a while and headed down to Argentina for some rest and relaxation. But rest isn't really part of an entrepreneur's make-up. It's in their nature to keep having good business ideas, and it wasn't long before Mycoskie had hit upon the one that would come to define him as a social entrepreneur.

On a visit to a village outside Buenos Aires, he was shocked to see that many of the children didn't have any shoes or, if they did, the shoes were ill-fitting and badly worn. Since shoes – particularly the local farmers' canvas shoe, the alpargata – can be bought relatively cheaply in Argentina, Mycoskie's first instinct was to set up a charity to donate shoes to the children. But after giving it some thought, he realised that this was not a model that would work. One pair of shoes per child would not make that much difference, because they wear out. And if he asked people to donate repeatedly – to provide new shoes for the same child every six months – the donors' sympathy for the cause might also wear out pretty quickly.

Instead he came up with the idea of 'TOMS: one-for-one shoes'. He would take the alpargata to America, manufacture it and sell it as a high end fashion item at around US$50 a pair. (A pair of similar shoes with a well-known brand name costs around $30.) For each pair he sold he would donate one pair to shoeless village children. That way he could guarantee a continual supply. Also, rather than running a charity – something he had no real experience of – he could run the project as a business.

Several years on, the business is thriving, supplying shoes not only to children in Argentina but also other parts of the world where foot diseases are a problem. In southern Ethiopia, a high concentration of silicone in the soil can cause podoconiosis, a disease which severely swells the feet. The shocking appearance of the disease means sufferers are often ostracised from society. 300,000 people in Ethiopia suffer from it simply because they have no shoes. The same silicone-rich soil exists in parts of France and Hawaii, where people wear shoes and are not affected.

Mycoskie had no experience of manufacturing – let alone shoe manufacturing – but he understood that he had to learn fast. For the first eighteen months, by his own admission, he made 'a poor job of making shoes', but since then he has brought in help from people with experience in the industry. The vital element that Mycoskie added was his own passion. It is a passion he wants others to share with him. One criticism of initiatives like TOMS is that the money spent by customers might otherwise have been used to make direct charitable donations. So Mycoskie encourages his customers to become more involved with TOMS by inviting them to volunteer to hand-deliver the shoes to the children in need. It's an intimate giving experience and he hopes it might inspire some of the volunteers to develop similar projects.

But is the one-for-one model one that can be repeated with other products? Mycoskie is doubtful. TOMS is a for-profit business, but does not yet make a profit. He says one-for-one is not an offer that you can just add to your existing business model; you have to build it in from the beginning.

Some would also argue that the charity aspect is just a marketing tool, but in the end does that matter? TOMS is making a real difference to poor children all over the world and Mycoskie is enjoying being an entrepreneur more than ever.

The shoe giver

make-up (n) /meɪk ʌp/ composition, character

ostracise (v) /ˈɒstrəsaɪz/ to refuse to allow someone to take part in a social group

self-confessed (adj) /self-kənˈfest/ the person admits this themselves

swell (v) /swel/ to grow larger

Changing a life begins with a single step

TALK ABOUT ▶ WHAT YOU CAN'T LIVE WITHOUT ▶ ORIGAMI IDEAS ▶ BEING ON THE SPOT ▶ MAKING A SHORT PITCH
WRITE ▶ HOW THINGS WORK

51

4d An elevator pitch

Real life making a short pitch

1 Work in pairs. Look at the advice about public speaking. Discuss with your partner what it means.

" Be sincere, be brief, be seated.
Franklin D. Roosevelt, former US President

2 Do you know what *an elevator pitch* is? Read the text quickly. Then cover the page and summarise the key points.

The principle of an elevator pitch is really like that of a TV commercial. You're trying to sell an idea to someone whose attention you have for a limited amount of time – 30 seconds to a minute before they get out of the elevator. Just as with a TV commercial, the idea is to get the person in front of you interested enough to come back and have another look. So the key things to convey are:

- the problem that your idea solves
- the uniqueness or freshness of your idea

That's all. It's not about selling yourself at this point – talking about your own achievements and experience – and it's not about criticising the competition.

3 You are going to listen to a business proposal based on the idea of doing voluntary work in the local community. Before you listen, discuss the questions with your partner.

1 What motivates people to do voluntary work?
2 What kind of things might people volunteer to do?

4 🎧 **1.23** Listen to the proposal and answer the questions.

1 What is the unique idea that the speaker describes?
2 What problem(s) does it solve?
3 What phrases does the speaker repeat often?

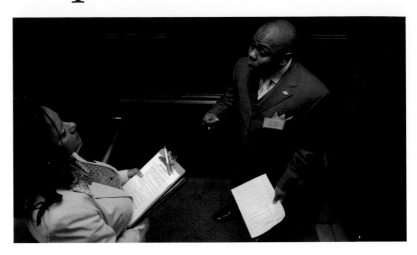

5 Speaking skill using rhetorical questions

🎧 **1.23** Look at the box. The speaker used rhetorical questions. Listen again and tick (✓) the phrases you hear. Then try to recall what he said directly after each question.

▶ USING RHETORICAL QUESTIONS	
What is it?	'So what?' I hear you say.
How does it work?	Isn't it going to be expensive?
Why is it necessary?	So, how do we achieve this?
What does it do exactly?	What's our ambition for …?

6 Pronunciation long and short vowels

a 🎧 **1.24** Work in pairs. Listen to the questions in the box and say if the stressed syllables in these words contain a long or short vowel sound. Then practise saying them.

is   <u>work</u>   <u>ne</u>cessary   do   <u>what</u>   ex<u>pen</u>sive
a<u>chieve</u>   am<u>bi</u>tion

b Underline the word in each pair that contains a long vowel sound. Then practise saying the words.

1 look	loop	5 bottle	both
2 scheme	skim	6 interactive	internal
3 father	fatter	7 forward	foreign
4 training	treasure		

7 Work in groups of three. You are each going to present your own elevator pitch for a new social enterprise. Follow the steps below.

Student A: Turn to page 153 and read the notes.

Student B: Turn to page 154 and read the notes.

Student C: Turn to page 155 and read the notes.

- Prepare your pitch carefully. Use the guidelines in Exercise 2 and the language in the box to help with the structure.
- Speak for no more than a minute.
- Write down the main message of each pitch and at the end compare your answers.
- Vote on who you think gave the most persuasive pitch.

4e Volunteer planner

Writing describing how things work

1 Work in pairs. Read the description of 'Volunteer Planner', a phone app to encourage volunteering in the community. Answer the questions.

1 Who is this description written for?
2 Which of the adjectives best describe this piece of writing?
   a friendly   b factual   c technical   d analytical

Volunteer Planner

Overview

Volunteer Planner is an easy-to-use tool that makes volunteering simpler. The application can be downloaded from the website www.volunteero.com and set up quickly: in five minutes or less. It consists of two main components: a database of volunteers and organisations; and the planner itself.

The database

For each geographical area, there is a register or database of both volunteers and organisations.

For each volunteer, details are listed of:
• their general availability e.g. one afternoon per week
• their contact number
• a brief description of qualifications (e.g. driving licence) and skills

For each organisation, details are given of:
• the type of activity and skills needed
• any special conditions relating to the work
• its precise location

The planner

The planner allows volunteers and organisations to fill slots for volunteers in a real-time calendar through their smart-phones. When a volunteer enters their name in a slot, the organisation is alerted automatically by a text message, inviting them to confirm the offer. By selecting 'accept' on the calendar, the organisation automatically sends confirmation to the volunteer. If the volunteer is forced to cancel this slot at a later date, they select 'cancel' on the calendar. A message is then sent automatically to the organisation; it is also sent to all the other volunteers who are eligible to work for it, inviting them to fill the slot.

2 How is the description organised to make it easier for the reader to follow? Did you find these features helpful?

3 **Writing skill punctuation**

a Find examples of these punctuation marks in the description of 'Volunteer Planner'.

   a colon :
   b semi-colon ;
   c dash –

b Match the punctuation marks in Exercise 3a (a–c) with their correct uses (1–5).

1 to separate items in lists where commas would be confusing
2 to explain the idea in a preceding clause or sentence
3 in place of parentheses ( ) to give extra information
4 to introduce a list
5 to separate two very strongly connected ideas

c Punctuate this passage correctly. Use a colon, two semi-colons and two dashes.

> The three good reasons to use the Volunteer Planner are to help you to plan your volunteering to help the organisation and this is our sincere hope to increase the number of volunteers.

4 Write a description of how something works for a potential investor. Use the idea that you presented in Exercise 7 on page 52 or another idea. Remember to organise your description using subheadings and bullet points.

5 Exchange descriptions with your partner. Use these questions to check your descriptions.

   • Have they written a clear, factual description?
   • Have they organised the description using subheadings and bullet points?
   • Have they used punctuation correctly?

4f Ethical Ocean

Ethical Ocean, a social enterprise

own
WHAT'S
good

ethical ocean ™

Before you watch

1 Work in pairs. What does a *social entrepreneur* do? Discuss with your partner.

2 David Damberger is a social entrepreneur and winner of a scholarship at the Skoll Centre for Social Entrepreneurship in Oxford. Look at the photo. What kind of activities do you think *Ethical Ocean* is involved with? Discuss with your partner.

While you watch

3 Watch the interview and check your ideas from Exercise 2.

4 Read these sentences about David Damberger's background. Then watch the first part of the video (to 01.22) and choose the correct option to complete the sentences.

1 David Damberger is from *Canada / Colorado*.
2 He helped start an enterprise called Engineers *Without Borders / With Ideas*.
3 Their idea was to help people in poor countries to improve *walls / wells* or bridges.
4 They realised that the problem was not a lack of technology or *engineers / know-how*.
5 The problem was *too much bureaucracy / a lack of business ability*.

5 Watch the second part of the video (01.23 to 02.06). Complete the table about *Ethical Ocean*.

1	Type of business:	An e-_____ for ethical goods
2	Description:	A one-_____ shop for everything ethical
3	Categories of goods:	_____ , fair trade, _____ friendly, sweat-shop labour _____
4	Product range:	clothing, _____ , home _____ products

6 Watch the third part of the video (02.07 to 03.12). Look at these words and listen to how *Ethical Ocean* ensures the companies on the site are ethical. Then summarise this to your partner.

1 certification   2 story   3 vote

7 Watch the fourth part of the video (03.13 to end) and answer the questions.

1 What category do the majority of products on the website fall into?

2 What particularly successful product does David Damberger mention?

3 What are the advantages of this product?

8 Work in groups. Discuss what you think of David Damberger's social enterprise idea, *Ethical Ocean*.

After you watch

9 Work in pairs. Look at these products and the list of ethical criteria (a–g). Which criteria are relevant to each product? Which do you actually consider when buying these products?

> car   clothes   cosmetics   electronic equipment
> fruit and vegetables   furniture   stationery   toys

a Are the materials used from sustainable sources?
b Was a lot of energy consumed to make this product?
c Where has it been transported from?
d Did the maker have good working conditions?
e Did the maker receive a fair proportion of the selling price?
f If it is a food product, is it organic (grown without the use of chemicals)?
g Will the product biodegrade or be recycled when it is finished with?

10 Roleplay a product pitch

Work in pairs.

Student A: Imagine you are a representative from a company who is going to pitch a product to *Ethical Ocean* to sell through their website. Look at these points and prepare your pitch.
- think what your product is
- think about what its ethical credentials are
- prepare to sell its benefits

Student B: Imagine you are a representative from *Ethical Ocean*. Look at these points and prepare your questions.
- think about the questions you will ask (price, ethical criteria, product benefits, etc.)

Act out the conversation. Then change roles and act out the conversation again with a different product.

---

accessory (n) /ək'sesəri/ an extra, supplementary item
bunch (n) /bʌntʃ/ a group
credentials (n) /krə'denʃls/ qualifications, proof of a thing's suitability
detergent (n) /dɪ'tɔːdʒənt/ washing powder or liquid
naively (adv) /naɪ'iːvli/ making a judgment that's too simple because you lack experience
sweat shop (n) /'swet ʃɒp/ a workplace where people work for very low wages

UNIT 4 REVIEW

Grammar

1 Read the article and complete it with these words.

chances	could	likelihood	likely	might
must	need	probably	should	unlikely

2 Answer the questions according to the author.

1   What is the problem with most innovations?
2   What is the answer to our future energy needs?
3   Is the writer optimistic or pessimistic about finding alternative ways of generating power?

What is the ^{1} _____ that in fifteen years' time we will still be burning fossil fuels like coal and gas and driving petrol-powered cars? Looking at the progress that has been made with alternative forms of energy, the ^{2} _____ are pretty high. The problem with innovation, especially green innovation, is that each time you think you ^{3} _____ have found the answer, you also find a catch. Wind turbines only work when the wind blows. The inventors ^{4} _____ have realised that, surely? Hydrogen is a clean alternative to petrol, but it is highly explosive and when the first accident happens, there is ^{5} _____ to be a strong public reaction against it.

The real innovation in energy ^{6} _____ will not come from a new means of power generation, but in how the energy network is organised. Advances in IT mean that rather than connecting big power stations to a network that delivers electricity to homes, factories and public buildings, in the future all these places ^{7} _____ be able to generate small amounts of energy, which they ^{8} _____ either use themselves or put back into the network for others to use. The question is: can we make that change? Some say that because it is not in the interest of big business, it is ^{9} _____ to happen any time soon. But look what happened to the music business. We didn't ^{10} _____ to change from a system of buying CDs to sharing music online. But that is what happened.

3 Work in pairs. Are you optimistic about finding a different way to manage our energy needs? Why?

I CAN	
express obligation and necessity, speculate and give advice in the past (past modals)	☐
talk about the probability of things happening	☐

Vocabulary

4 Complete the idiomatic expressions. The first letter has been given for you.

1   I'm not expecting you to produce an idea right now. Just give it some t_____ and see what you come u_____ with.
2   There's not a s_____ of evidence to suggest that this is going to work, but you can give it a g_____ anyway.
3   I came a_____ some old plans for an extension to the house. It was a real s_____ of luck, because I was about to employ an architect to do some drawings.
4   For a long time they were making no progress. Then Natalia had a f_____ of inspiration and suggested using hydrogen. It was then that they made the b_____ .
5   I don't really understand how the invention of the television came a_____ . It didn't really f_____ a particular need that people had.

5 Work in pairs. Have you ever had any experiences of the following? Discuss with your partner.

- an idea which needed some thought
- a flash of inspiration
- a stroke of luck
- an invention that didn't fill a particular need

I CAN	
use idioms	☐
talk about inventions and innovations	☐

Real life

6 Look at the statements from a short product pitch. Write a rhetorical question before each one.

1   _____ ? It's a vacuum cleaner that can clean any type of floor surface.
2   _____ ? Because there's no other machine that can perform all these functions.
3   _____ ? At the base, there's a rotary brush which cleans as it sucks up the dirt.
4   _____ ? Despite its sophistication, we're hoping to keep the cost down.
5   _____ ? By making it in China, where manufacturing costs are much lower.

7 Work in pairs. Think of a product that you use frequently. Present it to your partner as if it was a new product. Use at least three rhetorical questions.

I CAN	
give a short presentation for a new product	☐
use rhetorical questions in a presentation	☐

Speaking

8 Work in pairs. Discuss what device or technological gadget would most improve your life.

Unit 5 The writer's journey

A street at sunset in one of the world's most famous cities
Photograph by Fred Derwal

FEATURES

1 Work in pairs. Look at the photo. Discuss where it was taken and what you know about this place (its character, its landmarks, its people, etc.).

2 🔊 **1.25** Look at the questions and discuss them with your partner. Then listen to a travel writer's opinion and compare your answers.

1 What different factors influence how we experience a place when we travel?
2 What makes a good travel writer?

3 🔊 **1.25** Look at these adjectives. Which ones normally describe people (P), places (PL) or both (B)? Then listen again and say what the speaker uses each adjective to describe.

> romantic   cosy   officious   lazy   elegant
> affable   wary   grand   lively

4 Work in groups. Use adjectives to describe the following places. Use words from Exercise 3 if helpful.

* the city or town you are living in now
* a favourite city of yours

5a Where the Indus is young

Listening

1 Work in groups. Discuss the questions.

1 Have you read any travel books? What kind: travel guides, travel blogs, travel fiction, travelogues, adventure stories, accounts of expeditions?

2 What well-known books (travelogues or novels) have been written about your country? Do they give a true picture?

2 🔊 **1.26** Listen to an extract from the radio programme *The Book Club*, where a guest talks about and recommends a book. Complete the table.

1	Type of book	
2	Setting (time and place)	
3	Subject of book	
4	Adjectives used to describe it	w............... , g...............

3 🔊 **1.26** Listen again and choose the best option (a or b) to answer the questions.

1 Why did Sophie choose this book?
   a the writing is incredible
   b it's an amazing story
2 Who is the real hero of the book?
   a the mother
   b the daughter
3 What is frightening about the descent they make on horseback?
   a there is a deep drop on one side
   b the path is very steep
4 Why did this particular section sum up the Himalayas for the writer?
   a they make people seem insignificant
   b they are so beautiful
5 What does the writer blame for new diseases coming to this area?
   a western tourism
   b modern technology
6 What is Sophie suspicious about?
   a the author's political motives
   b western travellers who want places to remain untouched by western civilisation

> ▶ **WORDBUILDING** *-ing* adjectives
>
> We form *-ing* adjectives from verbs and we use them in descriptive writing to convey a dynamic feeling.
> *falling, gripping, raging*
>
> For further information and practice, see Workbook page 43.

4 What do you think of the decision to take such a young child on such a dangerous trip? Discuss with your partner.

Vocabulary roads and ways

5 Work in pairs. Find the following words in the audioscript on page 177: *ascent*, *path*, *track* and discuss what each word means. Then answer the questions about each pair of related words.

1	**ascent** and **descent**	Which is up and which down?
2	**path** and **track**	Which could not be for cars?
3	**way** and **course**	Which describes the route of a river?
4	**trail** and **route**	Which is only an overland way?
5	**road** and **street**	Which is only in a city, town or village?
6	**motorway** and **highway**	Which is American English and which is British English?

Language focus substitution

6 Work in pairs. Look at the highlighted words in the audioscript on page 177. What does each of the following substitutions refer to?

a the girl   *the daughter*
b This
c one
d to do so
e does
f this
g that
h others
i the former
j the same thing
k not

▶ **SUBSTITUTION**

Substituting lexis
It was a rough track, a path made of uneven stones.

Substituting nouns
It was a brave action, but not a sensible one.
Tea and coffee both contain caffeine; the former even more than the latter.

Substituting verbs and verb phrases
I love travelling in dangerous places, but Sophie doesn't.
I want to have a holiday, but to do so means taking time off work.

Substituting clauses
Not many people know this region.   Yes I'm aware of that.
The road was blocked. This meant we had to find another route.

Ellipsis (omitting words)
She wasn't the first person to write about this region. Others have also written books about it.

For further information and practice, see page 162.

7 Look at the language focus box. Then use the words below to make substitutions for the underlined phrases in the review so that it reads more naturally.

a lot	doesn't	it	one	others	this
to do so	a trip	–			

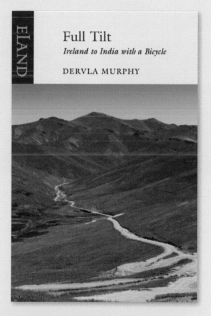

ELAND

Full Tilt
Ireland to India with a Bicycle

DERVLA MURPHY

Some people go out of their way to make travel convenient and comfortable. Dervla Murphy [1] *doesn't go out of her way*. Since she began writing, Murphy has shown a passion for travelling in an eccentric way. Luckily for us, she is also keen to share [2] *her passion for travelling* with us in her writing. Her first book, *Full Tilt,* describes her journey from Ireland to India with a bicycle. This was [3] *a journey* which she had been planning since she was ten years old. Where [4] *other travellers* might not have attracted so much attention, Murphy, being a lone woman travelling on a bicycle, attracted [5] *a lot of attention*. She took a revolver for protection and had to use [6] *the revolver* twice: once to scare off wolves in Bulgaria and once [7] *to scare off* people in Persia. To tell a story in an interesting way is one thing, but [8] *to tell a story* in such a humorous and good-natured way is another. As an example of good travel writing, I can't think of a better [9] *example*.

8 Pronunciation intonation in short responses

a Work in pairs. We often use substitution in spoken exchanges. Complete the answers to each question using one word in each case.

1 You have to be careful not to get ripped off in the local markets.
  Yes, I know _____ .
2 Would you like to drive?
  No, I'd rather you _____ .
3 Did he take warm clothes with him?
  I hope _____ .
4 Do you mind travelling alone?
  No, I actually prefer _____ .
5 Are there many good guidebooks about this region?
  Well, there are _____ .
6 Have you got an up-to-date map of Russia?
  No, but I've got an old _____ .

b 🔊 **1.27** Listen and check your answers. Pay attention to the stress and intonation in the responses. Read the exchanges aloud and imitate the pronunciation patterns.

Vocabulary and speaking a good read

9 Rewrite the phrases describing books using a noun in place of each word in bold.

1 It is **set** in …
  The _____ for the story is …
2 It **describes** a journey to …
  It's a _____ of a journey to …
3 What **appealed** to me about it was …
  Its _____ for me was …
4 The author **is commenting** on …
  It's a _____ on …
5 It's **about** two people who …
  It's a _____ of two people who …
6 It **deals with the subject of** …
  The main _____ is …

10 Work in groups of three. You are going to roleplay an edition of *The Book Club*.

Student A and Student B: You are the guests. Each choose a book to talk about and prepare what you are going to say about your book. Include these points: the genre of book, the author's name, the setting, the theme or basic plot, and what you liked about it.

Student C: You are the radio host. Prepare the questions you are going to ask your guests. Ask questions about their choices: what was different about the book, the style of writing, what they thought about the main characters, etc.

5b The adventures of Hergé

Reading

1 Work in pairs. What comics or cartoons did you read as a child? Do you still read any as an adult? Discuss.

2 Read the extract from an article about the author Hergé and the graphic novel, and answer the questions.

1 What is a graphic novel?
2 Why did readers particularly like Hergé's stories when they were first published?
3 What makes Hergé special among graphic novel writers?

3 Read the article again. Are the sentences true (T) or false (F)?

1 Cartoons are a good medium for readers today.
2 The idea of publishing whole books of Tintin's adventures came after Hergé's death.
3 Hergé did not want the stories to be entirely serious.
4 Hergé's account of a journey to the Moon was based only on his intuition and instinct.

4 Why do you think Hergé's books are so successful? What interests you about them, having read this article? Discuss with your partner.

THE ADVENTURES OF
★
HERGÉ
★

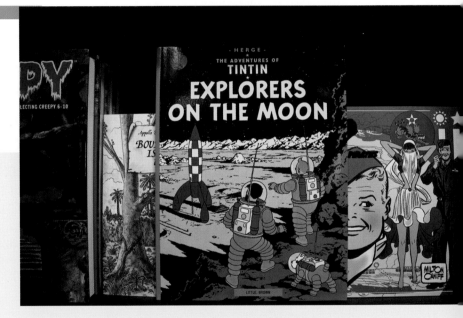

Cartoons suit the way we like information to be presented these days – graphically and in small chunks – and we are used to seeing in our newspapers and magazines cartoons and comic strips that take a wry look at modern life or provide a bit of escapism. But recently we have seen an increase in the number of graphic novels: book-length comics with a single, continuous narrative. Historically, graphic novels were not popular outside France, Belgium, Japan and the USA. The exception to this is the worldwide popularity of a young journalist-detective from Belgium, Tintin.

The creation of the Belgian cartoonist Hergé, *The Adventures of Tintin* first appeared in the Belgian journal *Le Vingtième Siècle* in 1929. Each story was originally read as a cartoon strip week by week, but appeared soon after in book form. One of the main attractions for readers was that they were taken to parts of the world that they had never seen and probably would never see: Russia, the Congo, America. Hergé himself only began to travel outside Belgium later in life, but he was passionate about educating his readers about other cultures and places.

Two things set Hergé apart as a graphic novelist. The first is his technical drawing skills: with just a few simple lines he is able to communicate a particular facial expression or movement. The second is the careful research he put into his stories. In *The Crab with the Golden Claws*, Tintin follows an opium smuggling ring to North Africa; in *King Ottakar's Sceptre*, he foils an attempt at a military coup in a central European country. While telling these stories, Hergé also steers a fine line between serious topics and humour.

Tintin had more than his fair share of adventures, but perhaps the greatest is his journey to the Moon told in *Destination Moon* and *Explorers on the Moon*. Written in 1953, sixteen years before the first Moon landing, the stories show a remarkable eye for technical detail and feeling for the nature of space travel. In the early 1950s, few could imagine what it was like to be looking down at our planet from outer space. And that is Hergé's true gift: to understand what a place was like without ever having travelled there.

foil (v) /fɔɪl/ stop a plot or crime
military coup (n) /ˈmɪlɪt(ə)ri kuː/ a takeover of the rule of a country by the army
wry (adj) /raɪ/ humorous, making fun of something

Idioms rhyming expressions

5 Work in pairs. In a rhyming expression, two words with the same sound are put together, for example, 'snail mail' = letters sent by post not email. Find two more examples of rhyming expressions in paragraphs 3 and 4 of the article and discuss with your partner what they mean.

6 Look at these expressions. Discuss what they mean. Which expressions truly rhyme and which just sound similar?

fair share	fine line	ill will	nitty-gritty*
no-go	real deal*	tell-tale	wishy-washy*

more colloquial

7 Complete these sentences using an expression from Exercise 6.

1 He got the job and I didn't. But there's no _____ between us.
2 Sneezing and feeling hot and cold are _____ symptoms of the flu.
3 It's not a _____ area any more: the war is over.
4 'It's OK' is rather a _____ answer.
5 We need to get down to the _____ : the exact price, quantity and so on.
6 As an example of a sportsman who never gives up, Rafael Nadal is the _____ .

Language focus nominalisation

8 Look at the pairs of sentences below (1–3). Answer the questions (a–d).

1 a Putting collections of cartoons into book form is <u>fashionable</u> now.
   b There is now <u>a fashion for</u> putting collections of cartoons into book form.
2 a The number of graphic novels <u>has increased</u>.
   b We have seen <u>an increase in</u> the number of graphic novels.
3 a Historically, graphic novels, <u>except</u> *Tintin*, were appreciated only in France, Belgium, Japan and the USA.
   b Historically, graphic novels were appreciated only in France, Belgium, Japan and the USA. <u>The exception</u> to this is *Tintin*.

a What part of speech has been changed to make a noun in each case?
b What part of speech follows the noun in these sentences?
c Is there any difference in meaning between the sentences in each pair?
d Which of the sentences (a or b) do you think is less conversational in tone?

> ▶ **NOMINALISATION**

Verb → noun nominalisation
Hergé recognised that his readers wanted to see the world.
Hergé recognised his readers' desire to see the world.

Adjective → noun nominalisation
The characters are original, which is one reason for the books' success.
The originality of the characters is one reason for the books' success.

Other types of nominalisation
The funny characters are partly why the books are so successful.
The funny characters are one reason (why) the books are so successful.

For further information and practice, see page 163.

9 Look at the language focus box. Find examples of nominalisation in the article which mean the following.

1 how popular Tintin has been
2 he was created by the Belgian cartoonist Hergé
3 the thing that attracts readers mainly
4 when the army tried to stage a coup
5 what space travel is like

10 Rewrite these sentences using nominalisation. Note that sometimes (as in items 4 and 5 in Exercise 9) you have to find a noun which isn't from the same root as the verb or adjective.

1 Hergé was inspired partly by Chinese drawings.
   One of Hergé's _____ .
2 He admired these drawings because they were so simple.
   He admired _____ .
3 In later life, Hergé started collecting modern art enthusiastically.
   In later life, Hergé became _____ .
4 Pop art interested him in particular.
   He had _____ .
5 Although he sometimes refers to the politics of the time, the books do not contain a political message.
   Despite _____ ,
   the books do not contain a political message.
6 Hergé has been recognised for all that he achieved with his own museum in Belgium.
   A museum in Belgium recognises _____ .

Speaking and writing speech bubbles

11 Work in pairs. Look at the cartoon strip on page 156. Discuss what you think the story is and complete the speech bubbles accordingly. Then work with another pair and read the dialogues to each other. Were your stories similar or very different?

5c In Patagonia

Reading and speaking

1 Work in pairs. You have two minutes to get an impression of Patagonia.

Student A: Look at the map and the photo.

Student B: Look at the fact file.

Then close your books and tell each other what you know.

2 The author Bruce Chatwin travelled through Patagonia in the 1970s and wrote a book about it, *In Patagonia*. In this extract from the book, he visits a poet. Read the extract and say which sentence (a–c) is true of the poet.

  a Living in Patagonia enables him to produce lots of poetry in peace and quiet.

  b His environment is harsh and he finds life a constant struggle.

  c He is passionate about the nature and history of Patagonia.

3 Read the sentences which summarise the extract and correct the underlined words.

  1 The poet had lived in Patagonia for <u>a few</u> years.
  2 Strangely, he kept <u>sheep</u> as domestic animals.
  3 <u>All the surfaces</u> were covered with Patagonian objects.
  4 He obviously liked to eat <u>seafood</u> while writing.
  5 One of his poems celebrated a <u>glacier</u> being <u>formed</u>.
  6 He was relaxed about his work and wrote <u>a large number of</u> poems.

Critical thinking analysing descriptive language

4 The writer uses descriptive language to paint a picture of the place and the person (the poet). Find the adjectives that describe the following.

  1 the surroundings of the house and environment
  2 the house itself
  3 the poet
  4 the poet's work

5 Work in pairs. Putting the adjectives you found in Exercise 4 together, what is the overall impression you have of this man and where he lives? Compare your answers with your partner.

6 What other descriptions in the passage also contribute to the impression you have?

PATAGONIA FACTS

Land area: 777,000 km² (France is 675,000 km²)

Population density: < 2 people per km²

Industry: sheep farming, whaling, oil and mineral mining

Geography: plains and lakes in the east; Andes Mountains in the west

Climate: cool and dry, wet in the west

Ethnic groups: Welsh, Spanish, other European, a few Indians

Attractions: dramatic landscape, rich in fossil remains

Word focus *cast*

7 *Cast* is a literary word meaning 'throw'. Find an expression with *cast* in the extract. What did the poet use it to describe?

8 Work in pairs. Complete these other phrases with *cast* using the words given. Then discuss their meaning with your partner.

doubt	eye	mind	net	shadow	vote

  1 I'd like you to cast your _____ back to when you first travelled abroad.
  2 They have cast the _____ wide by not asking job applicants for specific qualifications.
  3 Can you cast your _____ over this speech I've written?
  4 New video evidence has cast _____ on the defendant's claim.
  5 You should cast your _____ for the best candidate.
  6 Getting food poisoning cast a _____ over the rest of our holiday.

Speaking

9 Work in groups. Take turns to describe a meeting with someone when travelling and how that meeting affected your perception of the place. Include the following details.

  • a description of the place you were visiting and what you were doing there
  • how the meeting came about
  • a description of the person and the impression that they made on you

In Patagonia
by Bruce Chatwin

Anselmo told me to go and see the poet. 'The Maestro,' he said.

The poet lived along a lonely stretch of river, in overgrown orchards of apricots, alone in a two-roomed hut. He had been a teacher of literature in Buenos Aires. He came down to Patagonia forty years back and stayed.

I knocked on the door and he woke. It was drizzling and while he dressed, I sheltered under the porch and watched his colony of pet toads.

His fingers gripped my arm. He fixed me with an intense and luminous stare. 'Patagonia!' he cried. 'She is a hard mistress. She casts her spell. An enchantress! She folds you in her arms and never lets go.'

The rain drummed on the tin roof. For the next two hours he was my Patagonia. The room was dark and dusty. At the back, shelves made of planks and packing cases bent under the weight of books, mineral specimens, Indian artefacts and fossil oysters. On the walls were a cuckoo clock, a lithograph of pampas Indians, and another of the Gaucho Martin Fierro.

'The Indians rode better than the Gauchos,' he said. 'Brown limbs! Naked on horseback! Their children learnt to ride before they walked. They were one with their horses. *Ah! Mi Indio!*'

His desk was littered with broken almond shells and his favourite books; Ovid's *Tristia*, the *Georgics, Walden*, Pigafetta's *Voyage of Magellan, Leaves of Grass, The Poem of Martin Fierro, The Purple Land* and Blake's *Songs of Innocence*, of which he was especially fond. Smacking it free of dust, he gave me a copy of his *Canto on the Last Flooding of the Ghubut River*, privately printed in Trelew, which combined, in Alexandrines, his vision of the Deluge and a paean of praise

'Patagonia!' he cried. 'She is a hard mistress …! She folds you in her arms and never lets go.'

for the engineers of the new dam. He had published two volumes of poetry in his life, *Voices of the Earth* and *Rolling Stones*, the last named after the layer of glacier-rolled pebbles that cover the Patagonian pampas. The scope of his verse was cosmic; technically, it was astonishing. He managed to squeeze the extinction of the dinosaurs into rhymed couplets, using Spanish and Linnaean Latin.

He gave me a sticky aperitif of his own manufacture, sat me in a chair, and read, with gestures and clattering of false teeth, weighty stanzas that described the geological transformations of Patagonia. I asked him what he was writing at present. He cackled humorously. 'My production is limited. As TS Eliot once said: "the poem can wait".'

It stopped raining and I came to leave. Bees hummed around the poet's hives. His apricots were ripening, the colour of a pale sun. Clouds of thistledown drifted across the view and in a field there were some fleecy white sheep.

---

aperitif (n) /ə'perɪtiːf/ a drink taken before a meal
artefacts (n) /'ɑːtɪfakts/ objects of cultural interest
couplet (n) /'kʌplət/ two lines of a poem that go together
drizzle (n) /'drɪz(ə)l/ light rain
gaucho (n) /'gaʊtʃəʊ/ an Argentinian cowboy
hive (n) /haɪv/ a house for bees to live in
lithograph (n) /'lɪθəgrɑːf/ a print made from a drawing on a flat sheet of metal
oyster (n) /'ɔɪstə/ type of shellfish
paean (n) /'piːən/ a song or poem of praise
pampas (n) /'pæmpəs/ the plains of Argentina
pebble (n) /'peb(ə)l/ a small round stone
stanza (n) /'stænzə/ one verse of a poem

5d I'd like to read

Real life reading aloud

1 Work in pairs. Have you ever had to do any of these things? Tell your partner and then discuss the questions (1–4).

a read an essay at school or college
b recite a poem
c give a presentation from notes
d read at a book group
e read stories to children
f read a formal speech

1 When did you last listen to someone reading aloud? What did they read?
2 When did you last read something aloud to others? Where? What? Why? Do you think you did a good job?
3 Have you ever had to read aloud in English?
4 What tips would you give someone who has to read aloud?

2 Speaking skill engaging your audience

Look at the tips for engaging your audience when reading aloud. Complete the sentences with these words.

> background   dialogue   enthusiasm
> enunciate   pause   volume

▶ **ENGAGING YOUR AUDIENCE**

1 If you are reading from a book, prepare your audience by giving some _____ to the story or its author.
2 Read at a moderate pace and _____ the words clearly.
3 _____ from time to time to give the audience time to digest the information.
4 Vary your _____ , speaking more quietly for calm passages and more loudly when you need to stress words or when the action gathers pace.
5 When reading speech or _____ try to give different speakers a different voice.
6 Always read with expression and _____ .

3 🔊 **1.28** Listen to someone reading an extract from a book and answer the questions.

1 What type of book is the extract from?
2 What writing technique is the reader trying to illustrate with this extract?
3 Who does the character, Martins, think he sees in the shadows? Who is it in reality?

4 🔊 **1.29** Listen to the last part of the extract again and follow the reader's notes. Practise reading the extract to each other.

'… he began to believe that the whole thing was <u>an illusion</u> [stress] caused by shadow. He called sharply. [voice change] "Do you want anything?" [pause] and there was no reply. He called again. "Answer, can't you?" [express urgency] and an answer came, for a window curtain was drawn petulantly back by some sleeper he had awakened and [build volume here] the light fell straight across the narrow street and lit up the features [pause] … of Harry Lime.'

5 Pronunciation enunciation

a 🔊 **1.30** When quoting others it is important to enunciate their words clearly. Listen to two versions of this sentence. In which version are the words ~~enunciated~~ more clearly?

'Passing by the end of the street, he happened to turn and there just around the corner, pressed against a wall to escape notice, was a thick, stocky figure.'

b Practise reading the sentence in Exercise 5a with your partner. Make sure you enunciate the words clearly.

6 Work in pairs. You are each going to read an extract from Bill Bryson's *Neither here nor there*, about an American's first visit to Europe in the 1970s. Follow the instructions.

Student A: Turn to page 153.

Student B: Turn to page 156.

• First read the extract carefully and think about how you will introduce it and read it.
• Make notes on the text to help you read it, following the tips for engaging your audience.
• Read the extracts to each other.
• Then read your extracts again to another pair and compare the way each was read. Which reading did you prefer? Why?

TALK ABOUT ▶ A GOOD READ ▶ SPEECH BUBBLES ▶ DESCRIBING IMPRESSIONS ▶ **READING ALOUD**
WRITE ▶ A BOOK REVIEW

5e Book of the month

Writing a book review

1 Work in pairs. How do you normally choose what books to read? Discuss your answers.

a personal recommendation
b a book review in the press
c the blurb on the back cover
d seeing the film version of the book

2 Read the book review. What is the reviewer's opinion of the book? How does she justify this?

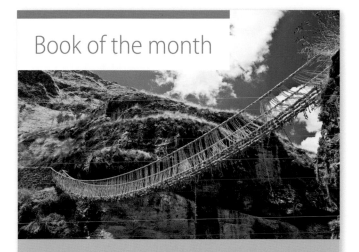

Book of the month

THE BRIDGE OF SAN LUIS REY
by Thornton Wilder

In 1714 a rope suspension bridge in Peru snaps and the five people on the bridge fall to their deaths. By chance Brother Juniper, a Franciscan monk, witnesses this tragedy. He is not only troubled by what he has seen but also troubled by why this should have happened. Why at this precise moment? Why these five people? Accordingly, he sets out to find out something about the lives of each person and so to make sense of the tragedy.

This short novel (only 124 pages long) is a beautiful reflection on the subject of destiny. It is not a true story, but some of the characters are based on real people. Written in elegant prose, each chapter describes the life of one of the five people on the bridge: from the aristocratic Marquesa de Montemayor, who longs to be back in her native Spain, to the wise Uncle Pio, whose lifelong ambition to make a star of a young actress is in the end frustrated. Our interest is not kept alive by the mystery of their deaths, but the compelling characters that Wilder has drawn so vividly: each eccentric in their own way, and each very human in their virtues and in their faults.

I cannot recommend this thought-provoking book highly enough.

3 Read the review again and answer the questions.

1 What type of book is it?
2 What is the main theme?
3 What tense is used to describe the plot?
4 What words describe the style of writing?

4 Look at the different ways to begin a book review. Which are most effective? Why? Which does the reviewer use?

a give your opinion about the book directly
b talk about the writer's background
c describe the opening of the story
d give a short summary of the whole story
e discuss the topic of the book

5 Writing skill descriptive words

a Underline the adjectives and adverbs in paragraphs 2 and 3 of the review. What does each describe? Which two are compound adjectives?

b Complete these compound adjectives.

| fetched | going | moving | packed |
| provoking | willed | written | wrenching |

1 thought-_____ e.g. book
2 far-_____ e.g. plot
3 heavy-_____ e.g. book
4 well-_____ e.g. book
5 action-_____ e.g. adventure
6 heart-_____ e.g. ending
7 fast-_____ e.g. plot
8 strong-_____ e.g. character

c Match the opposites with the correct compound adjective from Exercise 5b.

convincing	easy-to-read	happy	indecisive
poorly written	slow-moving	uneventful
uninspiring		

6 Write a review of a novel you have read (200–250 words). Follow this plan.

- Describe the setting and give a brief summary of the plot.
- Say what the theme of the book is.
- Describe the style of writing.
- Give your opinion or recommendation.

7 Exchange reviews with your partner. Use these questions to check your reviews.

- Is the review organised into clear paragraphs?
- Does it NOT reveal the whole story?
- Are you persuaded by the recommendation?

5f On the road: Andrew McCarthy

That trip changed my life.

Before you watch

1 Look at the photo and answer the questions.

1 Where do you think this is?
2 What kind of trip are these travellers on?

2 Work in pairs. What is the most memorable trip you have been on? What made it so special? Discuss with your partner.

While you watch

3 You are going to watch an interview with travel writer Andrew McCarthy. Watch the video and answer the questions.

1 What was the trip that changed Andrew McCarthy's life?

2 In what way did it change him?

4 Work in pairs. Watch the first part of the interview (to 02.09), where McCarthy describes how he became interested in this trip. Look at the words (a–e) and note why they are significant in the story. Then, with your partner, reconstruct the story.

a a bookstore
b a plane
c the Internet
d Harper's magazine
e a home phone number

5 Watch the second part of the interview (02.10 to 03.08) and answer the questions.

1 What adjectives does McCarthy use to describe:
   a this travel experience?

   b his feelings while on the trip? ....
   c what the experience was not? ....
   d what he felt for the first time? ....
2 What was the reason for the trip that he didn't know at the time but now realises?

6 Watch the third part of the interview (03.09 to end) and answer the questions.

1 What makes him unsure about going again with his children?

2 How long was the trip?

3 Where did he stay?

4 Complete this description of himself: 'a .... pilgrim'. What does he mean?

5 How did he justify being this kind of traveller?

7 Complete the summary of Andrew McCarthy's story using one word in each space.

About eighteen years ago, I was in a [1] .... and I picked up a book by a guy who had [2] .... the Camino de Santiago in [3] .... It sat on my bookshelf for months and one day I [4] .... it when I was looking for something to read on the plane. Having read it, I decided I wanted to do that. There was no [5] .... to research places in those days so I called the [6] .... up and I asked him questions about how to go about doing this trip. I went to Spain for a month and I had a [7] .... experience. I felt [8] .... and frightened but then something happened that [9] .... my life. And for the first time I felt [10] .... in the world. I stayed in little pilgrim [11] .... and to be truthful it wasn't very comfortable, so I sometimes stayed in *pensiones* instead and justified it by saying that this is the way to meet the [12] ....

After you watch

8 Roleplay an interview with a traveller

Work in pairs.

Student A: Imagine you are a traveller. Think of a place that you have always wanted to visit and imagine that you made this trip. Look at the points below and make notes.

Student B: Imagine you are a journalist. You are going to interview a traveller who has made an important trip. Look at the points below and prepare questions.

- what the place was like
- a significant event that happened while you were travelling there
- the effect that the trip had on you

Act out the interview. Then change roles and act out the interview again. Student B should choose a different place.

9 Work in groups. Make a list of five things that make people nervous about travel. Which ones make *you* anxious? Then discuss the items and how you deal with each one.

---

backpack (n) /'bækpæk/ a large bag carried on the back when travelling
bunkbed (n) /bʌŋk bed/ a pair of beds, one over the other
grab (v) /græb/ take hold of something strongly and suddenly
Moors (n) /mɔːs/ the Muslim peoples of northwest Africa
pilgrim (n) /'pɪlgrɪm/ a person who makes a journey to a religious destination

UNIT 5 REVIEW

Grammar

1 Read a travel writer's description of the Fiji islands in the South Pacific. Answer the questions.

   1 In what ways is Fiji an exclusive destination? In what ways is it not?

   2 What impression do you get of the Fijian people?

   3 What is the real Fiji?

Fiji is a collection of over a hundred inhabited islands in the South Pacific; most are the image of what a perfect desert island should be like. So it's no surprise to find a lot of upmarket hotels and beach cabanas catering for rich tourists and honeymooners. I went there hoping to experience this paradise more simply and wondering if it was possible to do so on a limited budget.

I shouldn't have worried about it. The Fijian's long experience of dealing with the needs of different types of tourists means they have provided for this by offering less expensive, youth hostel-style accommodation for backpackers like me in places like Yasawa. Here charming and hospitable locals will help you to feel part of their lives, inviting you to see their fishing villages and coral gardens – even taking you fishing with them, if you want to.

But beautiful and relaxing though these islands are, the feeling of being a tourist remains. It's not an uncomfortable sensation, but if, like me, your wish is to see a country's true way of life, then you should visit the main island of Viti Levu. This is the cultural hub of Fiji, where three-quarters of its population live and where you can experience real Fijian culture.

2 Look at the description again. What words or phrases have the following words from the article been substituted for?

a most (para 1)	e this (para 2)
b paradise (para 1)	f here (para 2)
c do so (para 1)	g want to (para 2)
d it (para 2)	h sensation (para 3)

3 Look at the sentences (1–4). Find similar sentences in the description and underline the part of each sentence that has been nominalised.

   1 It's not surprising that you find a lot of upmarket hotels.

   2 The Fijians are very experienced in dealing with the needs of tourists …

   3 … you still feel as if you are a tourist.

   4 … if you want to see how people really live in a country …

I CAN	
use substitution to avoid repetition and write more naturally	☐
form nouns from other parts of speech (nominalisation) to adjust register	☐

Vocabulary

4 Complete the sentences about travel and travel writing. The first and last letters have been given.

   1 We followed an old t_____l through the mountains.

   2 Following the earthquake, the area has become a n_____-_____o area.

   3 This part of the country was the s_____g for the novel *Rebecca* by Daphne du Maurier.

   4 We felt a little w_____y about taking the bus as the roads can be quite scary.

   5 The main t_____e of the book is the advantages of travelling alone.

5 Work in pairs. Describe a journey that you particularly enjoyed. What did you like about it?

I CAN	
describe places and journeys	☐
talk about travel writing	☐

Real life

6 Work in pairs. Discuss the best way to read this extract aloud. Then practise reading it to each other.

'Martins stood there, twenty yards away, staring at the silent motionless figure in the dark side-street who stared back at him. A police spy, perhaps, or an agent of those other men, those men who had corrupted Harry first and then killed him: even possibly the third man?'

7 Work with a different partner. Read the extract aloud to each other and compare your reading.

I CAN	
read a passage aloud with dramatic effect	☐
read in such a way as to engage an audience	☐

Speaking

8 Work in pairs. Tell each other about a place you visited that was not as you had expected it to be. What was surprising? Did you like the place? Why? / Why not?

Unit 6 Body matters

FEATURES

1 Work in pairs. Write a short caption to accompany the photo. Compare your caption with another pair.

2 🔊 **1.31** Listen to a woman discussing health and exercise with her friend, Rashmi, who is a doctor. What does Rashmi say about the following?

1 intensive exercise versus gentle exercise
2 the kinds of exercise that she does

3 🔊 **1.31** Look at the expressions to do with exercise and health. Four of the expressions need a preposition to complete them. Write in the prepositions. Then listen again and check your answers.

1 stay _____ fit
2 keep _____ shape
3 watch _____ your weight
4 work _____ at the gym
5 go _____ a walk/run/ride
6 stretch _____ your legs
7 take _____ exercise
8 go _____ a diet
9 keep _____ active

4 Work in groups. Ask each other questions about your fitness using the expressions in Exercise 3.

A: What do you do to stay fit?
B: I walk a lot and I go swimming a couple of times a week.
C: Don't you find swimming boring?
B: Just doing lengths is a bit dull, but it keeps me in reasonable shape.

TALK ABOUT ▸ EXERCISE TRENDS ▸ DESCRIBING AN INJURY ▸ DOES BEAUTY SELL? ▸ DISCUSSING PROPOSALS
WRITE ▸ A FORMAL REPORT

69

6a Exercise around the world

Reading

1 Look at this quotation by the professional swimmer David Walters. What point was he making about exercise? Do you agree?

> An hour of basketball feels like fifteen minutes. An hour on a treadmill feels like a weekend in traffic school.
>
> *David Walters, swimmer*

2 Read the sentences. Then quickly read the article about three people's different exercise routines. Match the sentences to the exercise they describe: Radio Taiso (RT), swogging (S) or yoga (Y). There is sometimes more than one possibility.

1 It's a fashionable form of exercise.
2 It benefits the mind and the body.
3 It is not a strenuous form of exercise.
4 Your body feels as if it is under attack.
5 People have been doing this form of exercise for centuries.
6 It's an enjoyable way to exercise.

3 Work in pairs. Write a suitable heading for each paragraph.

4 Work in groups. Discuss the main benefit of each form of exercise. Do you do any similar exercise yourself? Do any of them appeal to you? Why? / Why not?

> ▶ **WORDBUILDING** *off* and *up*
>
> There are certain phrasal verbs that use *off* and *up* to mean doing something completely or to the end. *dry off, eat up, finish off*
>
> For further information and practice, see Workbook page 51.

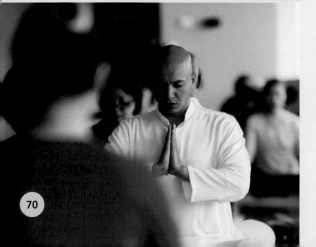

EXERCISE
AROUND THE WORLD

Here are a few of our readers' experiences.

KEVIN

Not many people outside Japan have come across Radio Taiso. Each day at 6.30 in the morning you hear this tinkly piano sound coming out of the radio and everywhere people start doing callisthenics – gentle warm up exercises – to get ready for the day ahead. They're group exercises that everyone can join in with – at home, in the park. That group ethic is very Japanese. People say the idea was copied from US factories in the 1920s. It's fantastic, because it's good fun and they're simple movements that anyone can do – old or young. Also, they get the brain working as well as the body.

JO

I do something called 'swogging': a mixture of jogging and swimming. The inspiration came from a book about people in the Caucasus mountains, who can live to well over a hundred and remain mentally and physically fit. For generations they've been walking down steep slopes each day to swim in cold mountain streams. The idea of freezing cold water might put a lot of people off, but it's scientifically proven to help your circulation and boost your immune system, because it triggers your body's self-defence mechanisms. Then they dry off and climb back up the mountain. I do the same thing in North Wales where I live, but I jog two miles to a lake. It's very exhilarating, but I've a little way to go before I get to a hundred!

NICKY

I went on a group yoga retreat last year in Tamil Nadu. To an outside observer, yoga doesn't look taxing – just slow stretching and holding certain positions. Yoga practitioners came up with their own version of the saying 'Don't just sit there, do something' which is 'Don't just do something, sit there'. But actually it's a very good workout. Like a lot of eastern exercise regimes, it offers a more holistic approach to health by combining bodily fitness with mental well-being. The idea is to concentrate on your breathing to make movement easier and reduce tension. Although it started out in India, only a small proportion of the population there practise yoga seriously. Recently more Indians have taken it up, partly because they've seen it become trendy in the West.

Language focus phrasal verbs

5 Look at the verb + preposition(s) combinations from paragraph 1 of the article and answer the questions.

> come across   come out of   join in with

a Which one(s) are not phrasal verbs: i.e. they simply combine the meanings of the verb and the preposition to give a more literal meaning (e.g. *go into* a room)?

b Which one(s) are phrasal verbs: i.e. they have a meaning different to the separate meanings of the verb and preposition and so have a more metaphorical or idiomatic meaning?

6 Look at the sentences (1–3) about yoga and answer the questions (a–b).

1 It started out in India.
2 In recent years lots of westerners have got into it.
3 Recently more Indians have taken it up.

a Which phrasal verbs have an object?
b What do you notice about the position(s) of the object?

> ▶ **PHRASAL VERBS**
>
> **Intransitive phrasal verbs**
> *We get along very well.*
>
> **Separable phrasal verbs**
> *I don't want to put off anyone.*
> *I don't want to put anyone off.*
> *I don't want to put you off.*
>
> **Inseparable phrasal verbs**
> *I came across a book on Tai Chi at the library.*
> *I came across it at the library.*
>
> **Three-part phrasal verbs**
> *Yoga practitioners came up with their own version.*
> *Yoga practitioners came up with it.*
>
> **Three-part phrasal verbs with two objects**
> *He put the pain down to his failure to warm up.*
> *He put it down to his failure to warm up.*
>
> For further information and practice, see page 163.

7 Look at the language focus box. Then read the descriptions of other exercise routines and put the objects of each phrasal verb in the correct position.

8 What do the phrasal verbs in bold in Exercise 7 mean? Discuss with your partner.

9 Put the words in the correct order to make sentences.

1 I'm thinking / of / up / Pilates / taking
2 I hurt my back playing tennis. It took / it / me / over/ ages / to get
3 My friend has his own dance school. He / up / set / last year / it
4 At school we had to exercise twice a week. We / of / it / get / couldn't / out
5 The doctor / out / some tests / is going / to carry / on my knee
6 How / hit / that idea / did you / on?
7 What do you / put / to / down / its success?
8 It takes / back / my childhood / to / me

Speaking

10 Work in pairs. Read the questionnaire and check you know the meanings of the phrasal verbs. Interview your partner using the questionnaire.

---

❶ How much time do you **set aside** for exercise each week?

❷ What kind of exercise do you **go in for**?

❸ Have you **taken up** any new forms of exercise in the last twelve months?

❹ Do you **keep up with** trends in exercise routines?

❺ Do you prefer to exercise alone or to **join in with** others?

❻ What **puts** you **off** exercising more?

---

11 Compare your findings with another pair. What conclusions can you draw about attitudes to exercise?

Sickness as a child left Joseph Pilates, born in Germany in 1880, frail and weak. To [1] ***get over*** (this), he developed a series of exercises to build core muscle strength. Some of his early students then opened studios using his methods, [2] ***setting up*** (them) in various cities. Pilates is now practised by millions all over the world.

The idea for Zumba ***came about*** by accident in the 1990s. Alberto Perez [3] ***hit on*** (it) when he was taking an aerobics class in his native Colombia. Having forgotten his usual music for the class, he

[4] ***fell back on*** (some Salsa dance music) he had with him. Zumba, a routine combining aerobics with Latin dance moves, was born. Since then it has ***taken off*** and become an international exercise craze.

Most people think Tai Chi is a form of meditation. In fact, it's an old Chinese martial art based on the idea of [5] ***getting out of*** (dangerous situations) by turning an attacker's force against him. The most common form of Tai Chi today is a routine of slow movements. You often see people [6] ***carrying out*** (them) in parks and public spaces.

6b No pain, no gain

Ultrarunner on the 161km
Ultra-Trail du Mont-Blanc
annual race, France

Vocabulary injuries

1 Work in pairs. Look at the photo and caption. What injuries do you think this runner risks?

2 Look at the collocations to describe common injuries. Choose the best noun to complete the collocations.

1 graze your *knee / voice / rib*
2 bump your *tooth / head / toe*
3 pull a *back / muscle / knee*
4 lose your *ankle / voice / back*
5 stub your *toe / ribs / knee*
6 sprain your *ankle / ribs / toe*
7 strain your *head / wrist / back*
8 chip a *tooth / voice / knee*
9 bruise your *head / ribs / muscle*
10 break your *knee / muscle / arm*

3 Work in groups. Put the injuries in Exercise 2 in order according to the following criteria.

a most/least painful
b most/least annoying
c most/least common

Listening

4 🎵 **1.32** Listen to an interview with ultrarunner Ben Newborn talking about sports injuries. Answer the questions.

1 How does he define ultrarunning?
2 What was Ben's biggest fear about doing the Ultra-Trail du Mont-Blanc?
3 What is the mistake many sportspeople make?
4 What is his answer to sports injuries?

5 🎵 **1.32** Listen again and complete the injuries and problems that Ben talks about.

1 He had to overcome _____ and the things that make you feel _____ .
2 A lot of sportspeople try to ignore small _____ or _____ in a joint.
3 Minor problems can develop into more _____ injuries.
4 His exercises have prevented him from getting ankle _____ , lower _____ pain and _____ knee.

Idioms health

6 Work in pairs. The ultrarunner used this idiom in the interview. What do you think it means?

'I'm not talking about when they**'re in a** really **bad way**.'

7 🎵 **1.33** Complete these idioms using the prepositions below. Then listen and check your answers. Discuss the meanings of the idioms with your partner.

down	in	off	on	out	under	up

1 A: I heard Sarah came off her bicycle. Is she _____ **a bad way**?
  B: Luckily she didn't break anything; she was pretty **shaken** _____ though.
2 A: Is it true that Jack nearly cut his finger off?
  B: Yes, he practically **passed** _____ when he saw what he'd done. It was quite a deep cut, but he's _____ **the mend** now, I think.
3 A: You look a bit _____ **colour**. Are you feeling _____ **the weather**?
  B: No, I'm not ill. I'm just **run** _____ from working too much.

8 Match these words with the correct idioms from Exercise 7.

> distressed　fainted　getting better
> lacking in energy　pale　suffering
> unwell

9 Pronunciation linking in idiomatic phrases

a 🔊 **1.33** Listen to the conversations in Exercise 7 again and pay attention to how the idioms in bold are pronounced, especially how they are linked.

b Act out the conversations with your partner, imitating this pronunciation.

Language focus verb patterns

10 Work in pairs. Match the verbs (1–6) with the verb patterns (a–f) that follow them. Then look at the highlighted verbs in the audioscript on pages 177–8 and check your answers.

1	involve	a	to do
2	require	b	someone to do
3	worry	c	someone do
4	make	d	doing
5	tend	e	about doing
6	discourage	f	someone from doing

11 Find one more example of each type of verb pattern in the audioscript on pages 177–8.

> ▶ **VERB PATTERNS**
>
> **Verb + to + infinitive**
> *Accidents seem to happen most when people are tired.*
>
> **Verb + object + to + infinitive**
> *The fallen tree caused the driver to stop suddenly.*
>
> **Verb + object + infinitive**
> *Drinking lots of water helps people feel less nauseous.*
>
> **Verb + -ing**
> *I don't recommend cycling without a helmet.*
>
> **Verb + preposition + -ing**
> *If you think about getting injured, it's more likely that you will.*
>
> **Verb + object + preposition + -ing**
> *She accused him of not paying attention.*
>
> For further information and practice, see page 164.

12 Look at the language focus box. Complete the sentences about sports injuries using the correct verb patterns. You need to add prepositions in some of the sentences.

1 These people often complain ＿＿＿＿ (suffer) 'pink eye' from the chlorine in the water. They also tend ＿＿＿＿ (be) susceptible to shoulder problems.
2 These people risk ＿＿＿＿ (damage) the joints in their legs. But they can avoid ＿＿＿＿ (get) long-term injuries by wearing the right shoes.
3 Since their sport relies so heavily ＿＿＿＿ (use) the arm, these people tend ＿＿＿＿ (have) problems with the elbow and tendons in the forearm.
4 Because these people pull muscles so often, they are encouraged ＿＿＿＿ (warm) up properly before a match. This can prevent such injuries ＿＿＿＿ (occur).
5 Neck pain is common among these people. Because they insist ＿＿＿＿ (bend) low over the handlebars, they are forced ＿＿＿＿ (raise) their heads to see ahead.

13 Which of these sportspeople are being referred to in the sentences in Exercise 12? Discuss with your partner.

> cyclists　footballers　runners　swimmers
> tennis players

14 Often verbs that express a similar idea are followed by the same verb pattern. Look at the sentences (1–8). Choose a verb from the box that could replace the verbs in bold without changing the verb pattern.

> appear　blame　convince　decide　expect
> mean　postpone　stop

1 We can't **prevent** people from having accidents.
2 The organisers were **criticised** for not having paid enough attention to track safety.
3 If the job **involves** straining my back in any way, I'm afraid I can't risk it.
4 I've **made up my mind** to get fit.
5 She **seemed** to pull a muscle as she stretched to reach the ball.
6 Don't **delay** going to the doctor. If you do, it'll take longer to recover from the injury.
7 I **hope** to be playing again in a few weeks.
8 The doctor **persuaded** him to take it easy for a while.

Speaking

15 Work in pairs. Choose one of the following incidents and describe what happened.

1 A time when you or a friend were injured doing a sport or in some other situation.
2 A time when you or a friend narrowly escaped being injured.

6c The enigma of beauty

Reading

1 Work in groups. Mark (B) the faces that you think are beautiful or handsome. Can you explain why? How many do you agree on? Discuss your findings.

2 Look at the sentences and discuss if you think each one is true or not. Then read the article and find out the author's views.

1 There are no universally agreed characteristics of human beauty.
2 Perceptions of a person's beauty can be connected to their social position.
3 Your character can have an influence on whether people think you are beautiful or not.
4 The search for beauty is superficial and vain.

3 Read the article again. Choose the meaning (a or b) that best matches the phrases from the text.

1 *meets the question with a composed reply* (para 1) means:
 a has a ready answer   b is calm
2 *we may as well dissect a soap bubble* (para 2) means:
 a delicate   b impossible
3 *… aesthetic … considerations* (para 2) means:
 a looking nice   b being healthy
4 *hanker after* (para 3) means:
 a you want something
 b you can't achieve something
5 *a shallow quest* (para 5) means the search is:
 a pointless   b trivial
6 *fussed over* (para 6) means:
 a made to feel special   b discussed a lot

Critical thinking identifying aims

4 Work in pairs. Look at this list of reasons for writing an article and discuss which best fits the article *The enigma of beauty*. Underline the parts of the article that support this view.

1 to persuade using objective or scientific facts
2 to persuade using subjective argument and anecdotal evidence
3 to inform and teach the reader something new
4 to inform and invite reflection on particular questions
5 to entertain by telling stories about real or imaginary characters

5 Compare your answers from Exercise 4 with another pair. Discuss the reasons for your conclusions.

Word focus *face*

6 Find two expressions with *face* in paragraphs 1 and 6 of the article which mean the following.

a to be honest   b to look sad

7 Look at the expressions with *face* in the sentences (1–6) and choose the meaning that *face* has in each one. Then explain the meaning of the expressions.

> attitude/expression   confront   credibility   surface

1 He couldn't admit he was wrong. He didn't want to **lose face** in front of the boss.
2 I'm sure she was disappointed not to be picked for the team, but she **put a brave face on** it.
3 I took her offer of help **at face value**. I don't think she had any hidden motive.
4 The actors had trouble **keeping a straight face** when Jon fell off the stage.
5 You should tell her that you scratched her car, because sooner or later you will have to **face the music**.
6 **On the face of it** it seems like a good idea, but I wouldn't rush into making a decision.

Speaking

8 Work in pairs. You work for an advertising company and you are planning an advertising campaign for a face cream that your company is launching. Read your role cards and prepare ideas for the campaign. Decide on the name of your product, then act out the meeting to agree on the advertisement you will run.

Student A: Turn to page 155.

Student B: Turn to page 156.

Sheli Jeffry is searching for beauty. As a scout for Ford, one of the world's top model agencies, Jeffry scans up to 200 young women every Thursday afternoon. They queue up and one by one the line diminishes. Tears roll and there are long faces as the refrain 'You're not what we're looking for right now' extinguishes the conversation – and hope. Confronted with this, one hopeful, Rebecca from Providence, asks: 'What are you looking for? Can you tell me exactly?' Jeffry meets the question with a composed reply. 'It's hard to say. I know it when I see it.'

Define beauty? Some say we may as well dissect a soap bubble; that beauty is only in the eye of the beholder. Yet it does seem that across different cultures we can agree on certain points. Psychologists have proven this by testing the attractiveness of different faces on children. Symmetry is one characteristic that meets with general approval; averageness is another: we seem to prefer features that are not extreme. Things that speak of strength and good health – a glowing complexion and full lips in women, a strong jaw in men – are also universal qualities. Scientists maintain that this is the true definition of beauty, because for them we are influenced not by aesthetic but by biological considerations: the need to produce healthy children.

At the same time we also observe cultural differences in how beauty is defined. The women of the Paaung tribe in Myanmar put copper coils around their necks to extend them because in their culture very long necks are considered beautiful. In China and Japan small feet are admired in women, though thankfully the ancient practice of foot-binding has long since disappeared. In cultures where people's skin is of a dark complexion, it is often seen as desirable to have a fair skin. Conversely, in the northern hemisphere among the naturally fair-skinned, people hanker after a tanned skin.

Perceptions of beauty also change over time. Historically in northern Europe, a tanned skin belonged to those who were forced to work outside – agricultural workers or other poorer members of society – and so a white skin was a symbol of status and beauty. Now a tan reflects status of a different kind: those that can afford time relaxing in the sun on a beach holiday in the Mediterranean or the Caribbean. Our idea of the perfect body shape is also different from 200 years ago. In almost all cultures a little fat was formerly seen as a positive trait, a sign of wealth and well-being. Nowadays a very different image stares out at us from the pages of fashion magazines: that of a long-limbed, impossibly slim figure. Whatever the perception of ideal beauty may be, the search for it has preoccupied people of all cultures for centuries, from ancient Egypt to modern China.

Is it a shallow quest? We all like to think that beauty is not only skin deep; that personality and charm contribute as much, if not more, to attractiveness as superficial beauty. Certainly, as we grow older, the more generous our definition of beauty seems to become. Experience teaches us to look for the beauty within, rather than what is on the outside.

But let's face it, most of us still care how we look. Until she was a hundred years old, my grandmother had a regular appointment at the beauty salon down the street. A month before she died, I took her there in my car. I stayed and watched as she was greeted and fussed over by the hairdresser and manicurist. Afterwards I drove her back to the nursing home. She admired her fire engine red nails every few minutes, patted her cloud of curls and radiated happiness. She is not alone is getting satisfaction from looking nice. It seems the quest for beauty goes deeper than vanity – maybe it fulfils a deep human need in all of us.

> **glowing** (adj) /ˈɡləʊɪŋ/ bright and healthy-looking
> **limb** (n) /lɪm/ an arm or a leg
> **manicurist** (n) /ˈmænɪkjʊərɪst/ someone who cleans, cuts and polishes fingernails
> **scout** (n) /skaʊt/ someone whose job is to search for people with certain qualities or talents

The
ENIGMA *of* BEAUTY

6d A bold initiative

Real life discussing proposals

1 Work in pairs. Read the ideas about how some governments around the world encourage their populations to keep fit and healthy. Answer the questions.

1 What are the pros and cons of each idea?
2 Which initiative would work best ? Why?
3 Are there any similar initiatives in your country?

1 JAPAN: Broadcast a national daily exercise routine on the radio each morning.

2 WASHINGTON STATE, USA: Make it compulsory for fast food chains to write the amount of calories contained in each item on the menu.

3 QATAR: Encourage companies to install gyms in the workplace so that workers can exercise, before or after work or during their lunchbreaks.

4 UK: Promote exercise activities that are quick and easy to do with public health campaigns.

5 SOUTH KOREA: Getting a good grade in Physical Education at school can help you get into university.

6 PHILIPPINES: Promote sports like karate in school that combine exercise with self-defence skills.

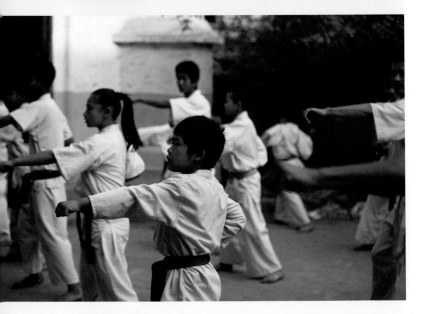

2 🔊 **1.34** Listen to a discussion between a group of human resources managers at a large company about ideas to promote health and fitness among their employees. Answer the questions.

1 Why is this of importance to the company?
2 What different ideas are proposed?
3 Were any of the ideas proposed similar to those in Exercise 1?
4 Which idea got approval from another member of the group? Which idea was rejected?

3 Speaking skill conceding a point

🔊 **1.34** The speakers tried to anticipate objections to each proposal. Look at the phrases in the box for conceding a point. Then listen to the discussion again and complete the phrases they used.

> ▶ **CONCEDING A POINT**
>
> I realise that [1] _____ .
> Admittedly, [2] _____ .
> It's not (a) particularly [3] _____ , I'll grant you, but _____ .
> I know [4] _____ , but _____ .
> I'm just thinking off the top of my head.
> I haven't worked this out exactly, but …
> I haven't thought through [5] _____ , but _____ .
> It wouldn't be so [6] _____ , but _____ .

4 Pronunciation toning down negative statements

a 🔊 **1.35** Listen to these two statements where the speaker tries to reduce the impact of a negative statement. Underline the words which are most strongly stressed in each sentence.

1 It's not a particularly original idea …
2 It wouldn't be so easy to monitor …

b 🔊 **1.36** Work in pairs. Practise saying these sentences where a negative sentiment has been toned down. Then listen and compare your pronunciation.

1 I know it's not a very practical solution.
2 It wouldn't be that simple to convince people.
3 I'm not actually sure of the exact figures.

5 Work in groups. Each think of another idea which will promote the health and well-being of employees in a company. Then present and discuss your ideas. Try to anticipate arguments against your proposal.

TALK ABOUT ▶ EXERCISE TRENDS ▶ DESCRIBING AN INJURY ▶ DOES BEAUTY SELL? ▶ **DISCUSSING PROPOSALS**
WRITE ▶ A FORMAL REPORT

6e A controversial plan

Writing a formal report

1 Work in pairs. Have you ever had to write a formal report? Who was it for and what was it about? Discuss with your partner.

2 Read the internal report about a public health initiative and look at the questions. Underline the parts of the report that answer the questions.

1 What is the aim of the report?
2 What are the main findings?
3 What action is proposed?

3 Read the description of reports in general and say which of the features in bold appear in the report.

> Formal reports present the **findings** of an investigation and make a **recommendation** based on these findings. The important thing is for the reader to be able to scan the document quickly for key information, so **bullet points**, **subheadings** and **short paragraphs** are all useful. Reports present **objective** facts, but internal reports between colleagues can also offer more **subjective** comments.

4 Writing skill linking adverbs and adverbial phrases

a Find the adverb or adverbial phrase in the report that has the same meaning as the words and phrases below. Which ones are used to introduce a more subjective comment?

> as might be expected
> clearly
> in view of this
> on the face of it
> on the other hand
> whatever the justification

PROPOSED INITIATIVE

Over 100 people of different ages and social backgrounds were interviewed to decide on the viability of a public health initiative.

The initiative examined was a proposal for smokers to pay higher health insurance premiums. *Ostensibly*, the proposal seems a logical one since insurance is based on the evaluation of risk. *Evidently*, if a person smokes, the risk of their getting ill is increased.

PUBLIC REACTION

30 per cent of the interviewees objected on the grounds that the initiative was discriminatory. A common argument was that, according to this principle, higher premiums should also be paid by people who overeat. *Rightly or wrongly*, these critics view smoking and overeating not as a question of personal choice, but as something beyond an individual's control.

Not surprisingly, there were many others (55 per cent) who took the opposite view: that smokers ought to pay for the consequences of their behaviour. However, when interviewees were asked if people should be helped to give up smoking, the response was 90 per cent positive.

RECOMMENDATION

Accordingly, we recommend that a pilot scheme be set up where smokers are given free help by their insurance company to stop smoking over a six-month period. During this time, they will be offered various solutions to stop smoking. If they succeed, they will be rewarded with a discount of 5 per cent on their insurance premiums for as long as they remain non-smokers. *Conversely*, if they fail, their insurance premiums will rise by 20 per cent.

---

b Work in pairs. Replace the expressions in bold in the sentences (1–6) with these adverbs.

> alternatively   apparently   interestingly   overall   specifically
> ultimately

1 **It seems that** this idea has already been tested in the USA.
2 **It was worth noting that** 15 per cent of the interviewees did not express a strong view.
3 **To be exact**, it was interference in their personal lives that smokers objected to.
4 **On the whole**, the response to the idea of a trial was positive.
5 **In the end** it will be the insurance companies who decide.
6 **Either that or** the government will take some other measures.

5 Write a short internal report for a company's health initiatives. You can use the ideas you discussed in Exercise 5 on page 76. Write between 200 and 250 words.

6 Exchange reports with your partner. Use these questions to check your summaries.

- Have they presented their aims, findings and recommendations?
- Have they divided the summary into clear sections?
- Have they been objective but at the same time presented a clear argument for the next step?
- Have they made use of linking adverbs and adverbial phrases?

6f Palestinian free running

The beauty of parkour is that you just
improvise with the environment around you.

Before you watch

1 Work in pairs. Look at the sports (a–f). Which are sports that people sometimes play or do in the street? Which are sports that people mainly do in the street? Think of other examples of each type.

a football ....

b volleyball ....

c skateboarding ....

d basketball ....

e roller blading ....

f climbing ....

....

....

2 Look at the photo and answer the questions.

1 What does the sport of parkour involve?

....

2 Who do you think it appeals to and why?

....

....

While you watch

3 Watch the video and check your answers from Exercise 2.

4 Watch the first part of the video (to 01.44) and choose the correct option to complete the sentences.

1 Parkour is an example of a performance art that is found in *modern cities / poor urbanised areas.*

2 Parkour originated in *London / Paris.*

3 Parkour is something you can do without *any equipment / any formal training.*

4 The young men in the video took up parkour *because they were bored / to keep in shape.*

5 Abed says without parkour he *would feel out of shape / wouldn't know what to do.*

5 Watch the second part of the video (01.45 to end) and complete the sentences using one word in each space.

1 Abed's mother feels .... about her son's involvement in parkour.

2 Common injuries include .... and broken arms and legs.

3 In order to avoid injury, practitioners have to learn how to ....

4 Mohammad feels that initially people were .... the sport.

5 It's possible that this .... sport will one day bring these young men wider recognition.

6 Work in pairs. Complete the summary using the correct verbs. Then watch the video again to check.

Since its creation in France, parkour has ¹ .... around the world and recently has ² .... on in Palestine. It's a creative sport, where participants ³ .... moves to negotiate obstacles in their environment. For the underprivileged youth of Gaza, it's a great way to ⁴ .... themselves and ⁵ .... fit at the same time.

Parkour is a risky sport because you can easily injure yourself if you ⁶ .... awkwardly. In spite of being just a sport, there is always the possibility that one day these men might be asked to ⁷ .... on a bigger public stage.

After you watch

7 Roleplay planning a sports campaign

Work in pairs.

Imagine you want to promote sport as a way for people in your city to keep healthy and fit. You think the best way to do this is with street sports. Look at these questions and then plan a campaign.

- What is the target age group or groups?
- What kind of sport would most appeal to this group?
- Where could they play or do this sport?
- What training, equipment and funds are needed?
- Are there health and safety implications?
- How could you encourage people to join in?

Present your plan to another pair. Ask each other questions about the practicalities of each plan.

8 Work in groups and discuss the questions.

1 Do you think sports like parkour should be regulated. Why? / Why not?

2 What are the advantages (and disadvantages) of 'street sports'?

3 If you had to nominate a sport to be included in the next Olympic Games, what would it be and why?

---

apathy (n) /ˈæpəθi/ a lack of interest, feeling unconcerned and unmotivated

awkward (adj) /ˈɔːkwəd/ uncomfortable, clumsy

improvise (v) /ˈɪmprəvaɪz/ compose or perform something without any preparation

poverty line (n) /ˈpɒvəti laɪn/ the minimum level of income needed to live

stunt man (n) /stʌnt mæn/ a person who simulates dangerous actions like falls and car chases in films

underprivileged (adj) /ʌndəˈprɪvɪlɪdʒd/ lacking social advantages, from a poor background

UNIT 6 REVIEW

Grammar

1 Have you or someone you know ever suffered from back pain? What did you/they do about it?

2 Read the blog. Who in the world suffers from back pain? What can be done about it?

Back pain is not a disease. However, it is a common health problem, which affects 80 per cent of us at some time in our lives. It prevents people [1] _____ (work), causes people [2] _____ (become) depressed and affects general well-being.
You could be forgiven [3] _____ (think) that lower back pain is a curse of our modern lifestyle. Many in the West blame our sedentary habits. But back pain is something that everyone around the world seems [4] _____ (suffer) from, whether they spend all day [5] _____ (sit) at a desk or [6] _____ (work) in the fields.
Scientists believe that back pain comes from our being bipedal, i.e. walking upright on two feet. So, unless you **go in for** regular posture training or have a physique that is not susceptible to it, you will suffer from back pain at some point.
What to do about it is another question. You can **look into** exercise classes that help to build core muscle strength. But they are mainly a preventive measure. Some countries have developed cures; in Madagascar, for example, Baobab tree bark is used. But mostly treatment for chronic pain consists of months of painkillers and manipulation before the practitioner can **turn around** the situation. It seems that for the time being, we will just have to **put up with** back pain.

3 Complete the first part of the blog by putting the verbs (1–6) in the correct form: infinitive, *to* + infinitive, *-ing* form or preposition + *-ing* form.

4 Look at the phrasal verbs in bold in the second half of the blog. Replace each noun object with a pronoun. Think carefully about the position of the pronoun.

I CAN	
use correct verb patterns (verb + *-ing* or infinitive)	
use different kinds of phrasal verbs	

Vocabulary

5 Complete the sentences about health and exercise by writing the correct preposition in each space.

1 If I am feeling run _____ , I always go for a long walk and then have a good night's sleep.
2 I fast one day a week. _____ the face of it, it doesn't sound much, but I feel amazing.
3 If I feel I am about to come _____ with a cold, I start taking lots of vitamin C.
4 A lot of sportspeople in their mid-thirties take _____ yoga to prolong their careers.
5 I think the secret to keeping _____ good shape is not eating too much.
6 It's difficult to set _____ time for exercise, but you just have to build it into your routine.

6 Work in pairs. Discuss the statements in Exercise 5. Which do you agree with?

I CAN	
talk about exercise and health	
use idioms and phrasal verbs	

Real life

7 Look at the proposal to install gyms in the workplace. Complete the text with these words.

admittedly	grant	head	out
particularly	through		

Workplace gyms are not a [1] _____ original idea, I'll [2] _____ you, but I think they could be very popular with employees. I haven't thought [3] _____ all the details but the basic idea is to get people exercising during the working day. [4] _____ , this isn't going to be a cheap option for companies. One possibility would be to offer companies tax relief on the investment they make. I'm just thinking off the top of my [5] _____ here. I haven't worked [6] _____ exactly the best way to help companies to fund this.

8 Work in pairs. Think of a health and fitness programme to help teenagers follow a healthier lifestyle. Present your proposal to another pair. Use phrases to anticipate arguments.

I CAN	
present and discuss a proposal	
anticipate arguments and concede a point	

Speaking

9 Work in groups. How are people in your country encouraged to stay fit? How are they encouraged to eat healthily? Discuss.

Unit 7 Stories from history

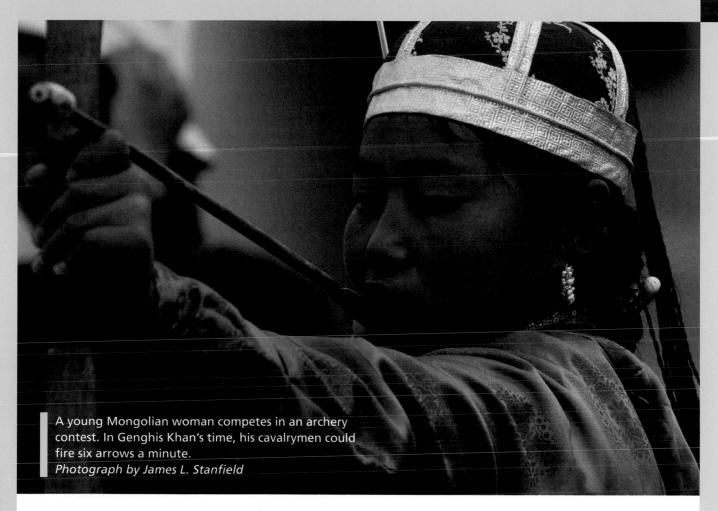

A young Mongolian woman competes in an archery contest. In Genghis Khan's time, his cavalrymen could fire six arrows a minute.
Photograph by James L. Stanfield

FEATURES

1 Look at the photo and the caption. What can you deduce about Genghis Khan?

2 🎵 2.1 Listen to an extract from a radio programme discussing how history views Genghis Khan. Then answer the questions.

1 What facts do we know about Genghis Khan?
2 What is people's opinion of Genghis Khan in his native Mongolia?
3 What is Genghis Khan's reputation in other countries?
4 What are his positive achievements, according to some western historians?

3 🎵 2.1 Work in pairs. The speaker mentions the element of storytelling when narrating history. Listen again and underline the expressions she uses. Then discuss with your partner what the expressions mean.

> there are two sides to every story
> it's always the same old story
> or so the story goes
> the evidence tells its own story
> he wanted to get the inside story

4 Who are the famous leaders in your country's history? What achievements are they remembered for? Discuss.

TALK ABOUT ▶ STORIES FROM HISTORY ▶ SOCIAL HISTORY ▶ HISTORICAL IRONY ▶ CONFIRMATION AND CLARIFICATION
WRITE ▶ DESCRIBING A PAST EVENT

7a The father of history

Reading

1 Work in pairs. Look at the quotation. What is the serious point it makes about history writing?

> Perhaps nobody has changed the course of history as much as the historians.
>
> *Franklin P. Jones, humorist (1908–1980)*

2 Read about Herodotus and his account of the Persian invasion of Greece and answer the questions.

1. Why did Xerxes of Persia invade Greece?
2. Who was Herodotus?
3. What is characteristic of his style of writing history?
4. What is Demaratus' message about the Greeks?
5. How will Xerxes act on this information?

3 Read the extract again. What can you say about the following?

1. how Greece was organised in this period
2. Xerxes' character
3. how Xerxes' subjects felt about him
4. the values that were important to the Spartans

4 What do you think of Herodotus' way of presenting historical facts? Is it effective? Is it accurate? Explain your reasons.

> ▶ **WORDBUILDING noun formation**
>
> Many nouns in English have the same form as the verb they are derived from. Others are formed with a suffix, e.g. *-ment*, *-ion*, *-ance*.
> *defeat, invasion, resistance*
>
> For further information and practice, see Workbook page 59.

The father of history

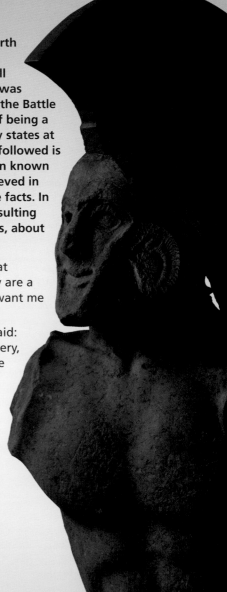

In 480 BC, the Persian king Xerxes I arrived in the north of Greece with an army of approximately 200,000 men, one of the largest armies ever amassed. As well as hoping to bring Greece under Persian control, he was determined to get revenge for his father's defeat at the Battle of Marathon ten years earlier. The Greeks, in spite of being a number of independent, and in some cases rival, city states at that time, united to face the common enemy. What followed is one of the great stories of history, recorded by a man known as 'the father of history', Herodotus. Herodotus believed in the power of storytelling as much as in detailing the facts. In this extract from Herodotus' *Histories*, Xerxes is consulting his Greek advisor, the exiled Spartan king Demaratus, about what he can expect from the Greek army.

'Demaratus, do you think the Greeks will make a stand against us? I imagine that even if they do, their resistance won't last long, on account of the fact that they are a divided people.' After hesitating for a moment, Demaratus answered, 'Do you want me to give you an honest answer or a pleasing one?'

Xerxes promised he would not punish him if he spoke honestly. So Demaratus said: 'All Greeks are brave, but the Spartans especially so. They'll never submit to slavery, even if you secure the surrender of the other Greeks. If only a thousand take the field, they'll still meet you in battle.'

Xerxes laughed at this. 'You don't seriously think that a thousand men, or even fifty thousand, could stand against an army like mine? With a single master, they might fight harder. However, left to their own free choice, they'll act differently.'

Demaratus replied, 'You asked for the truth and I gave it. The Spartans are as good as any men, but when they fight together, they are the bravest of all. Because although they are free men, they are not in all respects free. The law is their master and they fear it more than your subjects fear you. Whatever the law commands, they do; and the command is always the same: never flee in battle, stand firm, and conquer or die.'

Language focus linking words

5 Look at the sentences (1–6) from the extract and answer the questions (a and b).

1 **As well as** hoping to bring Greece under Persian control, he was determined to get revenge.
2 The Greeks, **in spite of** being a number of independent city states, united to face the common enemy.
3 Their resistance won't last long, **on account of** the fact that they are a divided people.
4 **After** hesitating for a moment, Demaratus answered.
5 **However**, left to their own free choice, they'll act differently.
6 **Although** they are free men, they are not in all respects free.

a Which highlighted linking words introduce: a contrast, a reason, an additional point, time?
b Which conjunction(s) are followed by a noun or gerund? Which start a clause or a new sentence?

> ▶ **LINKING WORDS**
>
> ***and, after, although, because, but, since, when*** (+ clause)
> *The Greeks had their differences, but they united against the enemy.*
> *Since his army was so large, Xerxes felt confident of victory.*
>
> ***after, as well as, despite, in addition to, in spite of, on account of*** (+ gerund or noun)
> *In addition to being skilled soldiers, the Spartans were fearless.*
>
> ***following, owing to*** (+ noun)
> *Following his father's defeat, Xerxes was set on revenge.*
>
> ***however, moreover, nevertheless*** (+ new sentence)
> *The Persian army was huge. Moreover, it was well equipped.*
>
> For further information and practice, see page 165.

6 Look at the language box and rewrite the sentences using the prompts so they have a similar meaning.

1 Herodotus is one of the world's most famous historians, but he only wrote one book.
   a Despite ....
   b Herodotus .... However, ...

2 Some people doubt that Herodotus' facts are reliable and have even called him 'the father of lies'.
   a In addition to ....
   b .... Moreover, ...

3 Some people are suspicious of Herodotus' *Histories*, because many of his stories are based on what others told him.
   a .... owing to ....
   b Since ....

4 When Herodotus had completed his *Histories*, he took them and read them aloud to the audience at the Olympic Games.
   a After ....
   b Following ....

7 Complete the description of Xerxes' first battle with the Greeks using these linking words.

> and   as well as   following   however
> in spite of   owing to   since   when

Xerxes was keen to reach and conquer the southern cities of Greece quickly. [1] .... , his army first had to travel through the pass at Thermopylae, which is extremely narrow, [2] .... the closeness of the mountains on one side and the sea on the other. [3] .... the Greeks heard of the Persian route, they put together a force of 7,000 men under King Leonidas of Sparta [4] .... sent them to protect the pass.

It was a battle the Greeks did not expect to win, [5] .... the Persian army was so much larger. [6] .... this, they still managed to hold the Persians off for seven days until a local man, Ephialtes, betrayed the Greeks by showing the Persians a mountain path that took them behind Greek lines. Leonidas, [7] .... keeping 300 Spartans with him, persuaded 700 other Greeks to fight to the end. Surrounded on all sides, they did not last long, but [8] .... this episode, Xerxes was forced to reassess his opinion of the Greeks, in particular, the Spartans.

Vocabulary and speaking stories from history

8 Match the words in bold (1–6) with the definitions in the box.

> achievement   a bad reputation   criminal
> explorer   personal loss   unlucky

1 a **pioneer** who made an amazing discovery
2 a lucky or **jinxed** leader
3 someone who achieved fame or **notoriety** from humble beginnings
4 an **outlaw** who helped people
5 an amazing **feat** in battle
6 someone who underwent a great **sacrifice** to help others

9 Work in groups. Each think of a story from history that you learned as a child. Use the ideas in Exercise 8 to help you. Make notes and then tell the story to the group. Ask each other questions about the story.

7b Microhistory

Listening

1 Work in groups. Think about your favourite toy(s) from your childhood and discuss the questions.

1 What was your favourite toy?
2 Was the toy particular to when you were a child, or can you still buy it now?
3 Did your parents pass down any toys or games to you from their childhood? What were they?

2 🎵 **2.2** You are going to listen to a radio interview about 'microhistory'. First read the definition. Then listen and answer the questions.

---

microhistory: the study of either the daily lives of individuals or communities, or of single events that helps us to understand life in the past. Microhistory asks questions like: Where did people meet socially? What did they eat? What were people's attitudes to children? How did they treat their elderly? What were the main festivals in the year?

---

1 Which question in the definition did the interview help to answer?
2 What was the answer that they found?

3 🎵 **2.2** Look at the questions. Listen again and choose the correct option to complete the sentences.

1 In the past, historians thought that childhood in the Middle Ages:
   a was an emotional time.
   b didn't really exist.
2 The interviewer isn't surprised that in the Middle Ages children went to work early in life because:
   a times were hard.
   b people did not live so long.
3 The objects were excavated:
   a from the river bed.
   b from an area next to the river.
4 When the archaeologist says they 'struck gold' he means that they:
   a found valuable objects.
   b are likely to become rich.
5 The objects they found were:
   a mostly small replicas of everyday objects.
   b mostly military toys.
6 The birdcage and stool tell us something new about:
   a what children were interested in.
   b what people had in their houses.

4 What example(s) were given of toys that still exist today? Can you think of other toys that have stood the test of time?

Idioms luck

5 Work in pairs. Look at this phrase from the interview and match it to the correct definition (a–d). Then do the same with the other phrases (1–5). Two phrases have the same definition.

'… you could say we **struck gold**!'

1 miss the boat
2 blow your chance
3 get your break
4 nothing goes your way
5 hit the jackpot

a have a big piece of luck
b achieve success through a lucky opportunity
c have a period of bad luck
d lose an opportunity

6 Work in groups. Complete one of these sentences using examples from your own experience. Then tell the group what happened to you.

1 I had a feeling nothing was going my way when …
2 I really hit the jackpot when I …
3 I blew my chance to … when I …
4 I got my break to … when …

Language focus subordinate clauses

7 Work in pairs. Look at the sentences from the interview (1–3) and the subordinate clauses in bold. Answer the questions (a–d).

1 **Compared to children today**, I imagine children then didn't have much of a childhood.
2 **As far as historians are concerned**, that is the accepted view of it.
3 **Considering people had much shorter lives**, you can understand why children were made to work.

a Can the sentences stand alone when the subordinate clause is removed?
b Can the subordinate clause stand alone without the main clause?
c Is the subject of the subordinate clause the same as the subject of the main clause?
d How does each subordinate clause give a more complete meaning to the sentence?

▶ **SUBORDINATE CLAUSES**

considering (that), assuming (that), in case + subject + verb
Considering (that) he found the object, I think he should be allowed to keep it.
They protected the objects in case they got damaged.

compared to, regardless of (+ noun or gerund)
It's an important object, regardless of its financial value.

as far as ... is concerned, thinking about it
Thinking about it, we should give these objects to the museum.

For further information and practice, see page 166.

---

8 Look at the language box. Match the two parts of the sentences from the interview.

1 **Insofar as** the objects have great historical value,
2 **Assuming that** these *are* all medieval toys,
3 **Regardless of** what they tell us about children at the time,
4 **In case** any listeners want to see these items,

a the collection will be going on tour around the country.
b some of these objects are things we didn't know existed in medieval households.
c you could say we struck gold!
d they paint a different picture of childhood in the Middle Ages.

9 Pronunciation intonation in subordinate clauses

a ◐ 2.3 Listen to the sentences in Exercise 8. Does the intonation rise or fall at the end of each subordinate clause?

b Work in pairs. Practise saying the sentences with the same intonation.

10 Complete the passage about a work of social history. Choose an appropriate subordinating conjunction.

as far as ... are concerned	contrary to
given that insofar as	in spite of
in view of the fact that	supposing that

Philippe Ariès' book *Centuries of Childhood* was revolutionary [1] _____ it told history from the point of view of the ordinary person, not the ruling classes. But [2] _____ ordinary people were generally illiterate, it was difficult for Ariès to gather documentary evidence about their lives.

[3] _____ some historians _____ , Ariès' research methods are unconventional and unreliable. But, [4] _____ this criticism, his work created a whole new interest in social history.

Ariès' main thesis is that in the Middle Ages there was no concept of childhood. [5] _____ there was no compulsory schooling, children were free to be trained for work around the age of seven. [6] _____ he is right, what does all this tell us? It tells us that, [7] _____ modern ideas about natural child development, it is actually society that chooses when a child becomes an adult.

Writing and speaking

11 Work in pairs. Think about your childhood, your parents' childhood and your grandparents' childhood. Look at the questions and discuss the answers with your partner.

• How much freedom were you given to do what you wanted?
• How much time did your parents spend playing with you?
• How much work were you expected to do (e.g. around the house)?
• When did childhood end and adulthood begin?

12 Write three or four sentences about how you think attitudes to childhood have changed over three generations.

TALK ABOUT ▶ STORIES FROM HISTORY ▶ SOCIAL HISTORY ▶ HISTORICAL IRONY ▶ CONFIRMATION AND CLARIFICATION
WRITE ▶ DESCRIBING A PAST EVENT

7c Diamond shipwreck

Reading

1 Look at the map showing shipping routes in the 16th century from Portugal to the East. Answer the questions.

1 Why did ships make these voyages?
2 What dangers did sailors face on voyages like this?

2 Read the article about the voyage of one of these ships. Discuss the following questions with your partner.

1 What was the purpose of the voyage?
2 What happened four months into the journey?
3 What was ironic about the way the voyage ended?

3 Read the article again and circle the word that does NOT fit in each sentence.

1 Among the objects on the *Bom Jesus* were … and … .
   a spices   b weapons   c treasure
2 The ships themselves were … vessels.
   a advanced   b well-built   c much travelled
3 Details of what happened are difficult to establish because of a lack of … evidence.
   a first-hand   b documentary   c new
4 This part of the Namibian coast is very … .
   a bleak   b hot   c unpopulated
5 The striking thing about the diamonds in this area is how … they are.
   a big   b accessible   c numerous
6 The voyage of the *Bom Jesus* ended in disaster because it was unable to resist the strong … .
   a tides   b currents   c winds

4 Find words in the article with the following meanings.

1 a great journey (para 2)
2 very strong and robust (para 3)
3 not very clear (para 4)
4 unfriendly (para 5)
5 a small suggestion or hint (para 8)

Critical thinking fact or conjecture

5 History is a mixture of known facts and conjecture (things which you guess might be true). Are the sentences fact (F) or conjecture (C)? Find evidence in the article to support your answer.

1 The wreck found on the Namibian coast was a 16th-century Portuguese trading ship.
2 The ship was in good condition when it set off.
3 The ship weas in contact with the authorities in Portugal.
4 The ship was blown off course because it was caught in a storm.
5 The ship sank after hitting some rocks.
6 The sailors managed to get ashore but died there.

6 Compare your answers in Exercise 5 with your partner. How believable are the sentences that you have marked 'conjecture'? Why is this?

Word focus *bear*

7 What is the meaning of *bear* in these phrases from the article?

a … **bearing** the coat of arms of King João (para 1)
b … **bearing** 300 sailors (para 3)

8 Work in pairs. Look at the other expressions with *bear* and discuss their meanings.

1 The sea wall **bore the brunt** of the storm, so that the boats suffered only minor damage.
2 The face on the coin **bears** little **resemblance** to the King himself.
3 He was never promoted and he **bore a grudge** against his employers for years.
4 The hole in the boat **bears witness** to the force of the storm.
5 Months of digging **bore fruit** when they uncovered the ship's mast.
6 **Bear in mind** that the ships of the day were made entirely of wood.

Speaking

9 Work in groups. You are each going to read two historical facts. After reading, ask each other to guess what the irony of each situation was.

Student A: Read the facts on page 154.

Student B: Read the facts on page 155.

Student C: Read the facts on page 156.

This improbable story would have been lost forever if it had not been for the astonishing discovery in 2008 of a shipwreck in the beach sands of Namibia. A company geologist working in the area came across a copper ingot. The ingot was the type traded for spices in the East Indies in the first half of the 16th century. Archaeologists would later find a staggering 22 tons of these ingots beneath the sand, as well as cannons, swords, ivory, muskets, chain mail and exquisite gold coins bearing the coat of arms of King João III of Portugal. From this, archaeologists and historians have pieced together the following remarkable story.

One fresh spring day in Lisbon in 1533, the great ships of the India fleet sailed grandly down the Tagus River and out into the Atlantic, flags flying. These ships were the pride of Portugal, the space shuttles of their day, off on a fifteen-month odyssey to bring back a fortune in pepper and spices from distant continents. Goa, Cochin, Mombasa, Zanzibar: once remote places that were now familiar ports of call, thanks to Portuguese ingenuity and skill.

The ships that sailed down the Tagus River in 1533 were sturdy and capable; two of them were brand-new and owned by the king himself. One was the *Bom Jesus*, captained by one Dom Francisco de Noronha and bearing three hundred sailors, soldiers, merchants, priests, nobles and slaves. She had on board a fortune in gold and ivory to trade at a famous spice port on the coast of India.

But four months or so after its grand departure from Lisbon, the fleet was struck and scattered by a huge storm. Details are sketchy. A report of the voyage by Captain Dom João Pereira, the fleet's commander, has been lost. All that remains is acknowledgement from a clerk in Lisbon that the report was received and a mention that the *Bom Jesus* disappeared in wild weather somewhere off the Cape of Good Hope. It is easy to imagine what happened next: the ship was caught in powerful winds and currents and driven helplessly northwards for hundreds of miles.

Somewhere near the Namib Desert, it struck rocks about 150 metres from shore. The shuddering blow broke off a big chunk of the stern, spilling tons of copper ingots into the sea and sending the *Bom Jesus* down.

And the sailors? 'In a storm, getting ashore would have been just about impossible,' says the archaeologist Dieter Noli. 'On the other hand, the storm might have blown itself out and the ship drifted ashore on one of those quiet, foggy days we also get around here.' And then what? This is one of the most inhospitable places on Earth, an uninhabited wasteland of sand and scrub. It was winter. They were cold, wet and exhausted. There was no hope of rescue, for nobody knew they were alive. No ship was likely to pass, since they were far off the trade routes. As for getting back to Portugal – they might as well have been shipwrecked on Mars.

Yet this place held an extraordinary secret. It was a desert so rich in high-quality diamonds that in the 1900s, the explorer Ernst Reuning made a bet with a companion about how long it would take to fill a tin cup with gems found in the sand. The job took all of ten minutes.

For long ages, millions of diamonds had been washed down to the shore from deposits in the mountains far inland. Only the hardest gems, some weighing hundreds of carats, survived the journey. They spilled into the Atlantic at the river's mouth and were washed up the coast, borne by the same cold current that would one day sweep the *Bom Jesus* to its end.

Whatever happened to the sailors of the *Bom Jesus*, none of them ever returned home. They died somewhere near this mysterious coast, unaware that beneath their feet were more than a hundred million carats of diamonds. They had no inkling of the irony to which they were victim. They had set off on a great journey in search of riches, and now here they were, on a shore of unimaginable wealth.

---

ingot (n) /ˈɪŋgət/ a bar of a precious metal such as gold or copper

musket (n) /ˈmʌskɪt/ an old-fashioned rifle

stern (n) /stɜːn/ the rear end of a ship

Diamond Shipwreck

7d I blame the weather

Real life asking for confirmation and clarification

1 Work in pairs. Discuss the questions.

1 What was the last lecture or talk you attended?
2 Why did you go?
3 What did you find out?

2 Quickly read the abstract of a history lecture. Then cover the text and answer the questions.

1 What will the lecture be about?
2 What general question will it try to address?

LET'S TALK ABOUT THE WEATHER

2.00 p.m. Forth Lecture Hall

Abstract: Weather affects events. Think how your own plans can be changed by snow or even just by a little rain. Then extend this to a larger scale, and you can imagine how more dramatic changes in the climate might have helped to shape human history. For example, how did a drought in Africa contribute to the decline of the Roman Empire? How did a cold spell in Europe lead to persecutions in the 17th century?

This lecture examines the connection between climate changes and specific events in world history and asks whether we pay too little attention to the environment in our studies of the past.

3 🎵 **2.4** You are going to hear four people asking questions after the lecture. Put the number of the questioner next to the topic they ask about.

a the meaning of the term 'Little Ice Age' ☐
b the connection between cold weather and punishment ☐
c the connection between the weather and the rat population ☐
d the connection between the weather and the fall of the Roman Empire ☐

4 Speaking skill prefacing a question and seeking clarification

🎵 **2.4** Work in pairs. Look at the box. The questioners prefaced each question with a comment. Listen again and tick (✓) the phrases they use to preface each question. What is the purpose of these phrases?

> ▶ **PREFACING A QUESTION AND SEEKING CLARIFICATION**
>
> **Prefacing a question**
> If I understood correctly, you said that …
> I'd just like to make sure I understood what you said about …
> I'd like to pick up on one thing you said about …
> The logical conclusion of your argument is that …
> You mentioned …
> Perhaps I missed something, but …
>
> **Seeking clarification**
> Am I right in thinking that ¹ _____ ?
> Can you expand a bit more on that?
> ² _____ . Is that what you're saying?
> Can you explain what you meant by ³ _____ ?
> How do ⁴ _____ fit in with _____ ?

5 🎵 **2.4** Complete the questions used to seek clarification in the box (1–4). Then listen again and check your answers.

6 Pronunciation intonation in questions

a 🎵 **2.5** Work in pairs. Listen to the questions. Does the intonation rise or fall in each one? What rule do they follow about *wh-* and *yes/no* questions?

1 Am I right in thinking that the drought was the cause?
2 Would you go along with that?
3 Can you explain what you meant by that?
4 How do punishments fit in with the Little Ice Age?
5 And what's your own opinion?

b Practise reading the questions in Exercise 6a with the correct intonation.

7 Work in pairs. You are each going to give a short talk about a historical event which was affected by weather. Look at the notes and prepare your talk. Then ask and answer questions. Remember to preface each question with a comment.

Student A: Turn to page 155.

Student B: Turn to page 156.

TALK ABOUT ▶ STORIES FROM HISTORY ▶ SOCIAL HISTORY ▶ HISTORICAL IRONY ▶ **CONFIRMATION AND CLARIFICATION**
WRITE ▶ DESCRIBING A PAST EVENT

7e Krakatoa

Writing describing a past event

1 Look at the photo and caption. What kind of island is this? Do you know any others like it?

2 Work in pairs. Read the short historical account about Krakatoa and answer the questions. Then discuss your answers with your partner.

1 What historical point is the writer trying to make?
2 What evidence does she give to support this?

In 1883, the volcano on the island of Krakatoa erupted with such force that the explosion could be heard 160 km away, sending ash as high as 6 km into the atmosphere. Until then, few people had ever heard of Krakatoa. It was just a small island passed by ships who navigated the straits between Java and Sumatra.

The major eruption took place on Monday 27th August, causing the deaths of tens of thousands of people on neighbouring islands, and destroying two-thirds of Krakatoa itself. But the lasting climatic effects were just as dramatic. In the preceding months the volcano had already been active, discharging so much ash into the sky that it blocked out the sun for miles around. However, the ash that entered the upper atmosphere after the main eruption was blown right around the globe on the trade winds. The following year, climatologists recorded a 1.2° C drop in global temperatures, which did not return to normal levels until some years later.

Unusual global weather patterns seem to have continued in the years following the eruption of Krakatoa. Nebraska, in the USA, suffered an extraordinary winter in 1888, when temperatures dropped 18 degrees in three minutes and up to 125 cm of snow fell in 36 hours – unheard of in those days, when 60 cm was the average for a whole year. Proving a direct connection between these events and the eruption is, of course, impossible, but the evidence is quite compelling.

Krakatoa erupting, Indonesia

3 Writing skill sequencing events

a Work in pairs. How does the writer sequence the different events surrounding the eruption of Krakatoa? Put these events in the order they appear in the text.

a events following the eruption of 1883
b the events leading up to the eruption of 1883
c the eruption itself

b Read the account again and find time phrases about the past which correspond to each of the present time phrases (a–d).

Present	Past
a up to now	1 ....
b in recent months	2 ....
c next year	3 ....
d nowadays	4 ....

c Complete the sentences with the correct time phrases. Use the words given.

Viewed from the present	Viewed from a point in the past
some days ago	They had met [1] .... (earlier)
tomorrow	There were further eruptions [2] .... (following)
at the moment	No one was living on Krakatoa [3] .... (time)
yesterday	Loud noises were heard [4] .... (previous)
from now on	Krakatoa became famous [5] .... (then)

4 Write about an event that happened in your town or region. Use the ideas below to help you. Describe the events leading up to the main event, the main event and the aftermath. Write 200–250 words.

- an extreme weather event
- the visit of an important person
- a sporting event or festival
- a special music event or festival

5 Exchange accounts with your partner. Use these questions to check your accounts.

- Is the sequence of events clear?
- Are the facts presented objectively?
- Are arguments supported by clear evidence?
- Have the correct time phrases been used?

Bringing a piece of
heritage home

Before you watch

1 Work in pairs. What is your favourite type of museum? Which of these categories does it fall into? What do you like to see there? Discuss with your partner.

art   design   ethnographical   general
natural history   science   transport   war

2 Look at the picture. Describe what it shows and where you would find it.

While you watch

3 Watch the video. Who is collecting objects like the one in the picture and why?

4 Watch the first part of the video (to 01.05) and choose the correct option to complete the table.

1	Period of objects in exhibition: *Qing dynasty / Ming dynasty*
2	Owner of objects: *Chinese state / private collector*
3	Where items were bought: *foreign auctions / foreign antique shops*
4	Location of exhibition: *a train station / a shopping mall*
5	Value of collection: *$25 million / $100 million*

5 Watch the second part of the video (01.06 to end) and answer the questions.

1 Who is competing for these objects?

2 What is happening to the price of this kind of item?

3 Where has this phenomenon been seen before?

4 What kind of items did people buy as the phenomenon evolved?

5 What are the two reasons people buy?

auction (n) /ˈɔːkʃ(ə)n/ a sale where items are sold to people who offer the highest amount
embroidered (adj) /ɪmˈbrɔɪdəd/ decorated with patterns or images sewn onto it
finery (n) /ˈfaɪn(ə)ri/ expensive and beautiful objects
hoard (n) /hɔːd/ a big collection of valuable items
lot (n) /lɒt/ an item for sale at an auction
repatriate (v) /riːˈpætrɪeɪt/ bring something/someone back to its/their home country
smash (v) /smæʃ/ break completely
stately (adj) /ˈsteɪtli/ dignified, grand

6 Complete the summary using one word in each space. Then watch the video again to check.

There are an increasing number of private Chinese [1] _____ who would like to [2] _____ objects that have ended up overseas. So they buy up pieces at [3] _____ all over the world and bring them back to China. Often it is one wealthy Chinese person [4] _____ against another to buy the piece and so prices have [5] _____ . But dealers say that there is also a market for more [6] _____ pieces which people buy as an [7] _____ or to help preserve their country's [8] _____ .

After you watch

7 Roleplay a meeting to negotiate a solution

Work in groups of four.

As part of its exhibits, a British museum has some treasure that was found on board a Portuguese 16th-century trading ship that had sunk at sea off the coast of South Africa (weapons, coins and art objects). The treasure was discovered by a British explorer in the 19th century and brought back to Britain. When the explorer died, his family gave the treasure to the museum. Portugal says this treasure is an important part of its cultural heritage and would like it returned. You are going to act out a meeting to try to negotiate what to do with the treasure.

Possible areas for negotiation:

- selling the pieces back
- loaning the pieces now and again
- sharing the pieces

Students A and B: Imagine you represent the museum. You think the treasure should stay in a world-famous museum. Read the information and the possible areas for negotiation and prepare your argument.

Students C and D: Imagine you represent the interests of Portugal. You would like the treasure returned. Read the information and the possible areas for negotiation and prepare your argument.

Act out the meeting to negotiate what to do with the treasure and try to come to a solution.

8 Work in groups. Think of three important objects in your country (e.g. monuments or artefacts in a museum) that best reflect your country's heritage. Describe them to your group and explain why you think they are significant.

UNIT 7 REVIEW

Grammar

1 Read the text about the history of four different geographers and answer the questions.

   1 What were these people's contribution to the field of geography?
     a George Everest   c George Custer
     b Homer   d James Whistler

   2 How is each of them remembered?

2 Choose the correct option to complete each subordinate clause.

Few geographers die famous. Take the geographer and surveyor George Everest. Considering [1] *he had / having* the world's highest mountain named after him, you'd think we would associate Mount Everest with him. However, compared to [2] *there are climbers / climbers* Hillary and Tenzing, who first conquered the mountain, Everest himself is relatively unknown.
There are also cases of people in history who were geographers but are remembered for other achievements. For example, although the Greek poet Homer [3] *is / being* sometimes referred to as 'the father of geography', he is best remembered for writing the *Iliad* and the *Odyssey*. George Custer, as well as [4] *he served / serving* as a cavalry commander in the US wars against the Plains Indians, where he suffered defeat at the Battle of the Little Bighorn, also served in the Corps of Topographical Engineers. Thanks to his skills, the army was able to map enemy positions during the Civil War. As far as his employers [5] *were / being* concerned, they would probably have preferred it if he had stuck to drawing maps!
My favourite unsung geographer, however, is James Whistler, the American artist best known for the painting 'Whistler's Mother'. Since [6] *he was / being* a talented draftsman, Whistler was employed by the US Coast Survey Engraving Division to make maps. He would often get bored by the work and start adding his own artistic flourishes to serious government documents, not to mention [7] *he doodled / doodling* on the office walls. Following [8] *there was one / one* such incident, when he added seagulls to a map of Anacapa, he was strongly disciplined.

I CAN	
use linking words to connect ideas	☐
make sentences with subordinate clauses	☐

Vocabulary

3 Complete the sentences about historical events using these words.

evidence   feat   ill-fated   old   outlaw
sacrifices

   1 Robin Hood was a(n) _____ who stole from the rich and gave to the poor.
   2 Napoleon's invasion of Russia was a(n) _____ expedition which ended in defeat.
   3 Some people dispute that there was ever a town on this site, but the archaeological _____ tells its own story.
   4 Alexander the Great's conquest of Persia was an amazing _____ for such a young man.
   5 Mother Theresa of Calcutta made great personal _____ to help the poor and sick.
   6 It's always the same _____ story. Once people gain power, they forget about the people who helped to put them there.

4 Work in pairs. Use phrases from Exercise 3 to describe four historical events (e.g. the sinking of the *Titanic*, the first landing on the Moon).

I CAN	
describe events from history	☐
talk about luck and chance	☐

Real life

5 Complete the comments made by different members of the audience at a lecture.

   1 If I understood _____ , you said that the Portuguese ship was part of a fleet of ships.
   2 I'd like to _____ up on something you said about the design of the ship.
   3 Perhaps I _____ something, but I don't see why no one went to look for survivors.
   4 Am I right _____ thinking that no one found any of the wreckage?
   5 Can you _____ a bit more on what the ship was carrying?
   6 How do the weapons found on the ship _____ in with the fact that it was a peaceful mission?

6 Work in groups. Tell each other the name of a game that you know well. Then ask each other questions to check what you know about it already and to find out more information.

I CAN	
use phrases to preface a question	☐
ask for confirmation and clarification	☐

Speaking

7 Work in pairs. Describe an important recent event in your country's history.

Unit 8 Digital media

Van Gogh's self-portrait at the Musée d'Orsay
Photograph by Raul Touzon

1 Look at the photo. What are these people doing and why? Would you do the same? Why?/Why not?

2 ◉ 2.6 Work in pairs. Discuss the questions. Then listen to a journalist talking about digital technology and compare your answers. Do you agree with him?

  1 How do digital media change the way we experience the world?
  2 How do audiences use digital media at concerts and conferences these days?
  3 Does the use of digital media enhance our experiences or spoil them?

3 ◉ 2.6 What different digital media did the journalist mention? Listen again and check your answers.

4 Categorise the activities according to how you use them (a–c). Then discuss your answers.

  a things that you do yourself
  b things you benefit from others doing
  c things you never do

> chat online   download music   post comments on forums
> review products   tweet   upload photos
> use social networking sites   write a blog

8a Sinkholes

Reading

1 Work in pairs. Do you read blogs? Which ones? Discuss with your partner.

2 Look at the features of blogs (a–e). Discuss which features encourage you to read blogs and which don't. Explain your reasons.

Blogs offer:
a   an insider's view on a subject
b   a personal account
c   a writer's passion for a subject
d   a genuine, even if sometimes biased opinion
e   the chance of dialogue with the writer

3 Look at the photo below. Write questions that you would like answered about the photo. Then read the blog and see if it answered your questions.

4 Read the blog again and choose the best option to complete the sentences.

1   The blogger decided to go to Guatemala himself to *see the holes / understand what had happened*.
2   The hole looked *man-made / natural*.
3   He suggests that Guatemala City rests on *insecure foundations / saturated earth*.
4   The official explanation is that *the sewer system was faulty / it was caused by an unexpected weather event*.
5   This sinkhole in Guatemala City is *unlike any other / not the first of its kind*.

Sinkholes

I've spent ten years photographing sinkholes and heard all sorts of explanations – some plausible, some just wild – as to why they occur. (Check out my previous blogs via the link below.) So when I saw these dramatic pictures on the news of a new sinkhole in Guatemala City, I decided to head down there to look for myself rather than take anyone else's word for it.

It's quite a scary sight. The hole, which is 18 metres wide and is estimated to be 100 metres deep, looks like someone has taken an enormous drill and drilled down into the earth. It's not the first time this has happened here. In 2007, a similar sinkhole appeared in a residential district of Guatemala City and was reported to have swallowed about a dozen homes.

It is known that most sinkholes are caused by a build-up of water in the soil over a natural cavity in limestone rock. The weight of the saturated soil causes the roof of the cavity to collapse and all the earth above with it. But in this case, there's no limestone bedrock. In fact there's no solid rock underneath at all. The city is built on rather loose volcanic debris. What is believed to have happened here is that water leaked from the sewer system and caused the ground under the foundations of buildings to become hollowed out. Then at a certain point the ground just collapsed in this extraordinary pipe shape.

So strictly speaking, this isn't a real sinkhole. It's a different phenomenon that no one has a name for yet. Whatever you call it, the effect is both amazing and frightening. One local official said that it had happened after a freak tropical storm caused overload on the water system and that it is not expected to happen again. Local residents seemed less sure. One told me she wasn't waiting to find out. 'My family and I are getting out of here as soon as we can!'

Other sinkholes like this are known to exist and I'd be very interested to hear from any readers if you've seen anything similar.

---

cavity (n) /ˈkævɪti/ a hole in a natural structure
limestone (n) /ˈlaɪmstəʊn/ a type of porous rock

5 Look again at the features of blogs in Exercise 2. Which features do this blog offer the reader? Underline the parts of the blog that show you this.

> ▶ **WORDBUILDING compound nouns**
>
> Compound nouns are a combination of a noun + noun. They are often used for objects and materials.
> *bedrock, guidebook, limestone*
>
> For further information and practice, see Workbook page 67.

Language focus passive reporting verbs

6 Look at these two sentences (A and B) from the blog which use passive reporting verbs. Answer the questions (1–4).

Type A: **It is known that** most sinkholes **are caused** by a build-up of water.

Type B: The hole **is estimated to be** 100 metres deep.

1 What grammatical form follows the reporting verb in each sentence?
2 Do we know who the agent of each of the passive reporting verbs is?
3 Why is a passive verb used, rather than an active verb?
4 Why do we often find this type of verb in news reports?

7 Find four more type B sentences with passive reporting verbs in the article. What are the times of the events they refer to: present, past or future?

> ▶ **PASSIVE REPORTING VERBS**
>
> **Present**
> A: *It is known that sinkholes occur in limestone rock.*
> B: *Sinkholes are known to occur in limestone rock.*
>
> A: *It is believed that the hole is growing larger.*
> B: *The hole is believed to be growing larger.*
>
> **Past**
> A: *It is said that the sinkholes appeared recently.*
> B: *The sinkholes are said to have appeared recently.*
>
> A: *It was reported that the sewers were leaking.*
> B: *The sewers were reported to be leaking.*
>
> A: *It wasn't thought that anyone had been injured.*
> B: *No one was thought to have been injured.*
>
> **Future**
> A: *It is expected that repair work will begin soon.*
> B: *Repair work is expected to begin soon.*
>
> For further information and practice, see page 166.

8 Look at the language focus box. Rewrite the sentences with passive reporting verbs you found in Exercise 7 into type A sentences.

Example:

1 The hole **is estimated to be** 100 metres deep.
It is estimated that the hole is 100 metres deep.

9 Rewrite the sentences about sinkholes in Yucatán using passive reporting verbs.

1 People say that the cenotes in Yucatán are the most beautiful sinkholes in the world.
The cenotes in Yucatán _____ .
2 Historians think they were important to the Mayan people because there were so few rivers in the region.
They _____ .
3 We already knew that the Mayans built important settlements near the cenotes.
The Mayans _____ .
4 The Mayans believed that the cenotes led to the next world after death.
It _____ .
5 Tourist agencies report that these water holes are increasingly popular with tourists.
These water holes _____ .
6 In future, agencies expect that the more popular ones will be closed to the public.
In future, the more popular ones _____ .

Speaking and writing

10 Work in pairs. Choose one of the topics below to speak about and imagine you are describing it to someone who has never seen this. Then tell your partner about your experience of visiting this place/event.

• a place of historical interest (e.g. a building, an archaeological site)
• a place of geographical interest (e.g. a mountain, a national park)
• a cultural event (e.g. a festival, a ceremony)

11 Write your description in the form of a short blog. Use passive reporting verbs. Look at the features of blog writing in Exercise 2. Write about 150 words.

8b Creating a buzz

Speaking and listening

1 Work in groups. Answer this short questionnaire about brands and advertising. Then discuss your answers.

> 1 Think about things you have bought recently (clothes, food, household products, etc.). Which brands are you especially loyal to?
>
> 2 What keeps you loyal to these brands?
>
> 3 What kind of advertising do you think you are most likely to take notice of: TV, magazine, online, other?
>
> 4 Has any new company or product attracted your interest recently?
>
> 5 How did they do this?

2 Look at the photo and answer the questions.

1 What are they selling?
2 What benefits are they offering the buyer?
3 What advertising tools do they use to convey this?

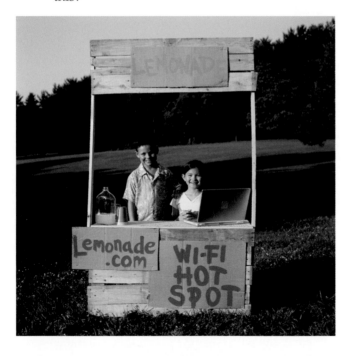

3 🔵 **2.7** Listen to an interview with a social media marketing specialist, Sarah Palmer, and answer the questions. According to Sarah:

1 What must your customers become if you are to be a successful marketer?
2 How often do companies manage to achieve 'a straight sell'?
3 What should companies encourage customers to do on the social networking site?
4 How can marketers of ordinary products engage their customers?

4 🔵 **2.7** Listen again. Are the sentences true (T) or false (F)?

1 It's not enough to be focused on the customer.
2 People aren't really interested in reading facts about the company.
3 *National Geographic* uses competitions to involve visitors.
4 *National Geographic* does not try to sell you anything directly.
5 Even with an everyday product, there are ways the seller can involve the customer.
6 The tea company has a website that educates the visitor.

Idioms business buzz words

5 Work in pairs. A *buzz word* is a word or expression that is fashionable at the moment. There are many examples in business. Look at the words in bold from the interview and discuss what they mean.

1 We hear about companies being **customer-focused** all the time these days.
2 And you, the company, want to get them to **buy into** your story.
3 We've been looking at examples of **best practice** in social media marketing.

6 Match the business buzz words (1–9) with the correct definition (a–i).

1 **At the end of the day**, it's your choice to decide whether to participate or not.
2 How much are we talking about? Give me a **ballpark figure**.
3 It's a great idea, but what's your **game plan**?
4 Keep me **in the loop**. I'd be interested to know what happens.
5 You can understand it, surely? It**'s not rocket science**.
6 Great. I'm glad that we**'re on the same page**.
7 Finding out we weren't the only ones developing this product was a big **reality check**.
8 We're looking for really fresh ideas, so try to **think outside the box**.
9 It's **a win-win situation**.

a advantageous to both sides
b be imaginative
c moment to face the true facts
d rough estimate
e simple
f strategy
g ultimately
h understand each other
i up to date with events

Language focus expressions with *no*

7 Match the two parts of the sentences. Then check your answers in the audioscript on page 179.

1 There's no point …
2 These days, a company has no hope …
3 There's no doubt …
4 Is there no mention …
5 They have no alternative …
6 No matter …

a of doing that unless they use social media.
b what you're selling, if you can involve people you'll find an audience.
c of selling at all?
d being focused on your customer if they're not focused on you.
e but to present the product in an ordinary way.
f that a straight sell can work occasionally.

> ▶ **EXPRESSIONS WITH *NO***
>
> ***no + noun + -ing***
> *There's no point (in) waiting.*
> *We had no difficulty (in) persuading them.*
>
> ***no + noun + of + -ing***
> *There's no way of telling.*
> *I had no intention of going there in person.*
>
> ***no + noun + that***
> *There's no question that it's a popular brand.*
>
> ***no … except/but to + infinitive***
> *We had no choice but to do what they said.*
> *We had no alternative except to invite them.*
>
> ***no matter + relative pronoun***
> *No matter where you go, you find the same thing.*
>
> Note: Only certain nouns are used in these expressions. See page 167.
>
> For further information and practice, see page 167.

8 Look at the language focus box. Then rewrite the statements made by a user of a commercial website using the words given.

1 It's definitely a very well-constructed website. (question)
There's _____ .
2 I found it very easy to navigate my way around the site. (difficulty)
I had _____ .
3 Also, whichever page I visited, there was always something interesting to look at. (matter)
Also, _____ .
4 I liked the fact that I didn't have to buy anything. (suggestion)
I liked the fact that there was _____ .
5 I was surprised that it didn't talk about shipping costs. (mention)
I was surprised that there was _____ .
6 You are forced to accept their delivery terms. (choice)
You have _____ .
7 I think that whatever the retailer does, they must make the buying process transparent. (matter)
I think that _____ .
8 Personally, I didn't intend to buy anything. (intention)
Personally, I had _____ .

9 Work in pairs. Think about a commercial website that you have visited recently. What was it? Why did you visit it? Was it a good or a bad experience? Complete these sentences in your own words. Discuss with your partner.

1 I had no problems …
2 There's no question that …
3 No matter …

Speaking

10 Work in groups. Look at the company profile below. Think of three suitable interactive elements for their social networking site that will attract and engage new customers. Use ideas that you discussed in Exercises 1 and 2 on page 96. Compare your ideas with other groups in the class.

Mosushi is a mobile vendor of Japanese snacks. Based in a large city it has five small vans which sell Japanese meals and snacks, teas and fruit juices from street locations. The company would like to get more of a following on social networks so that it can expand its business.

8c A hacker's life

Reading

1 Work in pairs. How do you (or could you) keep your internet use private and your personal details secure? Think of four ways, using the words to help you. Compare your ideas with another pair and discuss which are most useful.

> back up   download   identity   password
> theft   transaction   wi-fi

2 Look at the two definitions for a 'hacker'. Which definition fits your idea of a hacker? Then read the article about a hacker's conference on page 99. What is the author's view?

---

hacker (n) /ˈhækə/

1 an enthusiastic and skilful computer programmer or user

2 a person who uses computers to gain unauthorised access to data

---

3 Read the article again and answer the questions. Compare your answers with your partner.

1   What do DefCon hackers do to help improve internet security?
2   What are most hackers not?
3   What do hackers look at apart from online security?
4   What do they do with the information they find?
5   What does the writer like about the people at DefCon?
6   What two words sum up what *Capture the Flag* is?
7   What does the writer say about the majority of people who use the Internet?
8   What really motivates the hackers at DefCon?

4 Has your opinion of hackers changed after reading this article? How? Discuss with your partner.

Critical thinking identifying personal opinions

5 Work in pairs. Underline the adjectives and adverbs in the article that the writer uses to express his personal opinion.

Example:
But then comes the <u>worrying</u> realisation that …

6 What would you say, in summary, were the writer's personal opinions about the following?

1   the mixture of people he met at the DefCon conference
2   the security of personal data on the Internet
3   how we should feel about hackers

Word focus *break*

7 Work in pairs. Find three expressions with *break* (in paragraphs 1, 3 and 5) and discuss with your partner what each expression means.

8 Look at the sentences using expressions with *break* (1–6) and match the expressions with the correct definitions (a–f).

1   The manager called everyone together to **break the news** about the company closing.
2   During the first lesson, the teacher got us to play a couple of games to **break the ice**.
3   They are hoping that their new social networking site will really **break the mould**.
4   You really should buy a new pair of shoes. It won't **break the bank**.
5   It's a very big job but I think we**'ve broken the back of** it now.
6   We didn't make a profit but I think at least we **broke even**.

a   do something very different
b   do most of the (hard) work
c   help people relax
d   make neither a profit nor a loss
e   tell (someone) something important
f   use up all one's money

9 Write a sentence using one of the expressions with *break*. Read it to your partner, omitting the phrase, and ask them to guess what the missing phrase is.

Speaking

10 Work in pairs. Some important data has gone missing from an office computer. You are going to act out a meeting between a small business owner and an internet security consultant.

Student A: Turn to page 154. Look at the notes and prepare your answers.

Student B: turn to page 155. Look at the notes. Then prepare to ask questions and give advice.

A hacker's life

Hackers compete in
Capture the Flag.

Have you ever locked yourself out of your home and had to try to break in? First, you get a sense of accomplishment in succeeding. But then comes the worrying realisation that if *you* can break into your own place as an amateur, a professional could do so five times faster. So you look at the weak point in your security and fix it. Well, that's more or less how the DefCon hackers conference works.

Every year passionate hackers meet at DefCon in Las Vegas to present their knowledge and capabilities. Mention the word 'hacker' and many of us picture a seventeen-year-old geek sitting in their bedroom, illegally hacking into the US's defence secrets in the Pentagon. Or we just think 'criminals'. But that is actually a gross misrepresentation of what most hackers do.

The activities and experiments that take place at DefCon have an enormous impact on our daily lives. These are people who love the challenge of finding security gaps: computer addicts who can't break the habit. They look with great scrutiny at all kinds of systems, from the Internet to mobile communications to household door locks. And then they try to hack them. In doing so, they are doing all of us a great service, because they pass on their findings to the industries that design these systems, which are then able to plug the security holes.

A graphic example of this is when I attended a presentation on electronic door locks. Ironically, one of the most secure locks they demonstrated was a 4,000-year-old Egyptian tumbler lock. But when it came to more modern devices, the presenters revealed significant weaknesses in several brands of electro-mechanical locks. A bio-lock that uses a fingerprint scan for entry was defeated, easily, by a paper clip. (Unfortunately, although all the manufacturers of the insecure locks were alerted, not all of them responded.)

DefCon is a vast mix of cultures as well as a culture in itself. People in dark clothes and ripped jeans talk to people in golf shirts and khakis. Social status here is based on knowledge and accomplishment, not on clothing labels or car marques. It's kind of refreshing. There are government agents here, as well as video game enthusiasts. Not that people ask each other where they work – that would break the hackers' etiquette.

In an attempt to attract the brightest hackers, DefCon runs a competition called *Capture the Flag. Capture the Flag* pits elite hackers against each other in a cyber game of network attack and defence, that goes on 24 hours a day. In a large, dimly lit conference hall, small groups of hackers sit five metres from each other, intensely trying either to protect or to break into the system. There are huge video projections on the walls, pizza boxes and coffee cups are strewn everywhere. The room is mesmerising.

In another room, another contest is taking place. Here participants have five minutes to free themselves from handcuffs, escape from their 'cell', get past a guard, retrieve their passport from a locked filing cabinet, leave through another locked door, and make their escape to freedom.

If you're someone who dismisses the DefCon attendees as a group of geeks and social misfits, then you probably have the same password for 90 per cent of your online existence. Which means you are doomed. Because even if you think you're being clever by using your grandmother's birth date backwards as a secure key, you're no match for the people that I've met. There is no greater ignorance to be found online than that of an average internet user. I'm happy to admit that I'm one of them. I'm also aware that there are other people out there – big business among them – who are trying to get more and more access to the data of our personal online habits. Sadly, we have few tools to protect ourselves. But there is a group of people who are passionate about online freedom and have the means to help us protect our privacy. Many of them can be found at DefCon.

---

do someone a service (v) /duː ˈsʌmwʌn eɪ ˈsɜːvɪs/ help someone
etiquette (n) /ˈetɪket/ code of polite behaviour
handcuffs (n) /ˈhæn(d)kʌfs/ a pair of metal rings placed on the wrists to restrain someone
khakis (n) /ˈkɑːkis/ light-coloured smart casual trousers

A podcast

Vaadhoo Island in the Maldives

Real life making a podcast

1 Work in pairs. Discuss the questions.

1   How do you prefer to access news stories and reports?
    a   print   c   video
    b   Internet   d   audio

2   What kind of news stories and reports interest you particularly? Explain why.

> arts and culture   business   politics
> science and environment   sport   travel

2 ⊙ **2.8** Look at the photo and describe what you see. What kind of news report is this going to be? Listen to the podcast and check your answer.

3 ⊙ **2.8** Listen again and answer the questions.

1   What did scientists already know about the cause of these blue lights in the waves?
2   What more do they know now?

4 Speaking skill hedging language

⊙ **2.8** When we aren't absolutely certain of the facts, we commonly use 'hedging' language. Listen again and match the hedging expressions the speakers use with the facts (1–6).

1   … one of the most spectacular sights in nature.
2   … spend most of their lives in dark ocean waters.
3   … being able to light yourself up is useful.
4   … just lighting your way as you move around.
5   … electrical signals in the phytoplankton cause a chemical reaction.
6   … the electrical signal is generated by motion in the water.

> ▶ **HEDGING LANGUAGE**
>
> It seems / appears that …
> … tend(s) to …
>
> This suggests that …
> It's reasonable to assume that …
> We can probably conclude that …
>
> There are estimated to be …
> There are thought to be …
>
> Arguably …
> Probably / Possibly / Most likely / Perhaps …

5 Pronunciation word stress

a ⊙ **2.9** Listen again to the opening sentence of the interview. Underline where the stress falls in the words in bold. Where does the stress generally fall in a) two-syllable words and b) in words of three or more syllables?

'**Today** we're going to look at some new **evidence** about what is **arguably** one of the most **spectacular** sights in **nature**: the **phenomenon** where waves glow at night and **mirror** the stars with lots of **tiny**, blue lights.'

b Work in pairs. Where does the stress fall in the words in bold in this sentence? Practise reading it with the correct stress.

'It's **reasonable** to **assume** that the **electrical signal** is **generated** by **motion** in the **water**.'

c What do you notice about these two-syllable verbs with stress on the second syllable: *propose, confirm, describe, explain, include*?

6 Work in two groups of three. You are going to make a news podcast about a new discovery.

Group A: Turn to page 154. Read the information.

Group B: Turn to page 155. Read the information.

- Discuss what you are going to say and prepare the news story. Remember to use hedging language.
- Practise reading the story aloud, concentrating on stress and clear pronunciation.
- Deliver your podcast to the other group.

8e The invisible man

Writing an online news report

1 Look at the photo. What is the man doing? Why? Read the news report and check your answer.

2 After it was first published, this news story 'went viral', appearing on lots of different websites all over the Internet. Why did it have such wide appeal?

3 Work in pairs. Read the advice to news writers. Then read the report again and find the answer to the questions *Who? What? Where? When? Why?* and *How?*

> Like any good report, a news report includes the answers to the five *W*s and the *H*: *Who is it about? What did they do? Where did this happen? When did it happen? Why did they do it?* and *How did they do it?* The reader must be able to find the answers to these questions as easily and quickly as possible before the report gives other details and information.

4 Writing skill cautious language

a News reports (and academic reports) use cautious language when the information given cannot be verified 100%. Find an example of each of the following types of cautious language in the report.

1 the verbs *seem* or *appear*
2 passive reporting verbs
3 adverbs of degree or frequency
4 adverbs that speculate about a fact

b Rewrite these sentences using the words given to express more caution about each of the facts presented.

1 His pictures carry a strong social message. (generally)
2 He became internationally famous when a New York art dealer bought some of his works. (apparently)
3 His work makes people think more about their surroundings. (might)
4 He wants to draw our attention to what we cannot see in a picture. (seems)
5 Bolin used friends at first to help him paint his pictures. (said)

5 Write a short news report about something that happened in your town or school recently. Make sure your report answers the five 'Ws' and the 'H'. Write around 150 words.

THE INVISIBLE MAN

In his latest work created in the summer of 2011 at his Beijing studio, Chinese artist Liu Bolin blends into a background of a supermarket soft drinks display. When his assistants finished painting him in, he seemed to have disappeared. Entitled *Plasticizer*, the piece is supposed to express Bolin's shock at the discovery of plasticizer in food products. Plasticizers are additives generally used to make plastic and other non-food products less rigid.

Such pictures have made Bolin internationally famous, which is ironic because they started out as a statement about how unwanted he felt by society. Bolin loves the challenge of blending into any surroundings: a building site, a telephone box, a national monument. No trick photography or photoshopping is used and careful planning is needed for each image. First, before entering the scene, he tells the photographer how he would like the picture to look. Then he asks his assistant to paint him in. This process can take up to ten hours while Bolin stands completely still, presumably in some discomfort.

His pictures appear to have struck a chord with many people because more recently, Bolin has branched out from his Chinese roots and created a series of photos where he is camouflaged in other settings: New York, Paris, Venice, Rome and London.

6 Exchange news reports with your partner. Use these questions to check your reports.

• Does the report answer the six basic questions?
• Does it use cautious language appropriately?

Talking dictionaries

The Tuvan people have a very rich lexicon.

Before you watch

1 Work in pairs and discuss the questions.

1 Can you think of three languages which are spoken in more than one country? Which is the most widespread?
2 Is your language spoken in another country? If so, where?
3 Is another language, such as English, replacing your language or other languages in your country?

2 How can we save lesser spoken languages from being dominated or replaced by 'world' languages? Is it important to do this? Why? / Why not?

While you watch

3 Watch the video and compare your answers from Exercise 2 with what the speaker says.

4 Watch the first part of the video (to 01.02) and answer the questions.

1 How many of the world's languages are endangered?

2 Why are these languages dying out?

3 What are the 'savvy' communities doing to preserve their languages?

5 Watch the second part of the video (01.03 to 02.29) and then complete the summary of the Talking Dictionaries project using one word per space.

The aim of Talking Dictionaries is to give endangered languages a first-ever [1] .... on the [2] ....
An example is Siletz Dee-ni from Oregon, USA, which has only one [3] .... speaker .
This speaker has recorded [4] .... of words, which have been made into a talking dictionary. When you see the rich vocabulary of the language, it helps you appreciate the cultural [5] ....
The dictionary can then be used as a tool to [6] .... the language.

6 Watch the third part of the video (02.30 to end) and answer the questions.

1 What did the Papuan New Guinea villagers ask the Enduring Voices team?

2 What message did seeing the Matukar-Panau talking dictionary on the Internet send to people?

3 What is special about the Tuvan talking dictionary?

4 To whom do the Talking Dictionaries team want to spread the message of the importance of linguistic diversity?

7 Which words do you remember from the two talking dictionaries that you saw? What did they tell you about those particular cultures? Watch the video again to check.

1 Siletz Dee-ni (Oregon, USA)

2 Matukar-Panau (Papua New Guinea)

After you watch

8 Roleplay creating a talking dictionary

Work in groups of three or four.

You are going to make your own small talking dictionary. Follow these steps.

- Think of words or short phrases which are typical of your language and culture (e.g. social life, food, geography, weather).
- Make a list of five or six of these and write an English translation for each.

Read your phrases and their translations to your group. Then ask each other questions about why you chose these particular phrases.

9 Work in groups. Do you think that the Internet helps promote cultural diversity or does it make cultures more similar and homogenous? Discuss. Give examples to support your arguments.

---

collaboration (n) /kəlæbə'reɪʃn/ working together with someone
devalue (v) /diː'væljuː/ make something less valuable than it is
indigenous (adj) /ɪn'dɪdʒɪnəs/ native to a particular country or location
migratory (adj) /maɪ'greɪt(ə)ri/ moving from one place to live in another
pertaining (to) (v) /pə'teɪnɪŋ/ describing, related to
platform (n) /'plætfɔːm/ a computer software framework in which you can run other programs
revitalise (v) /riː'vaɪt(ə)laɪz/ put the life back into something
savvy (adj) /'sævi/ knowledgeable
worthwhile (adj) /wɜːθ'waɪl/ there's value in doing this

Grammar

1 Read the blog about the Mariana Trench and make passive reporting verbs from the words in italics.

2 Read the blog again and answer the questions.

1 Where and what is the Mariana Trench?
2 What was Cameron's aim in visiting it?

[1] *It / say / be* one of the greatest achievements in exploration since we put a man on the Moon. James Cameron recently made the headlines by diving eleven kilometres in a one-person submersible to what [2] *think / be* the deepest part of the ocean, the Mariana Trench. This great chasm, 120 times larger than the Grand Canyon, is where the Earth's Pacific plate slides under the Philippines plate.
Better known as the Hollywood director of the films *Titanic* and *Avatar*, Cameron is one of just three people to dive to Earth's deepest point, and the only one to be able to stay long enough to look around. Although [3] *it / already / know* how [4] *the Mariana Trench / be / form*, Cameron and his team hoped to discover more about the biology of the Mariana depths.
In 1960, Swiss engineer Jacques Piccard and US navy captain Don Walsh [5] *report / spend* twenty minutes in the Mariana depths, but they were unable to see anything because their submarine disturbed too much mud from the ocean floor. Cameron's submersible was equipped with stereo digital cameras to take 3D shots, and a large bank of LED lights. [6] *It / hope / that / his film / shed* new light on life in one of the most extreme environments on our planet.

3 Complete the statements which use phrases with *no*. Write one word in each space.
1 No matter _____ you rank it in the history of exploration, there's no doubt _____ James Cameron's achievement is a remarkable one.
2 Cameron had no way _____ telling what he would find, but he had no intention _____ letting that deter him from diving.
3 He had no difficulty _____ getting funding for the project, but with so many people backing him, he had no choice _____ to go through with it.

4 Work in pairs. Think of a place that someone discovered or explored for the first time. Make a sentence describing what people thought about this place using a passive reporting verb.

I CAN	
report what has been said (passive reporting verbs)	☐
use phrases with *no*	☐

Vocabulary

5 Choose the best option to complete the sentences.
1 I *position / post* a lot of comments on car forums.
2 He *puts on / writes* a weekly blog about interesting local events.
3 People think social media marketing is complicated but it's not *space / rocket* science!
4 By thinking outside the *box, / frame,* they came up with a really innovative website.
5 Their *match / game* plan is to sell a lot of advertising space on the website.
6 The customer is happy and the company is happy. It's a *win-win / gain-gain* situation.

6 Work in pairs. What's your favourite website? Is it interactive? Why do you like it?

I CAN	
talk about digital media	☐
understand business buzz words	☐

Real life

7 Rewrite the statements to make them less certain.
1 James Cameron has an obsession with exploring the deep seas. (seems)
2 The most difficult thing was going down alone in the submersible. (arguably)
3 He tweeted: 'Hitting bottom never felt so good.' (reported)
4 People who usually undertake such missions are scientists, not film directors. (tend)
5 In future these missions will be manned rather than unmanned. (likely)
6 The Mariana Trench is 11 km deep. (estimated)

8 Work in pairs. Make a short podcast about James Cameron's exploration of the deep sea. Then present your podcast to another pair.

I CAN	
make a news report	☐
use hedging language	☐

Speaking

9 Work in pairs. Describe to your partner how you make use of digital media a) in your work and b) in your social life. How would your life be different without it?

Unit 9 The music in us

A young boy watches a jazz band busking.
Photograph by Greg Dale

FEATURES

1 Look at the photo and answer the questions.

1 What is a *busker*?
2 Is it common to see them in your country? Where?
3 What kind of music do they play?

2 2.10 Work in pairs. Listen to a busker and make notes on the following. Then compare answers with your partner.

1 why she started busking
2 how her career developed
3 what kind of music she plays

3 Put the words in the right category (a–e).

> ballad   busker   dance   eclectic   folk   instrumental
> melodic   solo artist   soothing   sophisticated

a genres of music   d describing music
b musicians   e describing taste
c compositions

4 Work in groups. Discuss these questions.

1 How important is music to you? What kind of music do you listen to? Where and when?
2 Do you prefer live music or recorded music? Why?

9a World music

Reading

1 Work in groups and answer the questions.

1 How important is music in your culture?
2 Is there one style of music that dominates in your country?
3 How different are musical tastes across different generations?
4 Do you listen to music from other countries and cultures? If so, who or what?

2 Read the interview with a musician and say which of these statements best sums up his view of music and culture.

a Music isn't really very different from one culture to another.
b It's fascinating to study cultural differences in music.
c Fortunately, music is becoming more standardised across the world.

3 Match the types of music (1–4) with the point they are supposed to illustrate (a–d).

1 American teenagers and Sitar music
2 international pop music
3 Mexican-Irish songs
4 80s rock

a There's a wealth of diverse musical styles out there.
b Each generation believes it owns the music of its time.
c There is music out there with universal appeal.
d Music doesn't always have universal appeal.

4 Work in pairs. Has western pop music influenced traditional music in your country? Is this a good thing or not? Discuss with your partner.

WORLD MUSIC

INTERVIEW OF THE WEEK

He's been travelling for just under two years, away from recording and performing, so we thought it was time we caught up with musician Justin Cape.

WM: **Justin, you've spent a lot of time studying other musical styles and traditions. Are you trying to make music that has a more universal appeal?**

JC: No, not just a wider appeal – that's not my goal really. Global commercial forces have already homogenised music styles quite a lot. I noticed that on my travels. So we already have a brand of international pop with mass appeal. I just get excited by exploring different types of music.

WM: **But you have sophisticated tastes. For many people, different styles of music aren't always very accessible, are they?**

JC: No, they can seem alien, but I don't think that's so surprising: it's just to do with habit, like the food you eat. Not many American teenagers listen to Indian sitar music, just as not many nomads in the Sahara eat hamburgers and fries. But I think often, if you give it a chance, it can be incredibly rewarding.

WM: **And what are you listening to at the moment?**

JC: I listen to a group from Mali, called Tinariwen, a lot – they play a very upbeat mix of Middle Eastern and African music. I'm also a big fan of Ry Cooder, who's also a bit of a musical nomad. He really mines the world's diverse music styles. He started out exploring different kinds of American music: blues, gospel, R&B. Then he worked with musicians in Cuba and Mali. And he's just produced a CD of Mexican-Irish songs, which are fantastic!

WM: **And do you find the things people sing about vary a lot from culture to culture?**

JC: Not really. What you do find is that differences are as much generational as cultural. Each new generation has the feeling that 'their' music is speaking just to them; that it's addressing their hopes and heartbreaks, as if these things had never been experienced before. In western music, that idea's deeply ingrained. So we speak about music in generational terms: 60s soul, 80s rock and so on. But to answer your question, I think even if music is very different from place to place, the themes it treats are often pretty universal.

Language focus the adverb *just*

5 *Just* has a lot of meanings and is used often in spoken English. Look at the examples from the interview and match the sentences (1–6) with the correct meaning of *just* (a–f).

1 He's been travelling for **just** under two years.
2 It's **just** to do with habit, like the food you eat.
3 Not many American teenagers listen to Indian sitar music, **just** as not many nomads in the Sahara eat hamburgers and fries.
4 I **just** get excited by exploring music.
5 And he's **just** produced a CD of Mexican-Irish songs, which are fantastic!
6 Each new generation has the feeling that 'their' music is speaking **just** to them.

a very recently
b simply
c only
d exactly
e a little
f no particular meaning

> ► **THE ADVERB *JUST***
>
> **just + main verb**
> *They've just finished a tour of Asia.*
> *I'm just waiting for the song to download onto my computer.*
>
> **just + preposition**
> *She's just under 80 years old, but you wouldn't know it.*
> *He has just about finished recording the album.*
>
> **just + noun**
> *He hasn't got a bad throat. It's just the way he sings!*
>
> **just + adjective**
> *It's just sad that she doesn't play live more often.*
>
> **just + conjunction**
> *The concert was just as you said it would be.*
> Notes
> 1 *just* is placed before the word it emphasises
> 2 *just about = almost*
>
> For further information and practice, see page 168.

6 Work in pairs. Look at the language focus box and notice the position of *just* in each sentence. Then put *just* in the most appropriate place in the sentences below. There is sometimes more than one possibility. What is the meaning of *just* in each case?

1 If you took the time to listen to Ry Cooder, you'd definitely like him.
2 I've heard his new single on the radio.
3 It's over ten years since they last performed.
4 You saw her live? Wow! Hearing her sing gives me goosebumps.
5 The concert is in an old theatre behind the bank in the High Street.
6 Thank you for the CD – it's what I wanted.
7 I can't understand why so many people like his music!
8 I'm as interested in the lyrics as the music.

7 Pronunciation word stress: *just*

a 🔊 2.11 Listen to how *just* is pronounced in these phrases. In what situations would you hear each phrase?

1 Just a minute.
2 Phew! Just in time.
3 I just don't get it, I'm afraid.
4 Thanks, I just had one.
5 Thanks, I'm just looking.
6 Hello. You just tried to call, I think.
7 We're just friends.
8 I just wondered.

b Work in pairs. Make short conversations using these phrases and practise pronouncing them with the appropriate stress.

Speaking and vocabulary themes of songs

8 Work in groups. The list below contains the hundred most used words in pop song titles in the last hundred years (with common words like *the*, *to*, *I*, *you*, *my*, *don't*, etc. filtered out). First check you know what the words mean. Then follow this procedure.

1 Each think of three of your favourite pop song titles in English and two in your own language.
2 Check if the song titles contain one or more of these words.
3 Discuss what the most common themes are in the songs that you thought of.

> ain't alone angel arms around away
> baby bad beautiful believe blue boy
> change christmas comes crazy cry
> dance days dear dream ever everybody
> everything eyes fall feel fire fool forever
> girl gone gonna goodbye happy heart
> heaven hey hold kiss la lady leave life
> light lonely love lover mama man mind
> mine miss moon moonlight morning mr
> music night nobody oh people play
> please rain red remember river rock roll
> rose sing smile somebody something song
> soul star stay stop street summer sun
> sweet sweetheart talk tears theme things
> think tonight town true walk wanna
> wish woman wonderful world young

9b Healing music

Listening

1 Work in pairs. Answer the questions.

1 How do different types of music affect your mood?
2 Think of examples of when you use music to affect your mood (e.g. when driving a car).

2 Which of the following therapeutic properties do you think music has? Explain your reasons.

a relieving stress
b relieving pain
c acting as an anaesthetic
d helping sleep
e helping with learning difficulties
f preventing heart disease
g helping with speech difficulties
h combating memory loss

3 🎵 **2.12** Listen to a talk by a neuroscientist about music therapy. Which therapeutic properties in Exercise 2 does she mention?

4 🎵 **2.12** Complete the notes. Then listen and check your answers.

---

1 Area of the brain activated by music:
_____

2 The body releases endorphins to _____ and produce _____

3 Same parts of the brain are used to process _____ and _____ .

4 Music could help people with _____ and other _____ .

5 Gottfried Schlaug treated people who _____ .

6 The results of Schlaug's music therapy were really _____ .

7 Music therapy for memory loss is important because _____ .

▶ **WORDBUILDING negative prefixes**

We can use a number of different negative prefixes in English as well as the common *un-* and *in-* prefixes: *a-, dis-, dys-, non-*. *asymmetrical, dyslexia, non-toxic*

For further information and practice, see Workbook page 75.

Idioms music

5 Look at this idiom used by the speaker. What do you think it means?

'This news should be **music to our ears**.'

6 Match these music idioms (1–7) with the correct meaning.

---

accept responsibility   give a contrary opinion
know what's going on   make a fuss
seem very relevant to   shout about one's achievements
take things as they come

---

1 **You've changed your tune.** You said you didn't like rock music.
2 What she said about working long hours really **struck a chord with** the audience because they were mostly nurses.
3 It's a mistake to go to a job interview with a particular strategy. Just **play it by ear**.
4 Don't worry about John negotiating the deal for us. He **knows the score**.
5 I don't mean to **blow my own trumpet**, but I think my performance was the best.
6 Sooner or later someone will find out that I cheated and I'll have to **face the music**.
7 In the end he did help me tidy up, but he **made a big song and dance about it**.

7 Work in pairs. Describe examples of the following.

1 a person you know who likes to blow their own trumpet
2 a time when you made a big mistake and had to face the music
3 something you read recently that really struck a chord with you
4 a situation where it is best to play it by ear

Language focus expressing purpose

8 Work in pairs. Look at the sentences from the talk which express purpose (1–5) and answer the questions (a–d).

1 Endorphins are released at times of stress **to** help us deal with pain.
2 Hospitals now use music **for** pain relief after an operation.
3 Perhaps you are someone who has to strain **so as to** hear what people are saying in a noisy room.
4 I'm not saying you should take up the violin **so that** you can hear people better at parties.
5 I'm not saying you should take up the violin **in order to** be a better linguist.

a Which sentences use *to* + infinitive to express purpose?
b What modal verb follows *so that*? Can any other modal verb follow it?
c What part of speech must follow *for* when expressing purpose?
d Are *so as to* and *in order to* more or less formal than the simple *to* + infinitive?

▶ **EXPRESSING PURPOSE**

Infinitive of purpose
I gave up playing the piano (in order) to concentrate on my exams.
I turned down the music so as not to disturb the neighbours.

for
He listens to classical music for relaxation.
He plays in a band not for money but for fun.

avoid
We kept the music low to avoid annoying the neighbours.

so that / in order that
The extract of the song is there so that you can hear it before you buy it.
He wrote the lyrics down so that he wouldn't forget them.

For further information and practice, see page 168.

---

9 Look at the language focus box. Then use the prompts to rewrite the sentences so that they have the same meaning.

1 He took up the guitar because he wanted to join his brother's band.
   a He took up the guitar so that _____ .
   b He took up the guitar in order to
   _____ .
2 I play the trumpet because it helps me relax.
   a I play the trumpet to _____ .
   b I play the trumpet for _____ .
3 They sing familiar songs so that they don't confuse the patients.
   a They sing familiar songs so as _____ .
   b They sing familiar songs to avoid
   _____ .

10 Rewrite the phrases in italics using the words given.

When asked to pronounce new sounds in another language, we often prefer to pronounce sounds that we are already familiar with [1] *because we don't want to sound silly* (avoid). It seems that we have to lose our inhibitions [2] *if we want to pronounce another set of sounds properly* (order). But there are various things you can do [3] *if you want to improve* (to) your English pronunciation.

First, try to think of the sounds of a language as music. Secondly, try to exaggerate the sounds of the target language a little [4] *because then you get* (as) close to the reality of native pronunciation. Thirdly, practise singing songs in the target language [5] *because it helps you to lose* (so that) your inhibitions. It's amazing how much better someone can imitate pronunciation in a song than the ordinary spoken word.

Speaking

11 Work in groups. You are music consultants that advise companies and organisations on how to use music to achieve a particular effect or mood.

Group A: Think of a plan for how music could be used in schools.

Group B: Think of a plan for how music could be used in an airport.

Then present your ideas to the other group.

9c One love

Reading

1 Work in pairs. Look at the names of four famous pop artists (a–d). Which do you know and what do you know about them? Discuss with your partner.

- dead or alive
- nationality
- type of music played
- names of songs
- other things they are known for

a John Lennon
b Bob Marley
c Michael Jackson
d Elvis Presley

2 Read the review. Then look at the headlines about Bob Marley. Would the writer of the review agree, partly agree or disagree with them?

1 THE MAN WHO BROUGHT **REGGAE** TO THE WORLD

2 MILLIONS IN THIRD WORLD LOOK TO MARLEY AS A HERO

3 SOCIAL DISADVANTAGES INSPIRE MARLEY SONGS

4 MARLEY WAS AN **ABSENT FATHER**

5 NEW FILM REVEALS MUCH ABOUT REGGAE STAR'S LIFE

6 SINGER WHO SPREAD MESSAGE OF HARMONY

3 What makes Bob Marley stand out as a pop artist? Discuss with your partner.

4 Find words in the review with the following meanings.

1 sections or bits of film recording (para 2)
2 a disadvantaged and troubled area of a city (para 3)
3 a person who doesn't fit in to a group (para 3)
4 common, even dominant (para 5)
5 different sides or parties in a dispute (para 6)
6 in a state of great happiness (para 7)

Critical thinking identifying text types

5 Work in pairs. Look at the different types of review (a–c) and decide which best describes the one you have just read. Discuss your answer and reasons with your partner.

a a short description of a book, film or event with practical information for readers or viewers on how to read or see it
b an appraisal of a book, film or event with the reviewer's recommendation to the reader or viewer
c a description of the book, film or event and an analysis which adds the reviewer's own knowledge on the subject

6 In what situations is each type of review in Exercise 5 most useful? Discuss with your partner.

Word focus *hit*

7 Look at this sentence from the review. What does the word *hit* mean in this context?

'His first **hit** came when he was only eighteen years old.'

8 Look at the sentences using expressions with *hit*. Match the expressions in bold with the correct definition (a–f).

1 The recruitment process is **hit and miss**, I think: it doesn't really guarantee that we're going to get good people.
2 They **took** a big **hit** when the stock market crashed.
3 The video game that you bought was **a real hit** with Jack; he hasn't stopped playing it.
4 I think you **hit a nerve** when you told Benny that he needed to study harder. Did you see his expression?
5 I think I'd better **hit the road** or I'll be late home.
6 The joke he told didn't **hit the right note** with the audience. I think they were a bit offended.

a be appropriate
b a big success
c leave
d mention a sensitive point
e not consistently successful
f suffer a financial loss

Speaking

9 Work in groups. You are going to organise a charity concert to raise money for children in poverty. Decide on the following.

- the name and venue
- what age group you want to attract
- which artists you will invite to perform
- how it will raise money
- how you will link the event to the theme of children in poverty

ONE LOVE

What makes Bob Marley such an important figure in popular music? Globally, perhaps only Elvis, the Beatles and Michael Jackson are bigger names. Marley was not the first person to introduce reggae to a wider audience outside the West Indies, but he was, and remains, the only global reggae superstar. Yet, unlike the artists just mentioned, Marley and his music represent more than just great pop. Indeed, in many developing countries, he is celebrated as some kind of redeeming figure, a symbol of hope. To understand why this is, one needs to know more about the man and his background.

This is where the recent documentary, *Marley*, fascinates, even if it does not provide all the answers. Containing a lot of previously unseen footage – interviews, performances, recording sessions – the film provides an insight into the mind and motivation of a musician whose life was cut tragically short: Marley died of cancer in 1981 aged 36.

Born in a poor ghetto of Kingston, Jamaica, Marley had a passion for music and began recording at a young age, his first hit coming when he was only eighteen. His difficult environment instilled in him a keen sense of social justice, which came to be expressed in his music. The fact that he was of mixed race taught him what it felt like to be an outsider. His father was a white Jamaican who worked as a British marine officer; his mother was a black Jamaican who had married at eighteen.

His father was rarely present, travelling as he did for his work, and died when Bob was only ten years old. Did this absence have any bearing on Marley's behaviour towards his own children, of whom there were eleven in all? In the film, his daughter Cedella talks about her difficulty in getting her father to notice her. But neither she, nor any others in the family, has a bad word to say about him. There is no sense that he did not have time for them; simply that he was prioritising. Marley's calling was first and foremost to music and its power to effect change.

Shortly after his marriage to Rita Anderson in 1966, Marley became a Rastafarian, a faith that champions the right of Black Africans taken into slavery in the West Indies to return one day to Africa. So while themes of social injustice and hardship in the shanty towns of Kingston, Jamaica characterise early songs like *Trenchtown Rock* and *I Shot the Sheriff*, it is the theme of a displaced people that is prevalent in later songs: *Exodus* and *Redemption Song*.

Whether the songs deal with injustice or dislocation, they contain the sentiments of unity and love which run through almost all his work. Marley himself maintained that, 'People want to listen to a message. This could be passed through me or anybody. I am not a leader, but a messenger.' This is too modest. Marley experienced genuine hardship and even put his life on the line for justice. In 1976, he took great risks by organising a free concert in his home town of Kingston called 'Smile Jamaica'. The concert was intended to unite the warring political factions in Jamaica, but while preparing for it, he was the victim of an assassination attempt that left him wounded.

That his songs come from the heart and appeal to others who face hardship is certainly one key to Marley's enduring status as a songwriter. But what stays with you after watching this film is the magic of his performances. The music still sounds as fresh as it was when it was first recorded and Marley himself is lost in it, living each note as he spins and jumps ecstatically around the stage.

Even after two and a half hours of this documentary, you still feel there are many questions unanswered about this man who became the first Third World superstar. But isn't that the nature of great people who die young? They leave us wanting more. Kevin Macdonald's *Marley* is in selected cinemas from 3rd May.

TALK ABOUT ▸ THEMES OF SONGS ▸ MOOD MUSIC ▸ A CHARITY CONCERT ▸ YOUR FAVOURITE MUSIC

WRITE ▸ A DESCRIPTION

9d Desert Island Discs

Real life your favourite music

1 Work in pairs. Read the description of a popular radio show in the UK. Do you have a similar programme in your country? What is it? Discuss with your partner.

Desert Island Discs is a radio programme that has been running on BBC Radio since 1942. Each week a guest is interviewed about their life. The basis of the show is that the guest is 'invited' to be a castaway on a desert island. They are allowed to take with them eight pieces of music, a book and one luxury item. During the programme they talk about their life and the reasons for their choices of music.

2 🎵 **2.13** Listen to a 'castaway' talking about himself and answer the questions.

1 What is this man's job?
2 In what way has he been successful?
3 What kind of music is the first piece he chooses and why does he choose it?

3 Speaking skill responding to difficult questions

🎵 **2.13** Often when we respond to questions, we need to give ourselves a little time to think. Look at the phrases in the box. Then listen again and answer the questions.

a What questions does the interviewer ask?
b Which phrases does Frank Steel use in his answers?

> ▶ **RESPONDING TO DIFFICULT QUESTIONS**
>
> That's a good / an interesting question.
> I've never really thought about it.
> It's not (It isn't) something I've often thought about.
> I don't really look at it like that.
> I honestly don't know.
> I couldn't tell you, really.
> That's difficult to say.
> Frankly, I've no idea.

4 Pronunciation intonation to express uncertainty

a 🎵 **2.14** We often use a 'wavering' intonation – rising and falling in the same phrase or sentence – to express uncertainty. Listen to the phrases in the box and note which use a wavering intonation. Then practise saying the phrases.

b 🎵 **2.15** Say these phrases with a 'wavering' intonation. Then listen and check.

1 perhaps   3 I'm not sure
2 maybe   4 I can't say

5 Work in pairs. You are going to act out a *Desert Island Discs* interview. Follow these steps.

- Write down some details about yourself so that the 'interviewer' has some information to work with. Include your job and education, interests, and personal achievements.
- Exchange notes with your partner and each prepare questions to ask the other.
- Think of two pieces of music you would like to take to a desert island and your reasons for choosing these. Also think of one luxury item.
- Act out the interviews, taking it in turns to play the parts of interviewer and castaway.

6 Did you find out anything interesting or new about your partner? Tell the class.

9e Fado

Writing a description

1 Work in pairs. Describe a traditional form of music in your county to your partner, giving a few details: its style, its themes, its history, its popular appeal now.

2 Read the description of *Fado*, a traditional style of music from Portugal, and answer the questions.

1 How would you sum up what this style of music is?
2 With whom is it popular?

3 Look at the elements of a description and find an example of each one in the text.

1 It uses powerful adjectives.
2 It describes feelings.
3 It tries to convey an atmosphere.
4 It uses similes.
5 The author speaks to his audience as one of them.

4 Writing skill parallel structures

a Look at the sentences from the description. Notice how the words that follow the phrases in bold balance. For example, in 1, *either* and *or* are followed by a pronoun + verb. What parallel structures are used in the other sentences (2–4)?

1 … **either** you'll love it **or** you'll hate it.
2 **Like** the blues, Fado songs tell of …, **but unlike** the blues, the songs focus on …
3 … of being separated from **either** a loved one **or** your home, **or** something you can never regain.
4 Mariza has broadened Fado's appeal **by** fusing it with other musical traditions and **by** touring the world with her music.

b Rewrite these sentences using parallel structures.

1 Mariza is young, talented and she has lots of energy.
   Mariza is young, talented and energetic.
2 She sings both traditional songs and she sings more modern songs.
3 You can either book in advance or it's possible to pay on the door.
4 You can spend hours wandering around the old town, visiting cafés and you can listen to live music.
5 The music fuses traditional Spanish folk music and there are elements of North African music.

THE *FADO* OF LISBON by Jay Rowsell

People say about Fado that either you'll love it or you'll hate it. One thing is certain: you can't ignore it. It has been compared to the 'blues', because the songs are sad, but with Fado the intensity of the emotion is greater, piercing the listener's body like a knife. Like the blues, Fado songs tell of pain and hardship, but unlike the blues, the songs focus on the pain of separation: of being separated from either a loved one or your home, or something you can never regain. Perhaps that is not surprising when you consider that Portugal is a country with a long tradition of sailors and voyagers.

When I first saw a *fadista* perform in a dimly lit café one sultry evening in Lisbon twenty years ago, I was ignorant both of the Fado music tradition and of the Portuguese language. But that didn't matter, because the sheer drama of the music told its own story. In those days, Fado was a style of music that was known only in Portugal and a few of its former colonies: Brazil, Angola and Mozambique. Now, with the help of stars like Mariza, it has an international following. Mariza has broadened Fado's appeal by fusing it with other musical traditions – Spanish flamenco and Brazilian jazz, for example – and by touring the world with her music. But to hear traditional Fado, you should go where its roots are – the Alfama district of Lisbon. You may hate it, but I suspect you will love it.

5 Write a description of a traditional type of music or music and dance. Write approximately 200 words and include the following details.

- information about the history of this tradition
- a description of how it is performed, what its appeal is and the feelings it arouses
- where you can still find it being performed

6 Exchange descriptions with your partner. Use these questions to check your descriptions.

- Does the description give a sense of the atmosphere?
- Does it include strong descriptive language?
- Does it speak to the reader personally?
- Does it use parallel structures correctly?
- Would you want to listen to this kind of music?

9f A biopic

It's the story of the rags to riches tale in Jamaica.

Before you watch

1 Work in pairs. Read the quotations (a–f) by the singer Bob Marley. Then discuss with your partner what adjectives could describe his attitude to life.

a Just because you are happy it does not mean that the day is perfect but that you have looked beyond its imperfections.

b The truth is, everyone is going to hurt you. You just got to find the ones worth suffering for.

c Some people feel the rain. Others just get wet.

d Love the life you live. Live the life you love.

e The day you stop racing is the day you win the race.

f Better to die fighting for freedom then be a prisoner all the days of your life.

2 Work in pairs. If you were going to interview the director of a documentary about a famous musician's life, what questions would you ask? Write three key questions. Then compare your questions with another pair.

1 ....

2 ....

3 ....

While you watch

3 Watch the interview with Kevin Macdonald, the director of *Marley*, and compare your questions from Exercise 2 with the ones the interviewer asks.

4 Watch the first part of the video (to 00.54) and answer the questions.

1 What aspect of Marley's life did Kevin Macdonald feel had not been covered yet?

....

2 How does Kevin Macdonald describe the way people react when they hear Marley's music these days?

....

3 What does he hope the film will achieve?

....

5 Watch the second part of the video (00.55 to 01.52). Underline the adjectives and expressions Kevin Macdonald uses when he describes Bob Marley's life story.

> touching   fascinating   extraordinary   tough
> rags to riches   family troubles   racial issues
> personal suffering   crime   violence
> gangsters   political activity   amazing

6 Watch the third part of the video (01.53 to end) and complete the sentences about Bob Marley.

1 The first thing people like about him is that he is ....

2 More significantly he is very ....

3 He tries to offer people in hardship some ....

4 Because he's lived through tough times himself, you ....

5 He's the most listened to artist in the world because his message is ....

6 The things he sings about are things we can all ....

After you watch

7 Roleplay an interview with the director

Work in pairs.

Student A: Imagine you are a film director. You have made a documentary about the life of a famous person. Think about the reasons you chose this person and what story you wanted to tell.

Student B: Imagine you are a journalist. You are going to interview a film director about a recent documentary they have made about the life of a famous person. Prepare questions.

Act out the interview, then change roles and act out the interview again. Student B should choose a different famous person.

8 Work in groups and discuss these questions.

1 What situations can you think of where music brings people together?

2 What examples can you think of in your own culture?

---

afresh (adv) /əˈfreʃ/ from the start again, as if for the first time

numerically (adv) /njuːˈmerɪkli/ in terms of numbers

privilege (n) /ˈprɪvɪlɪdʒ/ an honour

rags (n) /rægz/ old, poor clothes

sincere (adj) /sɪnˈsɪə/ meaning what you say

solace (n) /ˈsɒlɪs/ comfort

tribulations (n) /ˌtrɪbjuˈleɪʃns/ difficulties, hardship

Grammar

1 Read the article about the 1971 *Concert for Bangladesh* and answer the questions.

1 What was the purpose of the concert?
2 In what three ways was it a success?

2 Rewrite the sentences (1–4) in the first two paragraphs of the article using these words.

1 so as to   3 for
2 to   4 so that

The *Concert for Bangladesh* in 1971 was the first large benefit concert of its kind, staged [1] *in order to help victims of a disaster*. It was organised by Beatle George Harrison and Indian musician Ravi Shankar at Madison Square Garden in New York and attracted an audience of 40,000 people.

The show's aim was to raise money [2] *for the relief* of the refugee crisis following the cyclone that hit the country in 1970 and the Bangladesh Liberation War. The concert itself raised over US$250,000 but further income was gained from the live album that was made from it. This money was passed to the charity UNICEF [3] *so that they could distribute it* to where it was most needed. Other famous music artists of the day, such as Bob Dylan, Billy Preston and Eric Clapton, also performed [4] *to ensure* as wide an audience as possible for the music.

But the aim of the *Concert for Bangladesh* wasn't only to raise money. The organisers wanted people to be more aware of Bangladesh and its problems. In this sense, according to organiser Ravi Shankar, 'It was fantastic.' It also turned out to be the start of a new movement in benefit concerts. Under fifteen years later *Live Aid*, a response to the Ethiopian famine, was staged in London and Philadelphia and attracted a global TV audience of almost two billion.

3 Work in pairs. Read the final paragraph again. Then insert the word *just* in the most appropriate place in each of the five sentences. In the first sentence you need to replace a word with *just*.

I CAN	
express purpose in different ways	
use *just* with different meanings	

Vocabulary

4 Match the words about music (1–8) with the correct definition (a–g).

1	eclectic taste	5	instrumental
2	strike a chord	6	face the music
3	a busker	7	a ballad
4	play it by ear	8	soothing

a accept responsibility
b liking different kinds of music
c take things as they come
d having a calming effect
e a person who plays music for money on the street
f seem relevant to
g a sentimental or romantic song
h (music) without singing

5 Work in pairs. Describe a song or a genre of music that you like and explain why you like it.

I CAN	
talk about music	
use music idioms	

Real life

6 Read the dialogue and complete the responses to the questions.

A: How often do you actively listen to music each day?
B: I couldn't [1] _____ you really. Well, if you count turning on the radio, then maybe three or four times.
A: Do you use music when doing certain things, like driving or working at your computer?
B: I've never really [2] _____ about it, but, yes, I do. I often listen to music when I'm working.
A: And does it help you work: make you more productive?
B: That's a(n) [3] _____ question. I suspect that it's probably a bit of a distraction, actually.
A: How do you think you would feel without music in your life?
B: That's difficult to [4] _____. It would be less fun, I imagine. No, I [5] _____ don't know.

7 Work in pairs. Act out a similar conversation by asking each other the questions in Exercise 6.

I CAN	
talk about (my favourite) music and why I like it	
give myself time to think when responding to difficult questions	

Speaking

8 Work in pairs. Describe a piece of music that you have heard being played a lot on the radio or TV recently. Explain why you like it / dislike it.

Unit 10 Social living

Cinco de Mayo, a festival celebrating the Mexican community in Denver, USA
Photograph by John McEvoy

FEATURES

1 Work in pairs. Look at the photo and caption. What festivals or public holidays in your country celebrate a spirit of community? How do they do this? Discuss with your partner.

2 🎵 **2.16** Listen to an extract from a radio programme talking about ethnic communities. Answer the questions.

1 Which cities are mentioned and what large ethnic populations do they have?
2 What do the communities have in common, apart from the one in London?
3 What values define Alejandra's ethnic community?

3 🎵 **2.16** Listen again. Which adjectives are used with these words to talk about communities?

groups	migrants	immigrant community	family
values	community	gatherings	heritage

4 Look at the questions and discuss with your partner.

1 Is there a strong sense of community where you live? What kind of social gatherings take place, e.g. street parties, meals with friends, dances?
2 Do you think it's confusing to have two cultures like Alejandra has, or is it a positive thing? Why?

10a Good citizens

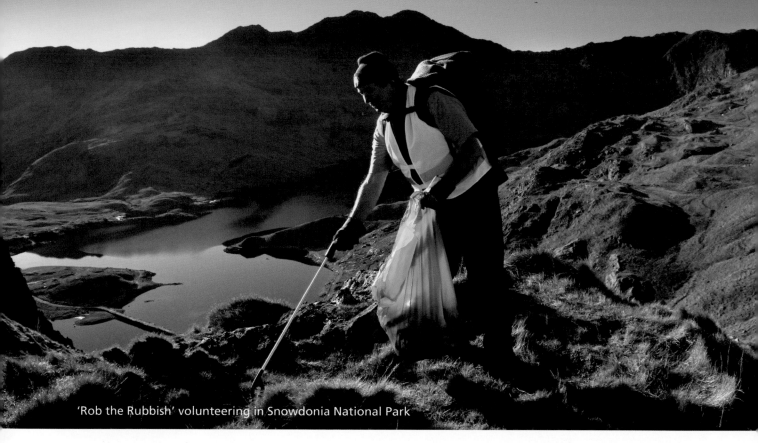

'Rob the Rubbish' volunteering in Snowdonia National Park

Listening

1 Work in pairs. Choose the correct option to complete each collocation.

1 .... **a part** in society
   a act   b play   c make
2 .... **one's bit** for the community
   a make   b do   c take
3 .... **a helping hand** to your neighbours
   a lend   b bring   c do
4 .... **responsibility** for your environment
   a hold   b keep   c take
5 .... **concern** for others who are less fortunate
   a take   b make   c show
6 .... **a say** in decisions that affect you
   a make   b take   c have

2 Look at the photo. In what way is Rob a good citizen? Which phrase(s) from Exercise 1 could be used to describe what Rob is doing?

3 🔊 **2.17** Listen to an interview with a sociologist about good citizenship and answer the questions.

1 What aspect of citizenship are schools focusing on?
2 What does the sociologist think young people should be encouraged to think about?
3 Do opinions of the duties of a good citizen vary from country to country?
4 What is an example of one of our basic duties to each other?

4 🔊 **2.17** Look at the phrases in bold used by the sociologist. Then listen again and write down what he is referring to or the example given in each case.

1 … **a hot topic** at the moment …
2 … I know **the intentions are good** …
3 … there were **some duties on a more human level** …
4 There were also **some unexpected findings**.

5 Work in groups. Think of three more examples of other public-spirited actions that people perform to help their communities.

> ▶ **WORDBUILDING compound adjectives**
>
> Compound adjectives which are a combination of an adjective + past participle are sometimes connected by a hyphen.
> *clear-cut, open-minded, public-spirited*
>
> For further information and practice, see Workbook page 83.

Language focus tag questions

6 🔘 **2.18** Listen to the questions from the interview (1–6). Which one(s):

a asks an open question?
b checks what you understand to be the case?
c isn't really asking a question but is just offering agreement?

1 Surely any training is better than none, isn't it?
2 And what is the point?
3 And you think that sort of duty is closer to the spirit of good citizenship, do you?
4 And how did people rate these duties?
5 I imagine there wasn't that much difference in the way different nationalities responded, was there?
6 That is surprising, isn't it?

7 🔘 **2.18** Listen again to the questions in Exercise 6 and answer the questions.

1 Does each question rise or fall at the end?
2 How would the meaning change in questions 1, 5 and 6 if the intonation were reversed?
3 What effect does the word 'surely' have on the meaning in question 1?

> ▶ **TAG QUESTIONS**
>
> **Tag questions: checking (rising intonation)**
> *You haven't seen my glasses anywhere, have you?*
> *He works for the council now, doesn't he?*
> *You think that's right, do you?*
>
> **Tag questions: agreement (falling intonation)**
> *People just want an easy life, don't they?*
> *It isn't fair, is it?*
>
> ***surely*: opinions**
> *Surely that would be a better solution?*
> *Surely everyone must make their own choices, mustn't they?*
>
> For further information and practice, see page 169.

8 Look at the language box. Then rewrite the statements in italics in these conversations as an appropriate tag question or *surely* question. There is sometimes more than one possibility.

1 A: *You follow the news a lot.*
  B: Yes, I do.
  A: *So you think it's important to keep up with political events.*
  B: Yes, very important.
2 A: *People aren't generally very public-spirited in our city.*
  B: No, I agree.
3 A: *It's up to each individual how much they participate in public life.*
  B: Not really. If everyone kept to themselves, there would be no community.
  A: *Yes, but there will always be some people who want to get involved.*
  B: *So you think it can just be left to others.*

4 A: *It isn't pleasant to live in run-down surroundings.*
  B: No, but what can you do?
  A: *But you care what your environment looks like.*
  B: Of course. I just don't have any time to do anything about it.

9 🔘 **2.19** Work in pairs. What are the tags for these questions? Discuss with your partner. Then listen and check your answers.

1 I'm disturbing you, _____? (negative tag)
2 Nothing bad happened, _____?
3 Let's go, _____? (affirmative tag)
4 Don't be late, _____? (affirmative tag)

10 Pronunciation tag questions

a Work in pairs. Look at the sentences and decide which ones probably have a rising intonation at the end and which a falling intonation. Explain your reasons.

1 You couldn't give me a hand, could you?
2 He would say that, wouldn't he?
3 You think I'm overreacting, do you?
4 Surely the answer is four, isn't it?
5 She didn't give a great performance, did she?
6 Let's go, shall we?
7 Nobody noticed I wasn't there, did they?

b 🔘 **2.20** Listen and check your answers. Then practise saying the questions with your partner.

Speaking

11 Work in groups. Look at the statements from an international citizenship survey and rank them in order of importance. Then ask each other questions about your answers.

> *Surely people shouldn't have to vote in elections if they don't feel inspired to?*

It is the duty of a citizen:

1 always to vote in elections.
2 always to obey laws and regulations.
3 to be active in social associations.
4 to try to understand the reasoning of people with other opinions.
5 to choose products for ethical or environmental reasons, even if they cost a bit more.
6 to help people in your country who are worse off than yourself.
7 to help people in the rest of the world who are worse off than yourself.

10b The civilised insect

Reading

1 Work in pairs. What is the first thing that comes to mind when you think of ants? What do you know about them (habitat, diet, grouping, predators etc.)? Discuss with your partner.

2 Look at these humorous quotes spoken by the main character, a disillusioned ant called Z, in the animated film *Antz*. What do you tell you about ants?

"When you're the middle child in a family of five million, you don't get any attention.

I wasn't cut out to be a worker. My whole life, I've never been able to lift more than ten times my body weight."

3 Read the article about how ant society works. What is the main reason why ants are so successful?

4 Look at the text again. Are these statements true (T) or false (F)?

1 Ants aren't found in very cold places.
2 Ants' bodies vary in shape and size according to the function they have to perform.
3 In some ways ants can be said to think before they act.
4 They use strength in numbers to overcome enemies.
5 Individually, ants are more intelligent than people give them credit for.

The civilised insect

Ants number approximately ten thousand trillion worldwide. Each individual ant scarcely weighs anything, but put together they weigh roughly the same as all of mankind. They are also ubiquitous, thriving everywhere except on icy mountain peaks and around the Poles. No one knows precisely how many species there are, but it is estimated at over 20,000. For an animal of its size, ants have been incredibly successful and this success owes much to the highly sophisticated social behaviour they exhibit.

In colonies that range in size from a few hundred to tens of millions, they organise their roles with a clear division of labour: a queen or queens whose job it is to reproduce; some fertile males who die shortly after mating with the queen; and the rest – sterile females who make up the main population of workers and soldiers, toiling away in a determined fashion. In some species, the bodies of these sterile females are adapted to the different jobs they have within the nest:

building and expanding the nest, foraging for food, defending against predators and so on.

How they achieve this level of organisation and synchronisation is even more amazing. Where we use sound and sight to communicate, ants depend primarily on pheromones, chemicals emitted by individuals and smelled or tasted by nestmates. A given species produces just ten to twenty signals, which unlike human language are entirely instinctive messages. A pheromone trail left by a foraging ant will lead others straight to where the food is. When an individual ant comes under attack or is dying, it sends out an alarm pheromone to alert the colony to mobilise as a defence unit.

In fact, when it comes to the art of war, ants are unsurpassed. They are completely fearless and will readily take on prey much larger than themselves, attacking in

deadly swarms and overwhelming their target. Such is their dedication to the common good of the colony that workers will also sacrifice their own lives to help others defeat the enemy.

Behaving in this altruistic and dedicated manner, these little creatures have flourished on Earth for more than 140 million years, long outlasting dinosaurs. Because they think as one, they have a collective intelligence greater than the sum of its individual parts; something you could hardly say of most species.

altruistic (a) /ˌæltruˈɪstɪk/ unselfish
colony (n) /ˈkɒləni/ a group of ants that nest together
forage (v) /ˈfɒrɪdʒ/ search for food
sterile (adj) /ˈsteraɪl/ not capable of reproducing

Language focus adverbs

5 Answer the questions about the adverbs and adjectives in the article.

1 What kind of word does *precisely* complement? (para 1)
2 What kind of word does *incredibly* complement? (para 1)
3 How would you say *scarcely weighs anything* using the word 'almost'? (para 1)
4 In paragraph 3, is *straight* an adjective or an adverb in this context?
5 Why does the author say *in a determined fashion* rather than adding *-ly* to the adjective? (para 2)

> ▶ **ADVERBS**
>
> **Adverb + verb**
> *Ants react **quickly** when they are in danger.*
>
> **Adverb + adjective**
> *Ants' nests are **carefully** constructed.*
>
> **Adverbs with the same form as the adjective**
> *When threatened, ants mobilise **fast**.*
> *Ants work **hard** to improve the colony.*
>
> **Adverbs meaning *almost ... not***
> *There is **barely** any place on earth that ants do not inhabit.*
>
> **Adverbs not formed with the *-ly* suffix**
> *They carry out their work **in a lively way**.*
> *They live **in an organised manner**.*
>
> For further information and practice, see page 170.

6 Look at the language box. Find one more example of each type of adverb form in paragraphs 4 and 5 of the article.

7 Transform the adjectives in brackets into adverbs or adverbial phrases and put them into the correct place in each clause or sentence.

1 Ants are sophisticated creatures. (social)
2 Ants are cooperative, but it would be wrong to say they act towards each other. (friendly)
3 An ant can lift up to twenty times its body weight, whereas most people can lift one time their own. (bare)
4 You could say an ant's brain was big (hard), but in fact it has the biggest brain-to-body-size ratio of any insect.
5 A worker ant doesn't live – on average 50 days – but a queen can live for decades. (long)
6 Some ants, when they attack other ant colonies, emit false pheromone signals to confuse the enemy. (clever)
7 Not all ants like to work. (hard)
8 The slave-maker ant steals eggs from other colonies. Then it makes the hatched ants work for it. (new)

Idioms animal verbs

8 Work in pairs. There are many verbs, used mainly in spoken English, that are derived from the names of animals. Each reflects a characteristic of that animal, for example, *to monkey around* = to play or fool around. Look at the 'animal verbs' and say what you think each means and the animal characteristic it reflects.

1 John's been **beavering away** all day to get his room tidy before he leaves.
2 Ever since he got that promotion, he's been **swanning around** the office as if he owned the company.
3 You **wolfed** that **down**. I haven't finished eating my first course yet!
4 He always tries to **duck out of** anything that involves hard work.
5 The press have **hounded** him day and night ever since he broke the world 100 metre record.
6 He's just **parroting** what the teacher said. Hasn't he got his own views on the subject?

9 What animal verbs do you use in your own language? Do they translate into English?

Speaking

10 Work in pairs. Look at the photos and the questions. Read the fact files then take turns to ask and answer the questions.

Student A: Turn to page 154.

Student B: turn to page 156.

a How and why do starlings flock together?
b Why do bees make honey and why are they so important to human beings?

TALK ABOUT ▶ CIVIC DUTIES ▶ **SOCIAL ANIMALS** ▶ A CONSERVATION PROJECT ▶ MAKING CONVERSATION
WRITE ▶ A DISCURSIVE ESSAY

121

10c Living free?

Reading

1 What is meant by the term *hunter-gatherer*? How is their life different from farmers?

2 Work in pairs. Look at the map. What does it tell you? Why do you think this is?

3 Read the article and say which statement best summarises what the author thinks about the Hadza way of life.

 a It's a good life but not practical for us nowadays.
 b It's a way of life that guarantees both health and harmony in society.
 c It's a sustainable way of life that we ought to imitate.

4 Read the article again quickly and find out which of these things the Hadza have, and which things they do not have. Then compare answers with you partner.

- working animals
- enemies
- sufficient food
- basic tools
- a lot of free time
- a government
- their own strict routines
- a difficult environment

5 Work in pairs. Explain what these phrases from the article mean.

 1 Agriculture's rise, however, came with a price. (para 2)
 2 they've left hardly a footprint on the land (para 3)
 3 this honour does not confer any particular power (para 4)
 4 the Hadza are such gentle stewards of the land (para 5)
 5 the Hadza have lost exclusive possession of much of their homeland (para 5)
 6 Their entire life is one insanely committed camping trip. (para 6)

Critical thinking reading between the lines

6 Sometimes in articles, an author's views are not explicitly stated, but have to be inferred by reading between the lines. Answer these questions by reading between the lines.

 1 Do you think the author admires the Hadza, or not especially?
 2 Do you think the author has particular views on the question of how land should be used?

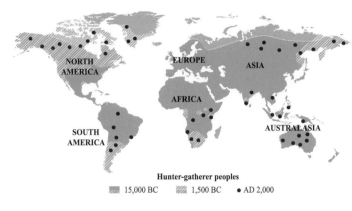

Hunter-gatherer peoples
▨ 15,000 BC ▨ 1,500 BC ● AD 2,000

7 Work in groups. Compare your answers from Exercise 6 and refer to parts of the text that support your view. Did you agree or not?

Word focus *free*

8 Look at this phrase from the article. What does it tell you about the Hadza?

'There are many things to envy about the Hadza – mostly what **free spirits** they appear to be.'

9 Work in pairs. Look at these other expressions using *free* and discuss what each one means.

 1 **Feel free** to make yourself a cup of tea or coffee.
 2 Did you really think he wouldn't want to be paid for his help? **There's no such thing as a free lunch**, you know.
 3 It was supposed to be a civilized debate but the chairman lost control and it became **a free-for-all**.
 4 They were very particular about the text, but they gave us **free rein** on the design.
 5 Although there was a lot of evidence to suggest he was guilty, he **got off scot-free**.

10 Choose two of the following and talk about them from your own experience.

- a discussion that became a free-for-all
- a time you were given free rein to do something
- a time you got off scot-free
- someone who is a free spirit

Speaking

11 Work in groups. You are going to take part in a discussion about the future of the Hadza lands. Look at the role cards and act out the discussion.

Student A: Turn to page 154.

Student B: Turn to page 155.

Student C: Turn to page 156.

The Hadza hunter-gatherers of Tanzania live a life that has not changed much in over ten thousand years. They have no crops, no livestock, no permanent shelters. In spite of long exposure to agriculturalist groups around them, who have domesticated both plants and animals, the Hadza have maintained their foraging lifestyle.

The story of the spread of agriculture is the story of growing population density. Villages formed, then cities, then nations. And in a relatively brief period, the hunter-gatherer lifestyle was extinguished in all but a few places. Agriculture's rise, however, came with a price. It introduced infectious disease epidemics, social stratification, intermittent famines and large-scale war. Professor Jared Diamond of UCLA has called the adoption of agriculture 'the worst mistake in human history' – a mistake from which we have never recovered.

Looking at the Hadza, you can see why he came to this conclusion. They do not engage in warfare. They do not live densely enough to be threatened by an infectious outbreak. They have no known history of famine. The Hadza diet is more stable and varied than that of most of the world's citizens. They live almost entirely free of possessions. The things they own – a cooking pot, a water container, an axe – can be wrapped in a blanket and carried over a shoulder. They enjoy an extraordinary amount of leisure time, 'working' – actively pursuing food – only four to six hours a day. And over all these thousands of years, they've left hardly a footprint on the land.

Hadza women gather berries and baobab fruit and dig edible tubers. Men collect honey and hunt. They will eat almost anything they can kill, from birds to wildebeest to zebras to buffalo. The Hadza recognise no official leaders. Camps are traditionally named after a senior male, but this honour does not confer any particular power. No Hadza adult has authority over any other. None has more wealth; or, rather, they all have no wealth. There are few social obligations – no birthdays, no public holidays, no anniversaries. People sleep whenever they want. Some stay up much of the night and doze during the heat of the day.

Living free?

The chief reason the Hadza have been able to maintain their lifestyle so long is that their homeland is not an inviting place. The soil is briny; fresh water is scarce; the bugs can be intolerable. For tens of thousands of years, it seems, no one else wanted to live here. Recently, however, escalating population pressures have brought a flood of people into Hadza lands. The fact that the Hadza are such gentle stewards of the land has, in a way, hurt them – the region has generally been viewed by outsiders as unused, a place sorely in need of development. The Hadza, who by nature are not a combative people, have almost always moved away rather than fight. But now there is nowhere to retreat. Over the past century, the Hadza have lost exclusive possession of much of their homeland.

There are many things to envy about the Hadza – mostly what free spirits they appear to be. Free from schedules, jobs, bosses, bills, traffic, taxes, laws, social duties and money. Free to grab food and run shirtless through the thorns. But who of us could live like them? Their entire life is one insanely committed camping trip. It's incredibly risky. Medical help is far away. One bad fall from a tree, one bite from a black mamba snake, and you're dead. Women give birth in the bush and nearly half of all children do not make it to age fifteen. They have to cope with extreme heat and swarming tsetse flies. The fact is that it's too late for us to go back to a Hadza lifestyle. Of greater concern is that soon it may be impossible for them to remain in one.

confer (v) /kən'fɜː/ give something (to somebody)
doze (v) /dəʊz/ sleep lightly
social stratification (n) /ˈsəʊʃ(ə)l ˌstrætɪfɪˈkeɪʃən/ different levels or classes in society
thorn (n) /θɔːn/ sharp needle growing from a plant or shrub

10d An interesting subject

Real life making conversation

1 Work in pairs. Which of the following points are characteristics of a good listener? Discuss.

a maintains eye contact
b shows appreciation
c tries to predict what the other person is going to say
d waits before giving their views
e asks questions
f relates what they hear to their own experience

2 Are you a good listener? Which of the points in Exercise 1 are you good or bad at doing?

3 🔊 **2.21** You are going to hear a conversation between two students about an assignment they've been given. Quickly read the task. Then listen to the conversation and answer the questions.

1 Why does the first speaker initiate the conversation?
2 What topic has the second student chosen for his essay?
3 Is the first speaker interested to know more? Why? / Why not?

> Throughout history, people have tried to establish alternative or 'utopian' societies: a perfect or ideal model society for others to follow. Research one of these and write an essay of 2,000 words, describing its principles and why you think it was an effective or ineffective model.

George Pullman

4 Speaking skill showing interest

🔊 **2.21** The speakers use phrases to show interest and keep the conversation going. Listen again and complete the phrases.

1 B: I've been researching a model society set up in the 1880s in Chicago by George Pullman …
   A: _____? _____ interesting.
2 B: … he based his society on capitalist principles, thinking that capitalism was the best way for a society to fulfil its material and spiritual needs.
   A: _____ .
   B: Yes, _____ ?
3 B: He owned all the buildings and rented them to the workers.
   A: _____ .
   B: No, _____ ?
4 A: So, it probably failed in the end then, _____ .
   B: I _____ – these things often do.

> ▶ **SHOWING INTEREST**
>
> **Showing interest**
> I got a 'B' for my essay. → Really?
> I'm going to Spain next month. → Are you?
> Lovely concert. → Yes, wasn't it?
> The weather doesn't look very promising. → No, it doesn't, does it?
> He left his job. → He didn't, did he?
> I'll give you a call some time. → Yes, do.
>
> **Responding naturally**
> What are you doing here? → Waiting.
> Are you going to the conference? → I expect / hope / think / suppose so.
> Will the shop still be open? → I think not. / I'm afraid not. / I doubt it.
>
> I've got a cold coming. → Me too.
> I can't wait for the holidays. → Me neither.

5 Pronunciation intonation and elision

a 🔊 **2.22** Look at the language box. Listen to the intonation in the first set of responses. Does the intonation rise or fall? Do they show interest, surprise or agreement?

b Work in pairs. Practise saying the responses in the same way.

c 🔊 **2.23** Listen to how these phrases are pronounced. Notice which sounds are elided. Then practise saying them with your partner.

1 I'm afraid not.   3 I expect so.   5 I doubt it.
2 I suppose so.   4 I hope so.

6 Imagine you are researching an essay on a particular topic. Choose a subject that you are familiar with. With your partner, act out two conversations like the one you heard in Exercise 3.

TALK ABOUT ▶ CIVIC DUTIES ▶ SOCIAL ANIMALS ▶ A CONSERVATION PROJECT ▶ MAKING CONVERSATION
WRITE ▶ A DISCURSIVE ESSAY

10e A good start in life

Writing a discursive essay

1 Look at the items (a–h). Choose the four items that you think most help people to achieve professional success in life.

a wealthy parents
b a strong work ethic
c good social connections
d supportive friends or community
e ambitious parents
f a good education
g a high social status
h something else?

2 Work in groups. Discuss your answers. Does social background (upbringing, education, parents' jobs, etc.) play a big part in determining a child's prospects in life?

3 Read the essay and answer the questions.

1 What is the main argument?
2 Do you agree? Why? / Why not?

4 Writing skill critical thinking in writing

Look at the four steps we use when writing a discursive essay (1–4). Which of the ideas from the essay (a–c) is the hypothesis, which is the thesis and which is part of the analysis?

1 think first about what the probable answer / your position is (your hypothesis)
2 develop this into your main argument (your thesis)
3 find evidence to support your argument (the analysis)
4 repeat your main argument in the conclusion

a A child's prospects are clearly connected to their own opinion of what they can achieve.
b Those from high-income families hoped to become lawyers or doctors.
c Social background is important for success because it shapes your expectations in life.

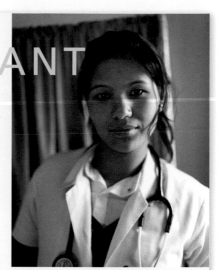

Is social background an **IMPORTANT FACTOR** *in success in life?*

It is generally thought that to have a good chance of succeeding in life you need to have certain social advantages: wealthy parents, a high social status and a privileged education. But I would argue that provided a child is given the basic necessities of life – being fed and clothed properly, and being loved and cared for – then their prospects are determined only by their own opinion of what they can achieve. And that is something that can be changed.

In a recent study, children in the city of Baltimore, USA, were interviewed about their prospects. Their ambitions reflected their own experience. Those from high-income families hoped to become lawyers or doctors, because those were typical professions of their parents' friends. Those from poorer backgrounds wanted to be professional sportspeople or music artists, because those were the people who had succeeded in their communities. However, they expected to be electricians or hairdressers. At school, the more privileged children performed better, because they knew that if they got good grades, their prospects of becoming a lawyer or doctor were good. The children from poorer backgrounds had no such incentive to do well at academic subjects and performed much worse. However, when their school offered cash prizes on condition that their grades improved, the improvement was immediate.

This shows that a child's prospects are clearly connected to their expectations. As long as children have low ambitions, they will see no benefit in working hard at school and, as a result, they will not succeed. Some people always start life worse off than others, but where they end up is a question of what they believe is possible.

5 Write an essay of 250–300 words on the topic *How does social background affect a child's prospects in life?* Use the ideas that you discussed in Exercise 2.

6 Exchange essays with your partner. Use these questions to check your essays.

- Is the main argument clear?
- Does the essay outline the main argument at the beginning and end of the essay?
- Does the analysis support the main argument?
- Do you find the arguments logical and convincing?

Initiation with ants

A gruelling initiation is about to begin.

Before you watch

1 Work in pairs. Look at the definition of *initiation*. Can you think of an example of ceremonies for these occasions (a–d)?

> **initiation (n)** /ɪnɪʃiˈeɪʃn/ a ceremony or task that gives a person formal admission or acceptance into a club, organisation, community or family

a being born
b passing from childhood into adulthood
c marriage
d another occasion

2 You are going to watch a video about an initiation ceremony. What part do you think ants will play in the ceremony?

While you watch

3 Watch the video and check your answer from Exercise 2.

4 Watch the first part of the video (to 00.50) and complete the table about the initiation ritual.

1	The signal for the start of the initiation:
2	Length of ritual:
3	Age of participants:
4	Animal used in ritual:
5	Purpose of ritual:
6	Number of times participant must perform ritual:

5 Watch the second part of the video (00.51 to end) and answer the questions.

1 How powerful is the sting of these ants?

2 How is it possible to place the ants in the gloves without being stung?

3 Why don't the ants escape from the gloves?

4 What is the purpose of the dance?

5 What happens after the gloves are removed?

6 How does the new initiate react to his ordeal?

6 What does the chief say about the wider purpose of this ritual? Do you agree with him? Why? / Why not?

7 Write a paragraph describing the ant initiation ritual. Use this structure. Then watch the video again to check.

The Sateré-Mawé tribe of the Amazon [1] .... an extreme ritual for [2] .... that acts as [3] .... into manhood. Bullet ants [4] .... gloves, which [5] .... by the initiates [6] .... ten minutes while [7] .... These ants [8] .... sting of a bee and the initiates [9] .... gloves [10] .... twenty times. After the gloves are taken off, [11] .... 24 hours. The chief of the tribe says that [12] ....

After you watch

8 Roleplay an interview about a ceremony

Work in pairs.

Student A: You are going to talk about a ceremony in your country. Choose a ceremony from the list or your own idea and prepare to talk about it.

- a naming ceremony for a child
- a rite of passage into adulthood
- a graduation ceremony
- a wedding ceremony

Student B: Imagine you are a foreign journalist. You are going to interview a local person about a ceremony in their country. Look at these points and prepare your questions.

- what the purpose of the ceremony is
- who participates
- what form the ceremony takes
- the origins and significance of the ceremony
- what it means for the person and what they like about it

Act out the interview, then change roles and act out the interview again. Student B should choose a new ceremony.

9 What's the most difficult thing you have had to do in front of a group of your peers?

> **carnivore** (n) /ˈkɑːnɪvɔː/ a person or animal who eats meat
> **excruciating** (adj) /ɪkˈskruːʃieɪtɪŋ/ very painful
> **medicine man** (n) /ˈmedɪsɪn mæn/ the person in a tribe who is supposed to be able to heal illnesses
> **mitt** (n) /mɪt/ a glove without finger compartments
> **neurotoxic** (adj) /ˈnjʊərəʊ ˈtɒksɪk/ poisonous to the nerves in the body
> **stab** (n) /stæb/ a wound made by a pointed object
> **stupor** (n) /ˈstjuːpə/ a state of near unconsciousness
> **swarm** (n) /swɔːm/ a large group of insects, e.g. bees
> **unfazed** (adj) /ʌnˈfeɪzd/ not troubled or bothered
> **writhe** (v) /raɪð/ move about in pain or trying to get free

UNIT 10 REVIEW

Grammar

1 Complete the interview about Cabo Pulmo National Marine Park.

   a Transform the adjectives in brackets (1–6) into their correct adverbial form.

   b Rewrite the questions (a–d) as tag questions.

2 Read the interview again and answer the questions.

   1 What was the key to saving the coral reef in this area?

   2 Why is the proposed new development a danger to the marine park?

I = Interviewer, J = Javier Hernandez

I: Cabo Pulmo National Marine Park is a great example of how citizens can act [1] _____ (concerted) to effect change. We interviewed local environmentalist Javier Hernandez to find out more. Javier, [a] *was your main purpose to protect the coral reef?*

J: Yes, that's right. We were concerned because the reef was deteriorating [2] _____ (fast) and we needed help to save it.

I: And [b] *did you get the help of the government?*

J: Yes. They set up the conservation area. Basically, through campaigning and lobbying [3] _____ (hard), we were able to get fishing banned in this area. After all the intensive fishing of the last 25 years, there were [4] _____ (hard) any fish left. The fish were part of a fragile ecosystem that supports the coral.

I: And [c] *has that changed?*

J: Absolutely. The project has been [5] _____ (incredible) successful. Stocks of fish have risen by 450%. It's a great victory for the environment and also for the community.

I: So [d] *can you relax now that you have won this particular battle?*

J: No! There's now a proposal to build an enormous tourist complex right next to the marine park. With a new marina, countless hotels and shops, the footprint will be huge. We're negotiating with the developers to reach a good solution. The negotiations are being conducted [6] _____ (friendly), but if they fail, we are worried about the negative impact on the marine park.

I CAN	
use tag questions to check or seek agreement	☐
describe how something is done using appropriate adverbial forms	☐

Vocabulary

3 Complete the collocations.

   1 We are a very close-k_____ community.

   2 My father is a second-g_____ immigrant.

   3 I don't see a lot of my e_____ family: uncles, aunts, cousins and so on.

   4 I try to do my b_____ for the community by helping to coach the local youth football team.

   5 My neighbours are always willing to lend a helping h_____ when someone needs it.

   6 Big festivals are part of our cultural h_____ .

4 Work in pairs. Discuss which of the statements in Exercise 3 are true for you. Explain your answers.

I CAN	
talk about community life	☐
talk about social responsibility	☐

Real life

5 Match the statements (1–6) with the correct short response (a–f).

   1 I waited an hour to get a bus home last night.

   2 Are they going to close the street to traffic when we have our street party?

   3 I think the new community centre they've built is fantastic.

   4 The team played brilliantly.

   5 I'll let you know if I need any more details.

   6 We're going to Madagascar this summer.

   a Please do.
   b I expect so.
   c Are you? How exciting!
   d Yes, they did, didn't they?
   e You didn't, did you?
   f Me too.

6 Work in pairs. Tell each other your news: what has happened to you recently, what your plans are, what you think about a recent event. Show interest and ask questions to get more information.

I CAN	
use short responses in conversation	☐
show interest in a conversation	☐

Speaking

7 Work in pairs. Discuss what aspects of social living you like best and which aspects you think are the most important for a well-functioning society.

Unit 11 Reason and emotion

Tree branch swing, India
Photograph by Jhulan Mahanta

FEATURES

1 🔊 **2.24** Look at the photo. Describe the boy's feelings. Then listen to a photographer who specialises in photographing people and compare your answer.

2 🔊 **2.24** Work in pairs. What does the speaker say about the following? Listen again and check.

1 facial expressions among different cultures
2 different emotions
3 photographing children

3 Look at the adjectives for describing emotions. Put two adjectives under each heading. Which word in each pair has the stronger meaning?

astonished	content	cross	despondent	ecstatic	livid
miserable	petrified	scared	taken aback		

<u>Anger</u>   <u>Fear</u>   <u>Surprise</u>   <u>Happiness</u>   <u>Sadness</u>

4 Choose two of the adjectives from Exercise 3 and talk about the last time or a memorable time when you felt this emotion.

> *I was really cross when I turned up for a concert the other week and they told me it had been cancelled. They offered me a refund, but they should have contacted people beforehand!*

11a Emotional intelligence

Listening

1 Look at the definition of *emotional intelligence*. How emotionally intelligent do you think you are? Do you know anyone who is particularly emotional intelligent?

> **emotional intelligence (EI)** the ability to recognise, judge and control one's own emotions and those of others

2 🔊 **2.25** Listen to an interview with a psychologist and answer the questions.

   a   What service does she offer?
   b   Why do people need this service?

3 🔊 **2.25** Read the sentences. Then listen again and choose the correct option to complete them.

  1 EIQ's training helps people to distinguish between positive and negative *influences / emotions*.
  2 More and more people around the world suffer from being *confused / nervous and worried*.
  3 Hikikomori are young Japanese who avoid *other people / their parents*.
  4 EIQ can help people overcome their fear of public *speaking / places*.
  5 Micro-expressions appear on the face only for a few *seconds / parts of a second*.
  6 Micro-expressions often show people's *darker / hidden* feelings.
  7 The presenter's micro-expression revealed his *surprise / irritation*.
  8 The doctor wanted emotional intelligence training to be able to feel *more detached from / closer to* her patients.

4 Do you think Naomi is right that life has become more difficult to deal with emotionally? Why? / Why not?

Idioms feelings

5 The idiom *on edge* was used in the interview to describe people who feel tense and nervous. Match the idioms with the feelings they describe.

> **Idioms**
> a bit down   all over the place   done in
> on edge   hot under the collar   speechless
> thrilled to bits   upbeat

> **Feelings**
> angry   confused and disorganised
> optimistic   sad   tense and nervous
> very happy   very surprised   very tired

6 Work in pairs. Look at these sentences. Check your answers from Exercise 5.

  1 Sorry, I think I sent you the wrong document. And I've left my memory stick at home. I'm **all over the place** today.
  2 Don't worry about Paolo. He's just **a bit down** after failing his driving test.
  3 Carla's very **on edge** today. Is she worried about something?
  4 We're very **upbeat** about our prospects of winning.
  5 Sorry, I can't do anything tonight. I've been travelling all day and I'm completely **done in**.
  6 He got a bit **hot under the collar** when you suggested that he wasn't doing his fair share of the work.
  7 Frankly, I was **speechless** when she said she didn't think it would work. It was her idea in the first place!
  8 A: Did he like his present? B: Yes, he was **thrilled to bits** with it.

Language focus unreal past

7 Look at the extracts from the interview (1–6), where the speaker uses a past form to talk about hypothetical situations in the present or future. Match the extracts with the descriptions (a–d).

1 Do you wish that you **felt** more in control of things?
2 Perhaps it's time you **looked** into 'emotional intelligence training'.
3 Suppose you **were** someone who felt very on edge when speaking in public.
4 I'd rather your listeners **took** one of our courses.
5 What if I **were to tell** you that you'd already made one of these?
6 If only I **was** better at building rapport with my patients.

a a wish
b a picture of an unreal situation
c a preference for what someone would like to happen
d a sentence that says what should be done now

▶ **UNREAL PAST**

would rather / would just as soon
I'd rather you found someone else to give the talk.
I'd just as soon people decided for themselves.

I wish / if only
I wish / If only life was less stressful.
I wish / If only he would relax a bit more.

what if / supposing / suppose
What if we were to offer you a free trial?
Supposing he reacted badly. What would you do?

it's (high) time
It's (high) time that we got a new computer.

For further information and practice, see page 171.

---

8 Look at the language focus box. Then rewrite the sentences below using the words given.

1 I think he might be persuaded by more money.
   (Supposing / we / offer)
2 He really needs to organise his life better.
   (It's high time / he / sort out)
3 Driving an hour to work each day is really stressful.
   (I wish / have to)
4 I never have time to take a proper holiday.
   (If only / I / be / able)
5 Can you let me see the letter before you send it?
   (I'd rather / you / show)
6 People do everything in such a hurry these days.
   (I wish / people / slow down)
7 He might refuse. What would you do then?
   (What if / he / say)
8 Do you have any good advice for me?
   (What / you / do / if)

9 Complete the conversation with one word in each space.

A: What if someone [1]_____ to offer you emotional intelligence training? What [2]_____ you say?
B: I think I [3]_____ be a bit taken aback. I'd [4]_____ other people didn't tell me how I should feel or respond emotionally.
A: Don't you wish that you [5]_____ understand your own emotions better?
B: Perhaps. But that doesn't mean I [6]_____ go and get training for it. [7]_____ the person didn't have any real qualifications? I'd just as [8]_____ trust my own instincts.

10 Pronunciation word stress: wishes

a 🔊 2.26 Work in pairs. Look at these sentences with *wish* and *if only*. Discuss where you think the stress falls. Then listen and check.

1 I wish he would listen to me.
2 I wish you were coming with me.
3 If only it were true.
4 If only you would relax a bit.

b Practise saying the sentences with your partner.

Speaking

11 Work in groups. Discuss the list of things that irritate people about modern life. Think of two more things each and explain why they irritate you. Agree on the three that are most irritating.

1 being stuck in traffic
2 waiting for things to download on the computer
3 receiving unsolicited calls at home from sales and marketing companies
4 people who talk loudly on their mobile phones in public places
5 people pushing in front of you in a queue (on foot or in a car)
6 parents who embarrass you thinking they are trendy

11b Thinking fast and slow

Reading

1 Work in pairs and discuss these situations. Would you follow your instinct or intuition? Or would you take your time before you came to a decision?

1 deciding whether to rent a nice flat you have seen (it's the first one you have looked at)
2 expressing something in English that you are not sure of
3 giving money to someone collecting for a charity in the street
4 deciding what to wear to a party
5 giving your opinion in a debate

2 Read the article about rational and irrational thinking and say which statement (a–c) best summarises Kahneman's theories.

a We can often be irrational in our thinking.
b We are essentially rational in our thinking.
c We are completely unpredictable in our thinking.

3 Match the questions in the article (1–3) with what they tell us about the way we think (a–c).

a that we carry a lot of preconceptions about the world with us
b that we are not logical when it comes to taking risks
c that we can be influenced in our thinking by irrelevant information

Thinking
FAST & SLOW

Psychologist Daniel Kahneman's work on how rational minds sometimes think irrationally won him the Nobel Prize in Economics, because it is key to understanding people's behaviour. Kahneman researched our irrational traits by asking intriguing questions. Here are three examples from his book *Thinking fast and slow*. Answer each one without thinking too hard. Should you get them wrong, don't worry: most of us do.

1 Roughly, how many United Nations states are African?

2 Linda is a single 31-year-old, bright and concerned with issues of social justice. Which statement is more probable: a) Linda works in a bank, or b) Linda works in a bank and is active in the feminist movement?

3 a You can either have £500 for certain, or a 50% chance of winning £1,000. Which would you choose?

3 b You can either lose £500 for certain, or have a 50% chance of losing £1,000. Which would you choose?

The answer to the first question is 53, but that's not important. What is psychologically interesting is that had someone already mentioned that the temperature today was 82° Fahrenheit, your answer would have been a higher number than if you had been told it was 28° Centigrade. The answer to the second question is that neither is more probable. However, an overwhelming number of people answer b. Were the same question presented as a logical formula, few would make this mistake. But we are influenced by the plausible details, preferring the human story to the hard logic. Logically, you should choose the same option in both 3a and 3b, but it seems that most of us take fewer risks when there's a chance of winning something. However, offered a chance to get out of a losing situation, most of us will take the gamble.

What Kahneman is trying to demonstrate is that our intuition can be unreliable and irrational. He describes our brain as having two systems: System One, where we form intuitive responses, and System Two, where more conscious, deliberate thought occurs. The problem is that on many occasions, System One is always trying to help, often with imperfect information. And the result can be imperfect, such as when taking financial decisions. Some even say that had it not been for this irrational thinking, the banking crisis of 2008 may not have occurred.

4 Find adjectives in the article with the following meanings.

1 interesting (para 1)
2 very large (para 2)
3 believable (para 2)
4 slow and careful (para 3)
5 incomplete, unsatisfactory (para 3)

5 Have you taken any financial decisions that weren't based on rational calculation? What were they? Did they work out for you?

> ▶ **WORDBUILDING heteronyms**
>
> There are some words in English ending in -ate that have the same form as an adjective and as a verb. We use pronunciation to distinguish between them.
> *deliberate*: verb /dəˌlɪbəreɪt/; adjective /dɪˌlɪbrət/
>
> For further information and practice, see Workbook page 91.

6 Pronunciation heteronyms

🔊 **2.27** Listen to the pairs of sentences. What is the difference in the pronunciation of the final syllable of each word in bold?

1 a Was that a **deliberate** mistake?
   b Don't **deliberate** for too long.
2 a We need to **separate** my books from yours.
   b That's a **separate** issue.
3 a He's very **articulate**.
   b He couldn't **articulate** what he meant.
4 a Let's not **duplicate** the work.
   b I have a **duplicate** copy.

Language focus inversion in conditionals

7 Look at these sentences from the article. Can you express exactly the same idea, beginning each sentence with *if*?

1 Should you get them wrong, don't worry.
2 Had someone already mentioned that the temperature today was 82° Fahrenheit, your answer would have been a higher number.
3 Were the same question presented as a logical formula, few would make this mistake.
4 Some even say that had it not been for this irrational thinking, the banking crisis of 2008 may not have occurred.

> ▶ **INVERSION IN CONDITIONALS**
>
> **should**
> *Should you get more information, please tell me.*
> *Should you need to contact me, I'll be at the Astoria hotel.*
>
> **second conditional**
> *Were the price lower, I wouldn't hesitate to buy it.*
> *Were you to decide to stay, we would give you the training.*
> *Were it not for me, you wouldn't be living here.*
>
> **third and mixed conditional**
> *Had I known earlier, I would have informed you.*
> *Had he not written the book, no one would know about this.*
>
> Notes
> 1 We use inversion in slightly more formal speech or writing.
> 2 The use of *for* + noun or *for* + *the fact that* is quite common in second and third conditional inversions.
> 3 We use the *were to* form only to talk about future possibilities, not unreal present situations.
>
> For further information and practice, see page 171.

8 Look at the language focus box. Then rewrite these conditional sentences using inversion.

1 If someone asks who told you, don't give them my name.
2 If I had thought about it for longer, I would have got the answer right.
3 They wouldn't be in this situation now if they had taken my advice.
4 If we took the risk, I am sure that we wouldn't regret it.
5 Would the world be a better place if everyone thought more carefully before acting?
6 If something is unclear, you can always call me on this number and ask.

9 Work in pairs. Write five sentences about yourself using inversion. Use the sentence stems below or make up your own. Then compare sentences with your partner.

1 Were it not for my parents …
2 I wouldn't be living here …
3 Had it not been for the bad weather …
4 I wouldn't have reached such a high level of English …
5 Had it not been for the fact that I was too young at the time …
6 I would have become a …

Speaking

10 Work in pairs. Look at these other Kahneman puzzles, taking no more than 30 seconds to answer each one. What point is Kahneman trying to make about the way we think in each case? Can you think of other situations where it isn't helpful to be an intuitive thinker?

1 A bat and a ball cost $1.10. The bat costs one dollar more than the ball. How much does the bat cost?
2 Imagine that you bought a ticket to see a play for $30. As you enter the theatre, you discover that you have lost the ticket. The theatre keeps no record of ticket purchasers. Would you pay $30 for another ticket to see the play?

11c Us. And them.

Reading

1 Look at the photos of the robots and answer the questions.

1 Which is real? Which are science fiction?
2 What do you think robots are able to do? What things can't they do?

2 Read the article about the new generation of robots. At the current stage of their development, what can robots do? Choose the correct option (a–c).

a They can only carry out industrial tasks.
b They can replace people in some simple jobs.
c They can already think and feel emotion.

3 Work in pairs. Write notes about what each robot can and can't do.

a Actroid-DER (Yume)
b HERB
c Vanderbilt prototype

4 Find words in the text with the following meanings.

1 make a sudden movement (para 1)
2 go to sleep temporarily (para 2)
3 a great flow, a waterfall (para 4)
4 propelling or throwing an object at speed (para 6)
5 people who have no experience of something (para 7)
6 copying (para 9)

Critical thinking understanding style

5 The author uses various techniques to keep this scientific subject light and prevent it becoming too serious. Match the extracts from the article (1–6) with the technique used (a–c).

1 … a role that admittedly is not the most demanding. (para 2)
2 … like a person who has lost interest in a conversation. (para 2)
3 … HERB isn't going to win first prize in a beauty contest. (para 5)
4 … a necessity if he is to help an elderly widow to the bathroom without catapulting her through the door. (para 6)
5 Picking up a drink is not a very difficult task for most of us. (para 7)
6 … he takes the safest course of action and simply stands there, honking at everybody. (para 8)

a an amusing image
b an understatement
c a comparison with human appearance or behaviour

6 Work in pairs. Compare your answers from Exercise 5 with your partner. Did these techniques improve the article for you or not? Explain your reasons.

Word focus *move*

7 Work in pairs. Look at this expression with *move* from the text and discuss what it means. Then complete the other expressions with *move* using the words given.

'HERB is **on the move** but he still has his limitations.'

| the goalposts | a muscle | to tears |
| up a gear | up in the world | |

1 Her story of having to look after her sick brother **moved everyone** _____ .
2 That's your Ferrari? You**'re moving** _____ .
3 Don't **move** _____ ! There's a bee on your collar. I'm going to brush it off.
4 They've **moved** _____ . They are now saying candidates must have worked for at least two years.
5 When his opponent started playing better, he just **moved** _____ and won the match easily.

Speaking

8 Work in pairs. Which of the following occupations do you think robots should *not* be allowed to participate in and why?

a police work
b healthcare
c childcare
d public transport

9 Ethical issues are always raised by technological progress. Look at these technologies and say what rules should govern their use.

- applications on phones that allow you to know where the user is
- genetic modification of foods
- open access to books and music on the Internet

U S . AND T H E M .

Someone types a command into a laptop, and Actroid-DER jerks upright. She raises her arms and the corners of her mouth lift to form a smile. She blinks, then turns her face toward me. 'Are you surprised that I'm a robot?' she asks. 'I look just like a human, don't I?'

Her comment has the effect of drawing my attention to the many ways that she does not. Developed in Japan by the Kokoro Company, the Actroid-DER android can be rented to serve as a kind of receptionist at corporate events, a role that admittedly is not the most demanding. But in spite of the $250,000 spent on her development, Yume, as she is known, moves jerkily, and her inelastic features give her lovely face a crazed look. She also appears to nod off between remarks, like a person who has lost interest in a conversation.

Actroid androids are part of a new generation of robots, designed to function not as industrial machines but as agents that we can more easily feel emotionally connected to, capable of taking on roles in our homes, schools and offices: cooking, folding the laundry, even babysitting our children. 'In five or ten years robots will routinely be functioning in human environments,' says Reid Simmons, a professor at Carnegie Mellon.

Such a prospect leads to a cascade of questions. How much everyday human function do we want in our machines? What should they look like? Do we want androids like Yume in our kitchens or are they just creepy? Will these robots change the way we relate to each other?

In another building not far away, HERB sits motionless, lost in thought. Short for *Home Exploring Robotic Butler*, HERB is being developed by Carnegie Mellon as a prototype service bot that might care for the elderly and disabled in the future. With Segway wheels for legs and computers for a body, HERB isn't going to win first prize in a beauty contest. But unlike Yume, HERB does have something like a mental life.

Traditional robots can be programmed to carry out very precise actions, but only within a very structured environment, like a factory production line. HERB is being programmed to 'think' for himself: to negotiate human spaces and move around without bumping into people who are themselves in motion. HERB's perception system consists of a video camera and a laser navigation device which control his mechanical arm. The arm is pressure-sensitive: a necessity if he is to help an elderly widow to the bathroom without catapulting her through the door.

HERB can pick up a juice box, hold it upright and place it down again gently. He can tell its shape and how easily it can break. To the uninitiated, these accomplishments might seem unimpressive. Picking up a drink is not a very difficult task for most of us. It's also a simple act for an industrial robot programmed for that specific action. But the difference between a social robot like HERB and a conventional factory bot is that HERB knows the object is a juice box, and not a teacup or a glass of milk. This understanding involves a great deal of mathematics and computer science, but it boils down to 'taking in information and processing it intelligently in the context of what he already knows about his world'.

So HERB is on the move but he still has his limitations. To function in human spaces, at the moment he just has a digital bicycle horn that he honks to let people know he's getting near them; if a room is crowded, he takes the safest course of action and simply stands there, honking at everybody.

Other robots are now probing the world of human emotions. One prototype developed at Vanderbilt University plays a simple ball game with children. The robot monitors a child's emotions by measuring minute changes in heartbeat, sweating and gaze. When it senses boredom or irritation, it changes the game until signals indicate the child is having fun again. There is no linguistic interaction, but it is a first step toward replicating a key aspect of humanity: recognising others' feelings, and adjusting your behaviour accordingly. But of course, as Yume confesses, 'I'm not human! I'll never be exactly like you.'

android (n) /ˈændrɔɪd/ a robot with a human form
bot (n) /bɒt/ abbreviation for robot
prototype (n) /ˈprəʊtətaɪp/ a first version of a machine

11d A sensitive subject

Real life **recognising feelings**

1 Work in pairs. Read this extract from a guide about communicating with people. Think of a situation where you didn't follow this advice. What happened? Discuss with your partner.

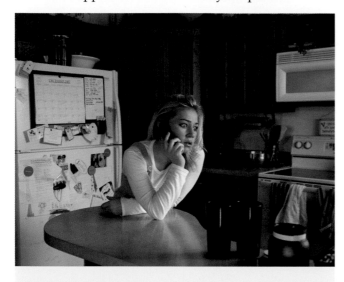

There are many opportunities for misunderstandings to arise in communication with others, whether in work relationships or simply between friends. And there is also a lot of advice about how to avoid these. But there is one simple tool in all types of communication that we should all bear in mind: if you feel something is wrong, ask. So if something strikes you as funny or strange or rude, or you think you have upset or offended the other person, just ask … sensitively, of course. Otherwise you will be left wondering what someone meant by a gesture or expression, or whether they were offended by or misunderstood something you said.

2 🔊 **2.28** Listen to three conversations. Answer the questions.

1 What is the relationship between each pair of speakers?
2 What is the subject of each conversation?

3 🔊 **2.28** Listen again. In each conversation there was a point of misunderstanding between the speakers. What was it?

a Conversation 1: ....
b Conversation 2: ....
c Conversation 3: ....

4 Speaking skill **recognising others' feelings**

🔊 **2.28** Look at the box. Then listen to the conversations again. Which expressions were used in the following situations?

1 Fernando asked Phil if everything was OK.
2 Alicia recognised Becky's feelings.
3 Becky corrected the impression she gave.
4 Megumi asked Paul about his feelings.
5 Paul corrected the impression he gave.

> ▶ **RECOGNISING OTHERS' FEELINGS**
>
> You look a little puzzled / surprised / troubled.
> You seem concerned / worried.
>
> Sorry, I didn't mean to offend you.
> Did I say something to upset you?
> Did I say something funny?
> Sorry, I don't understand what's so funny / what the joke is.
>
> Sorry, perhaps that sounded a bit abrupt.
> I'm sorry, that came out wrong.
> Please don't think me rude / ungrateful / nosy, but …

5 Pronunciation adjectives ending in *-ed*

a 🔊 **2.29** Work in pairs. How are these adjectives pronounced? Listen and check.

alarmed	concerned	distressed	embarrassed
insulted	offended	shocked	surprised
worried			

b What are the rules about the pronunciation of adjectives ending in *-ed*? Think of three other adjectives describing feelings that end in *-ed*. How are they pronounced?

c Practise saying the words again in Exercise 5a with the correct pronunciation.

6 Work in pairs. Improvise a conversation based on one of the situations below. Use phrases from the box in Exercise 4.

- a misunderstanding between colleagues about who was supposed to do a certain job
- a friend finding something funny that was not intended to be a joke
- a discussion between colleagues about some work that was not done properly

TALK ABOUT ▶ MODERN LIFE ▶ MIND GAMES ▶ TECHNOLOGY ETHICS ▶ RECOGNISING FEELINGS
WRITE ▶ AN EMAIL MESSAGE

11e Don't get me wrong

Writing an email message

1 Work in pairs. Discuss the questions.

1 It's said that up to 40 per cent of all emails are misinterpreted in some way. Why do you think this happens?
2 When was the last time you had a misunderstanding in an email exchange with someone? What happened?

2 Read the extract from a business communications forum and compare the answers you discussed in Exercise 1.

It's very easy to be misunderstood in an email. That's because people treat email like face-to-face conversation, where exchanges can be very short and to the point. But of course they are *not* the same. In face-to-face conversation we communicate our feelings with gestures, expressions and tone of voice, as well as words.

In email writing, both the writer and reader imagine the tone. So if the reader is feeling particularly sensitive, he or she might take offence at something that the writer intended to be a joke. Or if the writer tries to express urgency about something that needs doing, the reader might interpret this as impatience, frustration or anger, when really it's nothing of the kind.

3 Read the emails which caused misunderstandings. Match each email (A–F) with how it was interpreted by the reader (1–6).

1 You have ignored my wishes.
2 You are asking for my advice on something I am not included in.
3 You think I can't spell.
4 You think I'm always slow to get things done.
5 You think my ideas are worthless.
6 You think I am ignoring you.

A I got your report. I honestly didn't expect to see it until the end of the month.

B Thanks for letting me know about Jessica's farewell party next Saturday. I had hoped that you would change the day of the party to one that I could manage, but never mind.

C I read your suggestions and I think we will stick to the original plan.

D As you know, five of us have been offered the chance to visit the new Williams factory next week. There are two other people who I want to invite, not to include you – Fergus and Marcin. What do you think?

E Thanks for the email. I don't know about the 'optinos' because I don't know what the word means! But if you want my opinion, I think the Berkeley chairs are the best option.

F You haven't replied to the email I sent you two days ago. Please reply today or we'll miss the deadline.

4 Writing skill avoiding misunderstandings

Look at the phrases used for avoiding or clearing up misunderstandings (1–8). Then use the phrases to rewrite the emails and make them clearer. In some cases you can use more than one phrase, but in D you only need to correct the grammar mistake.

1 Don't take this the wrong way.
2 No offence intended.
3 I don't want to pressure you.
4 I'm joking, of course.
5 It took me rather by surprise.
6 Many thanks for getting back to me so quickly.
7 I do appreciate all your work on this.
8 I am not offended in any way.

5 You work for a company which publishes books. A colleague has told you that your department, foreign dictionaries, is going to be closed down. Write an email to your boss to find out: why the decision has been taken, if he had anything to do with it, and what is going to happen to the employees in your department.

6 Exchange emails with your partner. Use these questions to check your emails.

- Is the email clear in its purpose?
- Does it contain any mistakes (grammar or spelling)?
- Is the tone clear, i.e. it cannot be misinterpreted?

11f Self-teaching robots

This robot solves problems like we do.

Before you watch

1 Work in pairs. Look at the list (a–d) of machines and programs that are 'intelligent', i.e. they make decisions for themselves. Which do you find useful and which do you find annoying?

a a parking sensor on a car
b a warning system in a car that tells you when you are not wearing a seatbelt
c an automatic spelling checker on a computer
d speech recognition systems in a car or computer

2 How do you think a robot could 'learn' new things? Discuss with your partner.

While you watch

3 Watch the video and answer the questions.

1 How does the robot teach itself?
   _____

2 What are the creators' ambitions for this type of robot?
   _____

4 Watch the first part of the video again (to 01.22) and complete the notes.

Name of robot: 'The Real World ¹ _____ (RWGPS)'
Creator: Tokyo ² _____
³ _____ **of project:** Dr Osamu Hasegawa
Aim of project: to ⁴ _____ robots and the real world
Task given to robot: serving ⁵ _____
Information NOT given to robot: prior knowledge of ⁶ _____
How the robot solves the problem: analyses ⁷ _____ and applies filters

5 Read these sentences. Then watch the second part of the video (01.23 to end). Are the sentences true (T) or false (F)?

1 The robot was pre-programmed to pick up a cup.
2 The robot uses information from the Internet to make an 'intelligent' decision.
3 The robot uses Google to research specific items, much like we do.
4 Learning moral values is not a realistic ambition for this robot.

After you watch

6 Roleplay presenting an idea for a household robot

Work in pairs.

Imagine you have been asked to present an idea for a robot which can do some household chores. Look at the list of chores (a–h) and decide which one would be most useful. Design the concept for a robot to do this chore. Consider how sophisticated the robot would have to be and how it would work (in simple terms). It could be either an android-type robot or a simpler more industrial-type robot. Try to anticipate potential problems with the robot.

a ironing
b vacuum cleaning
c sorting and taking out the rubbish
d making the beds
e watering the plants
f walking the dog
g dusting/wiping surfaces
h cooking

Present your ideas to another pair and answer their questions.

7 Work in groups and discuss these questions.

1 Has your opinion changed about the possibilities for robots helping humans after watching the video and listening to your classmates' ideas? Why? / Why not?
2 What other chores or tasks in your daily life would you be most grateful for robot help with? How realistic do you think it is that this will be a possibility in the future?

core (n) /kɔː/ the heart or centre of something **educated guess** (n) /ˈedjʊkeɪtɪd ges/ a speculation based on a reasonable amount of knowledge or information **invaluable** (adj) /ɪnˈvæljʊbl/ very valuable **irrelevant** (adj) /ɪˈrelɪv(ə)nt/ unimportant, not related to the subject in question **moral values** (n) /ˈmɒrəl ˈvæljuːs/ a set of beliefs about what is right and wrong **scour** (v) /ˈskaʊə/ search a place very thoroughly

Grammar

1 Complete the article by putting the verbs in the correct form. Note that the last two are examples of inversion in a conditional sentence.

2 Answer the questions about the article.

1 What is the problem with this type of test?
2 Is this the participants' fault? Why? / Why not?

3 Work in pairs. Answer the statements (1–6) in the article. Discuss what you think each answer tells you about a person's emotional intelligence.

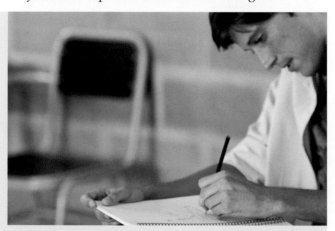

Look at these statements from a test of emotional intelligence and choose one of the following answers: *certainly true*, *probably true*, *probably untrue* or *certainly untrue*.

1 I'd rather not _____ (give) my opinion if it risks offending someone.
2 I'd rather others _____ (tell) me the truth even if it is sometimes painful.
3 I wish I _____ (can) control some of my bad habits, but I can't.
4 If I _____ (have) to list my main strengths, I'd have no trouble thinking of them.
5 Unless _____ (someone / praise) my work, I am not happy with it.
6 _____ (I / be asked) to do something unethical, I would refuse.

Now ask yourself: 'Did you answer them honestly?' The answer is probably 'not altogether'.

[7] _____ (you / be instructed) to be as honest as possible before you started, your responses might have been more truthful, but only a little. Why is this? Like other personality tests, the problem with measuring emotional intelligence is that it relies heavily on the respondent a) knowing their own feelings, and b) being truthful in their responses. Many of us would be inclined to give untruthful responses when asked about our weaknesses, not because we want to mislead, but because we all have a natural tendency to play down our faults.

I CAN	
talk about hypothetical or 'unreal' situations in the present/future using the past tense (unreal past)	
use inversion in conditional sentences	

Vocabulary

4 Choose the correct option to complete the sentences about feelings.

1 I'm not panicking. I just feel a bit *on edge / upbeat*.
2 I wasn't just cross. I was absolutely *hot under the collar / livid*.
3 To say I was surprised is an understatement. I was completely *ecstatic / speechless* .
4 I was *thrilled to bits / optimistic* to get the job. I've dreamed of working for UNICEF for years.
5 Don't worry. He's not miserable; he's just feeling *astonished / a bit down* at the moment.
6 I hate heights. I was absolutely *petrified / scared* that I would fall.

5 Work in pairs. Think about your first day in a new job or at a new university. Describe what happened and what your feelings were.

I CAN	
describe different emotions	
use idioms to describe feelings	

Real life

6 Work in pairs. Read the situations and complete the phrases that recognise other people's feelings.

1 *The other person is looking anxious.*
   _____ concerned. Is everything OK?
2 *You are aware that what you said was quite direct.*
   Sorry, perhaps that _____ .
3 *You want to decline an offer politely.*
   Please don't _____ , but I think I can manage.
4 *The other person looks a little hurt by what you said.*
   Sorry, I hope _____ .
5 *You said something that you didn't intend to say.*
   Sorry, that came _____ .

7 Work in pairs. Improvise a short conversation where there's been a misunderstanding. Use this situation or your own ideas.

- Your friend borrowed your laptop but hasn't returned it. You speak to them about it.

I CAN	
take part in a conversation where there's been a misunderstanding	
recognise others' feelings in a conversation and respond appropriately	

Speaking

8 Work in pairs. Are you a more rational person or someone who likes to trust their feelings? Discuss with your partner and give an example of this.

Unit 12 Landscapes

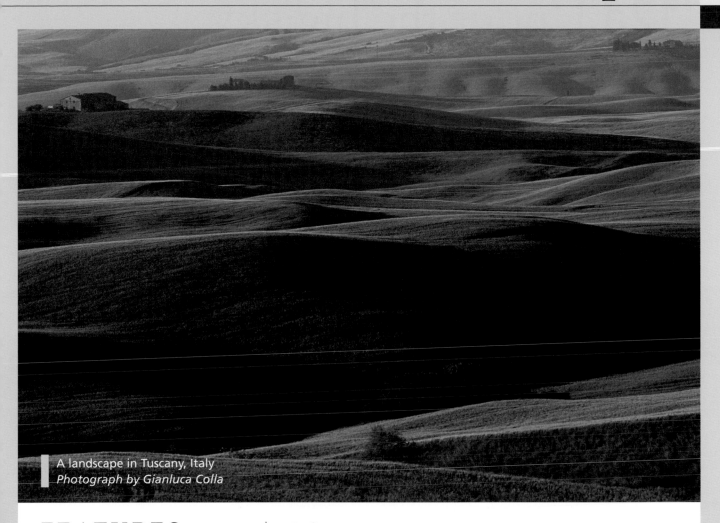

A landscape in Tuscany, Italy
Photograph by Gianluca Colla

FEATURES

1 🔊 **2.30** Look at the photo. Then listen to three people describing landscapes and answer the questions.

1 What kind of landscape does each speaker like?
2 Which speaker is describing the landscape in the photo?

2 🔊 **2.30** Listen again and write in the adjectives that are used to describe features of landscapes.

Speaker 1: a _____ environment, _____ vegetation,
a _____, flat landscape, a _____ sky

Speaker 2: _____-_____ mountains,
a pretty _____ scene,
a _____-_____ skyline

Speaker 3: _____ hills, _____ meadows,
_____ farmland, _____ plains,
_____, gentle countryside

3 🔊 **2.30** What were the reasons each person gave for liking each landscape? Listen again and check.

4 Work in groups. Think of examples of the following in your country and tell the rest of the group.

- a landscape that you associate with your childhood
- dramatic changes of scenery
- blots on the landscape

12a Under the big sky

Reading

1 Look at these two quotations about the American West. What do you think 'the West' represents for Americans? What do *you* associate with the word 'West'?

> Washington is not a place to live in. Go West, young man, go West and grow up with the country.
>
> *Horace Greeley, editor*

> So I pulled the sun screen down and … and kept on moving west. For West is where we all plan to go some day.
>
> *Robert Penn Warren, poet*

2 Work in pairs. Look at the photo and think of three adjectives or adjective + noun collocations you would use to describe this landscape. Discuss with your partner.

3 Read the article about the photographer William Albert Allard and answer the questions.

1 Where has Allard worked and what kind of photos does he take?
2 What does he feel about the American West?

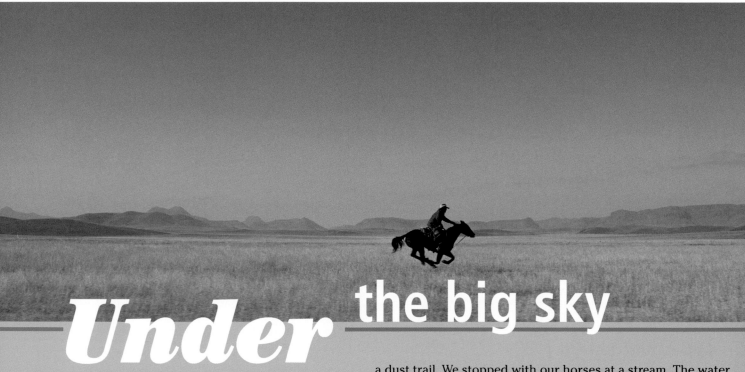

Under the big sky

In a career spanning fifty-odd years, American portrait and landscape photographer William Albert Allard has shown us people and places as he sees them. Much of his work, well over forty photographic assignments in fact, has been for *National Geographic*. One of his colleagues said about his work for *National Geographic*, 'Before Bill arrived, the stuff in the magazine was travel-postcard photography'. He claimed that Allard was instrumental in bringing a more intimate and personal style to photojournalism in the magazine. The assignments have taken him to dozens of countries all over the world, but Allard's heart was captured by his beloved 'West', as he explained in an article.

'It was a summer day in 1969. There had been no rain for weeks. A seventeen-year-old boy from a community in Stanford, Montana, said you can tell it's really dry when a single rider can kick up a dust trail. We stopped with our horses at a stream. The water was cool and tasted of the earth. "Do you ever feel like leaving your community here?" I asked.

'"No," the boy said. "It must be kind of rough on the outside, all alone, trying to make a living. Don't you think?" "Yes," I told him. "It can be all of that."

'Since that innocent exchange, I've spent much of my life travelling the world. I've seen a lot of wonderful places. But it was the American West that never left me. It kept drawing me back.

'Raised further east in Minneapolis, I didn't get my first look at the West until around 1965. I can still remember one early morning in Wyoming and the first light on high mountain meadows, the wisps of clouds within my reach. That look demanded another look, and another, until I found myself seeking any excuse, some idea for a story that would lead me back from the East, where I had moved, to that grand expanse.

'If we're lucky, we all find some place special to us. Even though it may change with time, if we love it deeply enough, there is a part of it within us to the end. That's how I feel about the West.'

4 Look at the statements. Then find and underline phrases in the article which support these statements.

1 Allard brings his own individual perspective to his photography. (para 1)
2 *National Geographic* photos used to be unexceptional. (para 1)
3 Riding horses is part of Montana's culture. (para 2)
4 The West had a magnetic pull on Allard. (para 4)
5 Land and sky seem close together in the West. (para 5)

Language focus approximation

5 Compare the pairs of sentences. What effect do the words in bold have on the meaning of each sentence?

1 a In a career spanning fifty years.
  b In a career spanning fifty-**odd** years.
2 a Before Bill arrived, the photos in the magazine were travel-postcard photography.
  b Before Bill arrived, the **stuff** in the magazine was travel-postcard photography.
3 a It must be rough on the outside.
  b It must be **kind of** rough on the outside.
4 a I found myself seeking an idea for a story.
  b I found myself seeking **some** idea for a story.

6 Find examples of the following in the text.

1 two more approximate numbers (paragraph 1)
2 an approximate date (paragraph 5)
3 one more use of *some* (in paragraph 6) to mean an unspecified thing

---

▶ APPROXIMATION

Numbers
fifty-odd years; fifteen or so people
some forty magazine articles
around / about / roughly six houses
dozens of letters; in the next day or two
(well) under / over a hundred messages

Adjectives
it's kind of* difficult
a greyish colour

some
We all have some place which is special.
Can you give me some idea when you will arrive?

Vague words
One moment. I'll just get my things.
There's some strange stuff* in my coffee.

* more colloquial
Note: The suffix *-ish* is usually added to words describing physical features: size, colour, etc. or time.

For further information and practice, see page 172.

---

7 🎧 **2.31** Look at the language focus box. Read the text below and think about what expressions of approximation might go with or in place of the underlined words. Then listen and note which expressions are used.

[1] Five years ago, I took a trip to Madagascar to photograph the landscape. An amateur photographer I had met at [2] a party told me it had the most wonderful scenery. Normally, I spend [3] two months researching a place before I go there. But in this case, I had only a [4] short amount of time before I had to be back. So, I packed my [5] belongings and left the next day. During the course of the assignment, I took [6] 2,000 pictures. The photographer that recommended Madagascar said the landscape was [7] varied. That was a huge understatement. There's desert, marshes, rainforest, sandy beaches and rocky coves; and all of this is home to [8] more than 200,000 different species of plants and animals.

8 Work in pairs. Use expressions of approximation to describe the following.

• how near you live to the sea (about)
• the number of months / years you've been living here (odd)
• the colour of some aspect of the landscape around you (hills, trees, buildings, etc.) (-*ish*)
• the number of high-rise buildings in your town or city (over)
• the sort of leisure activities people can do in this area (stuff)

Speaking

9 Work in pairs. What place is special to you? Prepare a description of it to include the following items. Then tell your partner about it.

• where the place is and its main features
• what the land is used for
• your favourite season (or time of day) to be there
• what you do there
• why it is special to you

12b Nature close up

Listening

1 The 17th-century Japanese poet Basho is famous for his haikus about nature. Look at the haiku and say what the form of a haiku is: how many lines, how many syllables per line and how many syllables in total.

2 **2.32** Listen to an extract from a radio programme where a biographer of Basho is being interviewed. Answer the questions.

1 What attracted her to write about Basho?
2 Why did Basho make his long journey across Japan?
3 Why does she think haikus are good at describing nature?

3 **2.32** Work in pairs. What did the biographer say caught the attention with each of the things below? Discuss with your partner. Then listen again and check.

1 a particular flower
2 the spray from a waterfall
3 a floating leaf
4 a frog
5 an avenue of trees

> ▶ **WORDBUILDING suffix *-ity***
>
> We add *-ity* to some adjectives to form a noun describing a state.
> *intense → intensity*
> Note that there are some irregular formations.
> *celebrated → celebrity, simple → simplicity*
>
> For further information and practice, see Workbook page 99.

Idioms adjective collocations

4 Look at the expression from the interview. Does the expression 'crystal clear' mean *extremely clear* or *moderately clear*?

'reflections in a **crystal clear** stream'

5 Look at these other expressions which all have an intense meaning. In all cases except two, the first word does the intensifying. Underline the two expressions where the second word intensifies.

bone dry	rock hard
brand new	scared stiff
fast asleep	sopping wet
freezing cold	stone cold
lightning quick	wide open
pitch black	worried sick

An old silent pond ...
A frog jumps into the pond,
splash! Silence again.

Basho

6 Work in pairs. Choose three of the phrases from Exercise 5 and put them into sentences that describe situations from your own experience. Then tell your partner.

> *Once on holiday in France, we went out for a long walk. But we got lost on the way home and had to find our way back in the dark. It was pitch black and I was worried sick that we'd never get home.*

Language focus qualifiers

7 Look at the sentences from the interview (a–f) and the underlined qualifiers. Answer the questions.

1 What kind of word is being qualified in each case?
2 What effect does the qualifier have on this word?

a Observing nature is <u>a bit of</u> a luxury.
b That's <u>quite</u> interesting, because one of his preoccupations was observing nature.
c But <u>fairly</u> late in life, he decided he needed to get away from it all.
d Basho was actually already <u>quite</u> a well-known poet in his lifetime.
e So he travelled a distance of <u>slightly</u> less than 1,200 miles.
f It upset him <u>rather</u>.

> ▶ **QUALIFIERS**
>
> **quite, pretty and fairly**
> It's quite/fairly/pretty unusual to see a double rainbow.
> It's quite a steep path.
> It's a fairly/pretty easy climb.
> I quite enjoyed meeting her.
>
> **rather**
> It's a rather long way. OR It's rather a long way.
> The book was rather good, I thought.
> He misjudged the situation rather.
>
> **slightly, a little, a bit**
> I was slightly/a little/a bit disappointed to miss the sunset.
> It's a bit of a rocky road.
> The other beach is slightly / a bit / a little further away.
> I regret it slightly / a little / a bit.
> Notes
> 1 quite comes before 'a' when modifying adjective + noun
> 2 the meaning of these words can depend on the intonation
>
> For further information and practice, see page 173.

8 Look at the language focus box. Then cross out the qualifier which does not fit in each sentence.

1 Basho was *rather / quite / fairly* a modest man in many respects.
2 Basho also suffered *a bit / quite / slightly* from health problems.
3 It's *a bit of / pretty / quite* difficult to imagine how he managed such a journey.
4 The route he took has now become *a bit of / pretty / quite* a famous trail in Japan.
5 A haiku is a *fairly / pretty / quite* short poem: only 17 syllables.
6 Sometimes, when translated, they are *fairly / a bit / slightly* shorter.
7 I *pretty / quite / rather* like reading his poetry.
8 It's *quite / rather / a little* easy to see why it's so popular.

9 Pronunciation *quite*, *fairly* and *pretty*

a 🎵 **2.33** Whether the qualifiers intensify the word they go with or tone it down depends on where the stress is placed and the intonation. Listen and say which meaning each phrase has.

	Slightly intensifying	Toning down
1 It's quite a long way.	☐	☐
2 I feel pretty confident.	☐	☐
3 The water's quite cold.	☐	☐
4 It's fairly important.	☐	☐
5 He's a pretty well-known writer.	☐	☐
6 It's quite a big lake.	☐	☐

b Work in pairs. Practise saying the phrases with each pronunciation pattern. See if your partner can guess the meaning that you intend.

10 Make sentences about your feelings about the following. Use qualifiers from the language focus box.

- going for long walks
- reading poetry
- how easy it is to enjoy nature in your area

Speaking and writing

11 Work in pairs. Think of two more examples of 'nature close up', like the ones in the photos: small things that strike you as interesting or beautiful. Describe them to your partner and explain why you chose them.

12 Choose one of your ideas from Exercise 11 and try to put it into the form of a haiku. Follow the rules of a haiku from Exercise 1.

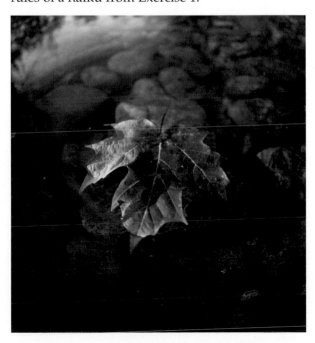

12c Room with a view

Reading

1 Work in pairs. Do you have pictures on your walls at home – paintings, posters or photos? What are they of? Discuss with your partner.

2 Look at the photo of a picture on a wall in a room. Then read the article about a camera obscura and note down the steps in the process used to make this picture. Compare notes with your partner.

3 Read the article again. Are the sentences true (T) or false (F), or is there not enough information to say if the sentences are true or false (N)?

1 The picture produced by a camera obscura is always clear.
2 The effect produced by a camera obscura has been known to people for centuries.
3 The modern camera is based on the same principle as the camera obscura.
4 The technical explanation for this phenomenon is not very complicated.
5 Vermeer used a type of camera obscura to achieve effects in his paintings that other artists were not able to.
6 Morell was the first person to try to photograph the effects produced by a camera obscura.
7 Morell's first photograph of a camera obscura image was of a toy shop outside his house.
8 Morell wanted to create a new movement within art photography.

Critical thinking identifying aims

4 Which of these things do you think it would be possible to do from the information given in the article? Give reasons.

1 make a camera obscura
2 make a shoebox camera
3 take a photo of an image in a camera obscura

5 Which of these were the author's aims in describing the camera obscura?

a so the reader could do it themselves
b so the reader could appreciate both how it is done and the results
c so the reader could appreciate only the results

Word focus *space* and *room*

6 Work in pairs. Look at the extracts from the article (a–b). Are the words *space* and *room* interchangeable? What about in the other sentences (1–3)?

a … when light enters a dark **space** through a tiny hole. (para 2)
b … he chose a **room** in his own house in Quincy, a Boston suburb. (para 6)

1 Do you have any **room** in your bag for my laptop?
2 Sorry to take so long – I couldn't find a parking **space**.
3 I love the feeling of wide open **space** around me.

7 Look at the sentences and say a) which word (*space* or *room*) completes the expressions and b) what each expression means. Sometimes both words are possible.

1 I really think you should **give her some** _____ . She's very upset after the argument with Stuart.
2 We haven't found a design that we're happy with yet, but **watch this** _____ .
3 Everyone knows that he's unreliable, but no one wants to say it. That's **the elephant in the** _____ .
4 I think we should tell them that we're busy with other projects. That will give us a bit of **breathing** _____ .
5 His English has certainly got better, but there's still _____ **for improvement**.

Speaking

8 Work in pairs. Look at the photo below and discuss how you think this photographic effect was achieved. Then check the answer on page 153.

9 Choose from the list of subjects and prepare a description of a technique used to produce a particular effect. Then explain it to your partner.

- a cooking technique (e.g. cooking perfect rice)
- a dancing technique (e.g. moonwalking)
- a DIY technique (e.g. hanging wallpaper)
- a technique in a particular sport (e.g. tennis)

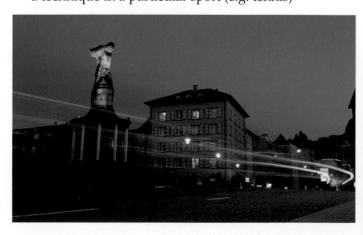

R O O M   W I T H   A   V I E W

It's 1988 and Cuban-born Abelardo Morell is in a classroom in Boston teaching an introductory photography course at an art college. On a sunny day, he covers the classroom windows with black plastic, making the space as dark as possible, cuts a dime-size hole in the plastic, and tells his students to watch. Almost instantly the back wall comes alive like a movie screen, its surface covered with a fuzzy image of people and cars moving along the street outside. The image is upside down, sky on floor, ground on ceiling, as if the laws of gravity have gone haywire.

Something strange and wonderful happens when light enters a dark space through a tiny hole. Aristotle described the phenomenon in the fourth century BC; Leonardo da Vinci sketched the process and in nineteenth-century seaside resorts, tourists queued up to see demonstrations of the magical results.

Morell had turned his classroom into a camera obscura ('dark room' in Latin), perhaps the earliest known imaging device, and the ancestor of the photographic camera. A camera obscura receives images just like the human eye – through a small opening and upside down. Light from outside enters the hole at an angle, the rays reflected from tops of objects, like trees, travelling downward, and those from the lower plane, say flowers, travelling upward, the rays crossing inside the dark space and forming an inverted image. It seems like a miracle, but in fact it's basic physics. The brain automatically rights the eye's image; in a regular camera a mirror flips the image. Here, it remains upside down.

A portable version of the camera obscura – a box with a small hole fitted with a lens – first became popular in the seventeenth century and was used by painters like Vermeer and Canaletto as a drawing aid. In Vermeer's case, some claim that he must have traced over the image to achieve such accurate perspective in his paintings. Scientists also used the camera obscura to observe solar eclipses, just as children do today with pinhole cameras made from shoe boxes. Then, in the early 1800s, innovators began inserting chemically treated paper or metal plates at the

back of the boxy camera obscura to capture the image, and the art of photography was born.

When Morell saw how fascinated his students were by the ghost-like images that appeared on the wall, he decided to try to photograph the effect. To his knowledge this had never been done before. It took months to master the technique, to figure out the right size of hole to allow both brightness and sharpness and to determine the right exposure time for the detail of the image on the wall to emerge on film.

He chose a room in his own house in Quincy, a Boston suburb. He set his large-format view camera on a tripod in his son's bedroom in front of the camera obscura image and opened the shutter. He left the room and waited. For eight hours. The result was mesmerising. The developed picture showed inverted trees and houses

across the street hovering over the boy's toys like a scene from a fairy tale. 'I was giddy,' Morell said. 'It felt like the moment photography was invented.' From that eureka moment, Morell has gone on to produce a series of original and enthralling photographs. His views range from New York City panoramas to warm Italian vistas.

Replacing film with a digital sensor, which is more light-sensitive, he cut exposure times from hours to minutes, permitting him to capture clouds, shadows and other atmospheric features. He is most excited about his work with a floorless tent: a portable camera obscura that he takes to rooftops or parks or city streets to project images directly onto the ground. By melting the boundaries between landscape and dreamscape, Morell's hope is that he will 'refresh how people see the world'.

---

dime (n) /daɪm/ a small American coin
eureka /jʊə'riːkə/ a Greek expression meaning 'I've found it!'
exposure (n) /ɪk'spəʊʒə(r)/ the time the light is allowed to enter the camera
flip (v) /flɪp/ turn over
giddy (adj) /'gɪdi/ a feeling (in your head) that you are losing your balance
lens (n) /lenz/ a piece of glass through which the image enters the camera
shutter (n) /'ʃʌtə/ the part of a camera that opens and shuts to allow the image in

---

12d A blot on the urban landscape

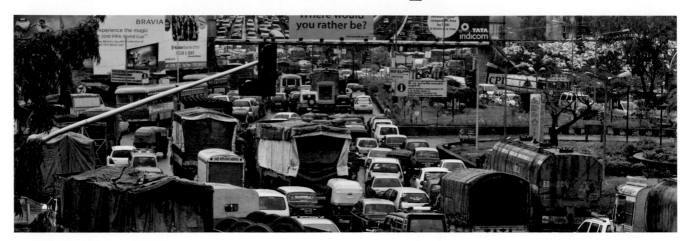

Real life a debate

1 Read the text and complete it with one word in each space.

> Although it's said the Great Wall of China is the only man-made thing you can see from space, in fact it is man-made pollution in our cities that is most visible on the landscape: ¹ _____ pollution in the day and ² _____ pollution at night.

2 Work in pairs. Look at the facts below about the world's top six most congested cities and guess which cities they are.

1 In 2008, this South American city had a record 265 km traffic jam.
2 In 2010, a 100 km traffic jam took ten days to clear in this Asian capital.
3 Europe's most congested city.
4 Europe's most romantic city also holds the record for the worst traffic jam ever: 18 million cars!
5 In this eastern European capital, 38% of the roads are always congested.
6 This city in Central America records the world's highest 'commuter pain' (stress, lost time and ill health).

3 Think of two ways traffic congestion could be reduced in big cities. Then exchange ideas with another pair.

4 Speaking skill interrupting

a 🔊 **2.34** Listen to an extract from a local meeting about traffic congestion in a city and answer the questions.

1 What two ideas to reduce traffic congestion are presented?
2 What are the two points of debate about the first idea?

b 🔊 **2.34** During the discussion, different speakers interrupted each other. Look at the box. Then listen again and underline the phrases that the speakers used to interrupt and prevent interruptions.

> ▶ **INTERRUPTING**
>
> **Interrupting**
> Sorry, can I just interrupt you there?
> Can I just say something in answer to that?
> No, hang on a minute …
> No, I'm sorry I have to stop you there …
> Yes, but …
>
> **Preventing interruptions**
> Sorry, can I just finish what I was saying?
> Just a moment, please …
> OK, you can make your point in a moment.

5 Pronunciation intonation in interruptions

a 🔊 **2.35** It is important when interrupting or preventing interruptions to be polite. Listen to how the phrases in the box are pronounced with a firm but gentle tone.

b Work in pairs. Practise saying the phrases to each other. Tell your partner if their tone sounds too hard or unfriendly.

6 Work in groups. Use the ideas you discussed in Exercise 3 and prepare to participate in a debate. Think about the main issues and possible objections or concerns. Take the roles of the chair and the participants at the meeting. Use the language in the box to help you interrupt each other.

12e A unique service

Writing a speculative letter

1 Work in pairs. Imagine you have just started a new business. What methods could you use to attract or win new customers?

2 Look at this list of tips for approaching clients cold (without any previous contact). Which do you think are most important and why? Discuss with your partner.

a focus on a specific group or type of customers

b decide which channel of communication these customers will prefer

c make sure the company is the right size (not too big or small in relation to what you offer)

d be conscious of how much they will want to spend

e be clear about your offer and what is different about it

f offer some 'bait' – a discount or extra service

3 Read the letter. Does it follow the tips in Exercise 2? Underline the parts of the letter that correspond to each tip.

4 Writing skill persuasive language

a Find examples of the following persuasive techniques in the letter.

1 making strong claims

2 using clear, short sentences

3 recognising what the other person wants

4 empathising with the other person by describing experiences you have in common

5 suggesting possible options or solutions

b Match the techniques (1–5) in Exercise 4a with these sentences.

a Clearly, no one wants to be a victim of computer fraud.

b And why not?

c You could try the system out for a week before you commit to paying anything.

d Our company offers a truly innovative approach.

e We know how frustrating it is to lose important data.

EXOSCAPE
Garden & landscape designs

Dear Ms Ciewinski,

Please excuse my direct method of approach. We are currently writing to a number of medium-sized local businesses like yours to see if you would like to join the growing number of businesses benefiting from the unique service we offer.

Exoscape is a young team of landscape gardeners and exterior designers. We specialise in transforming the outer appearance of buildings and grounds. Clearly, you don't want to spend a lot of money on this. But it is amazing what effects can be achieved at a low cost with a little landscaping and the addition of plants and well-placed lighting.

We all look at our surroundings from time to time and think they need freshening up. If you have recently, why not pick up the phone and give us a call? If you would like to know more about us first, please have a look on our website. It lists the services we offer and tells you what our clients are saying about us.

Currently we are offering an initial 30-minute consultation free of charge. You might like to take advantage of this offer before it expires at the end of the month.

I look forward to hearing from you.

Yours sincerely,

Lars Thielker

5 A lot of companies send out documents (letters, marketing literature, etc.) with poor English. These give a bad impression to customers and business partners. You are a translator and copy writer. You offer a service checking the English in documents. Write a speculative letter offering your services to local companies. Write between 150 and 200 words.

6 Exchange letters with your partner. Use these questions to check your letters.

• Is the letter persuasive?
• Is the service they are offering described clearly?
• Does it make a special offer?

12f Canada oil sands

Nothing, just nothing. Not even one stick.

Before you watch

1 Work in pairs. What do you know about where oil is normally found and how it is extracted? Discuss with your partner. Use these words to help you.

> deposits   drill   oil rig   pump out   rock

2 Look at the photo and the title of the video and answer the questions.

1 Where do you think the oil is found here?

2 What effect does extracting the oil have on the landscape?

3 Why has this method of extracting oil become popular recently?

While you watch

3 Watch the video and check your answers from Exercise 2.

4 Watch the first part of the video (to 02.13) and answer the questions.

1 What does the woman say you cannot see any longer on the landscape?

2 What is this area normally home to?

3 What level of oil reserves does Canada have?

4 What was photographer Peter Essick's mission?

5 Watch the second part of the video (02.14 to 2.37). Complete the description of the mining process using one word in each space.

First the ^{1} .... is cut down. Then the top ^{2} .... is removed and the sand ^{3} .... by enormous shovels. It's then carried by dump ^{4} .... to a processing facility. Each truck can carry almost 400 tons of oil-rich sand. After processing, the synthetic crude is shipped via ^{5} .... to refineries in the United States.

6 Watch the third part of the video (02.38 to end). Has Canada's oil boom had a positive (P), negative (N) or unknown (U) effect on the following?

a the cost of living in the area
b employment opportunities in the area
c local people's lives in general
d the soil
e the climate
f wildlife

After you watch

7 Roleplay an interview about the Canada oil sands

Work in pairs.

Student A: Imagine you are a journalist from a local newspaper. You are going to interview a spokesperson for an oil company that extracts oil from the Canada oil sands. Look at these points and prepare a list of questions to ask the spokesperson.

- the reasons why this kind of exploitation of oil is necessary
- what the company is doing to mitigate the impact of its activities

Student B: Imagine you are a spokesperson for an oil company that extracts oil from the Canada oil sands. A journalist from a local paper is going to interview you. Consider these points and prepare what you are going to say to the journalist.

- the arguments for defending what you are doing
- how you plan to protect the environment from lasting damage

Act out the interview, then change roles and act out the interview again.

8 Work in groups. Look at these other ways in which people exploit natural resources. Which are the most damaging to the environment? Which are the least damaging? Discuss what can be done to mitigate the effects of the damage in each case.

- growing trees for wood and paper
- large-scale fishing
- farming especially for meat
- hydro-electric power
- coal mining

---

bitumen (n) /ˈbɪtʃəmən/ tar, a thick black oil-based substance
bog (n) /bɒg/ a marsh or wetland
boreal (adj) /ˈbɔːrɪəl/ belonging to the Arctic climate zone
crude (adj) /kruːd/ not refined, in its unprocessed form
flare (v) /fleə(r)/ ignite suddenly with a strong flame
muskeg (n) /ˈmʌskeg/ an acidic type of soil
nesting spot (n) /ˈnestɪŋ spɒt/ a place where birds can make their nests
peat (n) /piːt/ soft, partly carbonised vegetable matter found in bogs and marshes
wilderness (n) /ˈwɪldənəs/ an area of wild, deserted land
strip mining (n) /strɪp ˈmaɪnɪŋ/ getting at material near the surface by removing the top soil
viscous (adj) /ˈvɪskəs/ thick, of a liquid

Grammar

1 Look at the photo. Where do you think this is? What is the man doing? Read the article and check your answer.

2 Use these words to qualify and approximate the expressions in italics (1–8) in the article. In some cases you may need to add other small words.

1	quite	4	-ish	7	rather
2	some	5	bit	8	kind
3	or so	6	dozens		

3 Work in pairs. Describe a sight you can commonly see in the countryside in your country.

In our increasingly crowded world, Iceland is an exception. Although it has a modern and cosmopolitan capital, Reykjavik, it is characterised by wild, unspoiled landscapes with some of the most dramatic scenery to be found anywhere on Earth. It is also [1] *a dynamic landscape*, a fact nowhere more in evidence than on the highly active volcanic Westman islands, a small archipelago [2] *ten kilometres* south of the main island. In the last [3] *fifty years*, these islands have seen enormous changes. One, Surtsey, only appeared in 1963 following a volcanic eruption, and another, Vestmannaeyjar, was evacuated in 1973 after its volcano devastated buildings and homes. Another attraction for visitors to these extraordinary islands is the puffin population. These [4] *small* black and white birds can be seen in their thousands perched on the cliffs and steep grassy slopes above the Icelandic sea that surrounds the islands. Lucky visitors can also witness the ancient and traditional art of puffin catching or sky fishing. Using large nets on long poles – [5] *like* butterfly nets – hunters stalk the puffins perilously close to the cliff's edge, and when they take flight, they catch them in their nets. [6] *Puffins* can be caught in this way each day. It's dangerous work, but this does not deter the local hunters, for whom puffin meat is a staple food. I was [7] *taken aback* by the fishiness of it at first, but the meat was [8] *tasty*.

I CAN	
use language of approximation	
modify the meaning of words using qualifiers	

Vocabulary

4 Complete the descriptions of different landscapes using these words.

bone	brand	lush	monotonous	rolling
rustic	skyline	wide		

1 The countryside is very green and gentle in this area: _____ hills and _____ meadows, with a few _____-looking buildings – barns and old cottages.

2 This is an area of _____ open plains with few buildings in sight. The summers are long and there is little rain, so the earth becomes _____ dry. Some find it a _____ landscape, but I love the feeling of space and the big sky.

3 It's a _____-new business district with tall, glass buildings and paved walkways. By day it's buzzing with people and the night-time _____ is dramatic.

5 Work in pairs. Describe the landscape around your home, university or workplace.

I CAN	
describe features of a landscape	
use adjective collocations	

Real life

6 Rewrite these phrases for interrupting and preventing interruptions so that they are less direct.

1 I must interrupt you there.
2 I have to answer that.
3 Stop there.
4 Let me finish.
5 Make your point in a moment.
6 One moment.

7 Work in pairs. Explain to each other what you think is most important when learning English. Try to interrupt when the other person is speaking and prevent interruptions when you are speaking.

I CAN	
participate in a debate	
interrupt politely and prevent interruptions	

Speaking

8 Work in pairs. Turn to the photo of a landscape or scene from nature that you liked best in Unit 12. Explain why you like it.

UNIT 1c Exercise 11, page 14

Group A

1 **misgiving** (n) /mɪsˈɡɪvɪŋ/ doubt or apprehension about something
2 **spurn** (v) /spɜːn/ reject
3 **zany** (adj) /ˈzeɪni/ eccentric and unconventional, even a little crazy

Example:
If the word was 'immortal', a correct definition would be: '*Immortal* means living forever, never dying. So we say, for example, "the immortal words of Shakespeare" or "Shakespeare has achieved immortal fame".'
A false definition would be: '*Immortal* means behaving in a way which is not right. So we say, for example, "Earning that much money when others earn very little is immortal."'

UNIT 2c Exercise 11, page 26

Quiz

How would you feel in the following situations? Read the questions and answer A, B or C for each one. Then look at the key on page 154 to find out what your comfort zone is. Discuss if you agree with the answers.

A comfortable and keen on the prospect
B a little uncomfortable, but willing to try
C uncomfortable and reluctant to do it

1 AT A KARAOKE CLUB, A FRIEND FORCES YOU TO GO ON STAGE TO SING FRANK SINATRA'S 'MY WAY'.
2 YOU ARE ASKED TO GIVE A 45-MINUTE TALK ABOUT YOUR ORGANISATION TO A GROUP OF 250 PRE-UNIVERSITY STUDENTS NEXT MONTH.
3 A FAMOUS PERSON YOU ADMIRE (E.G. A WRITER OR AN ACTOR) IS SITTING NEAR YOU ON A TRAIN READING A BOOK. YOU WOULD LOVE TO SPEAK TO THEM AND GET THEIR AUTOGRAPH.
4 A FRIEND, WHO IS A CYCLING FANATIC, HAS INVITED YOU TO GO ON A CYCLING HOLIDAY WITH THEM IN THE MOUNTAINS.
5 A GROUP OF YOUR FRIENDS HAS ORGANISED AN ADVENTURE WEEKEND INVOLVING CANOEING IN WHITE WATER RAPIDS, ROCK CLIMBING AND CAVING IN UNDERGROUND CAVES.
6 YOU ARE ASKED IF YOU WOULD MIND BEING FILMED AT WORK BY A TV CREW WHO ARE MAKING A FLY-ON-THE-WALL DOCUMENTARY ABOUT YOUR ORGANISATION.
7 YOU ARE UNEXPECTEDLY OFFERED A PROMOTION TO A JOB WITH MORE PAY BUT ALSO MUCH MORE RESPONSIBILITY AND LESS SECURITY (YOU WILL BE JUDGED BY YOUR RESULTS).
8 YOUR NEXT DOOR NEIGHBOUR'S DAUGHTER PRACTISES THE VIOLIN FOR TWO HOURS EVERY EVENING AND THE SOUND IS LOUD AND HORRIBLE. YOU NEED TO SPEAK TO THEM DIRECTLY ABOUT IT.

UNIT 3d Exercise 7, page 40

Student A

By Francesca Martelli: A children's carousel powered by wind and solar power. The carousel will have little carriages in the shape of historic cars made over the decades by the city's car manufacturer. Francesca hopes the project can be part-funded by the car manufacturer.

UNIT 4d Exercise 7, page 52

Student A

A typical coffee shop selling fresh coffee produces over two tonnes of waste coffee grounds each year. Your idea is to use these coffee grounds to grow mushrooms, which you can then sell to greengrocers and supermarkets. Currently, cafés simply throw away the used coffee grounds into the general waste. By using them to grow mushrooms, you would be a) recycling the waste coffee and b) reducing the cost of the compost you need to grow your mushrooms.

UNIT 5d Exercise 6, page 64

Student A: Extract 1

'When I told friends in London that I was going to travel around Europe and write a book about it, they said, "Oh, you must speak a lot of languages."
"Why, no," I would reply with a certain pride, "only English," and they would look at me as if I were crazy. But that's the glory of foreign travel, as far as I'm concerned. I don't want to know what people are talking about. I can't think of anything that excites a greater sense of childlike wonder than to be in a country where you are ignorant of almost everything. Suddenly you're five years old again. You can't read anything, you have only the most rudimentary sense of how things work, you can't even reliably cross a street without endangering your life. Your whole existence becomes a series of interesting guesses.'

Unit 12c Exercise 8, page 146

Light trails: This effect is achieved by leaving the camera shutter open for a prolonged period. A longer exposure time will give you more light trails, and make them longer. However, if the shutter is open too long, then the brightness of each trail will begin to fade.

UNIT 1c Exercise 11, page 14

Group B
1 **howl** (v) /haʊl/ let out a long, pained cry like a dog or wolf
2 **jaded** (adj) /ˈdʒeɪdɪd/ bored with something, lacking enthusiasm
3 **reprieve** (n) /rɪˈpriːv/ a temporary delay in a punishment

Example:
If the word was 'immortal', a correct definition would be: '*Immortal* means living forever, never dying. So we say, for example, "the immortal words of Shakespeare" or "Shakespeare has achieved immortal fame".'
A false definition would be: '*Immortal* means behaving in a way which is not right. So we say, for example, "Earning that much money when others earn very little is immortal."'

UNIT 2c Exercise 11, page 26

Answers to Quiz

Mostly 'A's: You feel confident with new challenges and are happy to be in the spotlight. That's great, but be careful not to over-extend yourself.

Mostly 'B's: You are careful, but you want to expand your comfort zone by doing things that challenge you.

Mostly 'C's: You are someone who likes to stay well within their comfort zone. That's OK, but remember that leaving your comfort zone now and then can be empowering.

UNIT 4d Exercise 7, page 52

Student B
Your idea is to make it easier for people to scrap their old cars. Currently, when a car has reached the end of its life, the owner has to pay a scrap metal dealer £100 to come and collect it from their house. You would like to offer to collect people's scrap cars for free. You will then a) try to recycle as many parts as possible before b) taking it to the scrap metal dealer to get money for the remaining metal or parts.

UNIT 7c Exercise 9, page 86

Student A
Read the facts. The underlined words give a clue, if needed.

1 Fact: Alfred Nobel was the man after whom the Nobel <u>peace</u> prize was named, but …
   Irony: he was also the inventor of dynamite.
2 Fact: Jim Fixx, the author of *The Complete Book of Running*, was the man who popularised jogging as a way to get <u>healthy</u> exercise. But at the age of 52, while out jogging …
   Irony: he had a heart attack and died.

UNIT 8c Exercise 10, page 98

Student A
You are a small business owner and you run a small travel agency which employs six people. Some data has gone missing but it is unclear whether someone hacked into the computer or an employee took the data or deleted the data by accident. Think about the following:
- how many computers your office uses
- how you protect your information (passwords, virus protection, etc.)
- what you use the Internet for (e.g. what external sites you use and what transactions you do)
- how you keep all sensitive documents, digital or written

UNIT 8d Exercise 6, page 100

Group A
Why do stars twinkle?
The traditional answer is that the light from them is disturbed by movement of air in our own atmosphere. If that is true, why don't planets twinkle too? Now some scientists think the real reason must be to do with the distance (planets are much nearer) and that there is something getting in the way. What that 'something' is no one knows yet.

UNIT 10b Exercise 10, page 121

Student A
The sight of starlings flocking is one of the most amazing sights in nature. Some time around dusk, starlings come together and circle in the sky in large groups for some minutes over the reed beds, where they make their nests. It is thought that they do this to be less vulnerable to predators. Flying in close formation, they change direction every few seconds. No one is quite sure how they manage to do this without colliding. One suggestion is that each bird follows the movement of the bird directly in front of it, and each bird has very quick reaction times. After circling in the air for some time, suddenly they all come down to ground together, as if being sucked down a hole.

UNIT 10c Exercise 11, page 122

Student A
You are an ecologist. You want to help the Hadza preserve their way of life. To do this you think that a large area of land needs to be strictly conserved, so that no development – building, farming – can take place there. You would also like the Hadza to be left in peace, i.e. not become a tourist attraction for visitors on safari.

UNIT 3d Exercise 7, page 40

Student B

By Rana Suweilah: A giant LED screen mounted on a black granite wall (granite being the rock found in the nearby mountains). In front of the wall will be a large paved area, where people can skate or play games, with seating around it. The screen will show video footage of construction workers in the 1950s, building skyscrapers in the city centre.

UNIT 4d Exercise 7, page 52

Student C

It is very annoying to return home in the evening and find the postman has been unable to deliver a package because no one was at home. Your idea is to provide an evening redelivery service for parcels and big letters. Currently, if no one is at home, the package is returned to a depot on the outskirts of town, which people have to visit in person to collect their post. Using your system, people would pay an annual fee for you to collect these packages and redeliver them at a more convenient time.

UNIT 6c Exercise 8, page 74

Student A

You are a marketing manager. Your company has developed a face cream for women in their 40s. It moisturises the skin, protects against the sun, and helps to prevent wrinkles forming.
Because women in their 40s are keen to remain looking young, you want the advertisements to feature a single young model in her 30s, who is fair-skinned and very beautiful: a universally recognisable image of beauty. It will also encourage men to buy the product for their wives. Beauty sells, as far as you are concerned.

UNIT 7c Exercise 9, page 86

Student B

Read the facts. The underlined words give a clue, if needed.

1   Fact: Henry VIII of England (1491–1547) had six wives because he desperately wanted a son and <u>strong male</u> successor. But his successor …

Irony: Edward, his only son, was a weak child and he died when he was fifteen, having been king for only six years. Henry's greatest successor was his daughter, Elizabeth I, who ruled for 45 years.

2   Fact: Einstein had one of the most <u>brilliant</u> minds of the twentieth century. Yet when he was seventeen, he …
Irony: failed his university entrance exam.

UNIT 7d Exercise 7, page 88

Student A

Studies have shown that high temperatures can have the effect of making people more aggressive. Many of the riots and violent protests that have taken place in the northern hemisphere have occurred in warm or hot weather. In the UK, summer riots took place in 1981 and 2011. In France, the student riots of 1968 took place in May, and the hot summer of 1967 sparked protests across the USA. The worst of these was the five-day riot in Detroit, which resulted in 7,300 arrests and property damage of $60 million.

UNIT 8c Exercise 10, page 98

Student B

You are an internet security consultant. Prepare to ask questions about how the owner (Student A) protects their small business' sensitive information. Ask these questions:

- how they use computers and the Internet
- how they use external sites, such as social networking sites
- whether they use the Internet for financial transactions

Then give advice. Think about these security areas: passwords, public computers, financial information, etc.

UNIT 8d Exercise 6, page 100

Group B
Why do people yawn?
People yawn not to show they are sleepy, but to try and stay awake. Research says that people yawn to cool the brain so it can operate better. That explains why others yawn when they see us yawning. It is part of ancient behaviour that helps groups to stay awake and be alert to danger.

UNIT 10c Exercise 11, page 122

Student B

You are a local politician. While you would like in principle to respect the Hadza way of life, you think that they present an image of Tanzania as a primitive country. You would like to encourage them to move into farming settlements on existing protected land. They will still be able to hunt, but as a hobby more than as a way of life.

UNIT 5b Exercise 11, page 61

UNIT 5d Exercise 6, page 64

Student B: Extract 2

'In the morning, I got up early and went for a long walk through the sleeping streets. I love to watch cities wake up, and Paris wakes up more abruptly, more startlingly, than any place I know. One minute you have the city to yourself: it's just you and a guy delivering crates of bread, and a couple of droning street-cleaning machines. Then all at once it's frantic: cars and buses swishing past in sudden abundance, cafés and kiosks opening, people flying out of Metro stations like flocks of startled birds, movement everywhere, thousands and thousands of pairs of hurrying legs.

By half past eight, Paris is a terrible place for walking. There's too much traffic. A blue haze of uncombusted diesel hangs over every boulevard. I know Baron Haussmann made Paris a grand place to look at, but the man had no concept of traffic flow.'

UNIT 6c Exercise 8, page 74

Student B

You are a sales manager. Your company has developed a face cream for women in their 40s. It moisturises the skin, protects against the sun, and helps to prevent wrinkles forming.

You think that women don't want to see an impossibly beautiful model in the advertisements, but women that they can identify with: that are average, with some wrinkles and blemishes, and that represent diverse ethnic backgrounds. You think you could even use members of the public in the advertisements.

UNIT 7c Exercise 9, page 86

Student C

Read these facts. The underlined words give a clue, if needed.

1   Fact: In the American Civil War, General John Sedgwick said to his soldiers, 'Don't worry. The enemy <u>couldn't hit</u> an elephant at this distance.' However, …
    Irony: he was shot by an enemy bullet.

2   Fact: Alexander Bell worked hard at creating new inventions. He came up with the <u>telephone</u>, for example. But he …
    Irony: refused to have one in his own study because he said that it got in the way of his work.

UNIT 7d Exercise 7, page 88

Student B

The Stradivarius is the world's most famous violin, producing a quality of sound that no other violinmaker has ever managed to achieve. For years, musicians and scientists have proposed different theories about what makes these instruments so special. Some said it was the varnish that Stradavari used; others that it was in their design. But more recently, two scientists, Henri Grissino-Mayer and Lloyd Burckle, have suggested that the secret lay in the quality of the wood that Stradivari used. They claim that the drop in temperatures during the Little Ice Age changed the nature of the wood in the trees that the violins were made from, producing an exceptional wood that the world has not seen since.

UNIT 10b Exercise 10, page 121

Student B

As the honey bees travel from flower to flower to collect nectar to make honey, pollen from each flower collects on their legs. Some of this pollen is then deposited at the next flower they visit, pollinating it. Human beings have long depended on wild honey bees to pollinate plants. In fact, about 75% of the crops we grow depend on bees for pollination. We also depend on bees for honey. Bees make honey to be able to feed themselves during the winter months when flowers are not in bloom. Humans can use the honey because bees make far too much for their own consumption.

UNIT 10c Exercise 11, page 122

Student C

You are a property developer. You believe that no one can fight progress, including the Hadza. You would like to build tourist centres around the national park where the Hadza live. These would be eco-lodges from which tourists could take safaris. The Hadza could then be employed as guides and workers on the site, exchanging their way of life for a more up-to-date, reliable and profitable existence.

UNIT 1

Time phrases
Form and use

Certain time phrases are often, but not always, used with certain tenses.

Present simple
every week, frequently, from time to time, generally, never, nowadays, often, time and again

Present continuous
at present, at the moment, at this moment in time, currently, now, this week

Past simple
at the time, in the past, in 2006, last week, previously, prior to, three days ago

Past continuous
as, at the same time as, at the time, while, whilst

Present perfect simple
already, ever, for, how long, in recent times/years, just, lately, never, only just, over the last two years, recently, since, so far, up to now, yet

Present perfect continuous
for, how long, lately, recently, since, up to now

Past perfect simple and continuous
already, before that, by then, for some time, previously, prior to that time, until then, up to then

will, *going to*, present continuous for future and future continuous
next week, in three days' (time), soon, on Friday, in a while, in the coming days/months/years, in the long term, sooner or later, this weekend

Practice

1 Choose the correct time phrase to complete the sentences.

1 It's hard to believe it's been ten years (since)/ *before* we moved to Canada.
2 Nelson Mandela became President of South Africa in 1994. *Prior to that time, / Since then,* he had spent 27 years in prison.
3 When I was younger I frequently came to blows with people. *Nowadays / At the moment* I avoid confrontation at all costs.
4 *Over the last few decades, / In a few decades' time,* businesses have become more concerned about the environment.
5 China is *currently / generally* experiencing an economic boom.
6 Forecasters are warning that temperatures will rocket *in the coming days. / lately.*

2 Complete the sentences. Put the verb in brackets in the correct tense.

1 Nobody ____has had____ (have) any contact with Jay since he arrived in Mexico.

2 Our car broke down on the motorway yesterday. It _____ (run) perfectly smoothly up to then.
3 My grandparents met in 1940. They _____ (live) in Cairo at the time.
4 I've worked hard to get this degree but I'm sure in the long term it _____ (be) worth it.
5 He _____ (save) money since he got his new job.
6 Ignore his calls. Sooner or later he _____ (realise) that you're not interested.

The perfect aspect
Form

The perfect aspect has three structures: present perfect, past perfect and future perfect. These can be combined with the continuous aspect to form present perfect continuous, past perfect continuous and future perfect continuous.

Name	Example
Present perfect simple	I have worked
Present perfect continuous	I have been working
Past perfect simple	I had worked
Past perfect continuous	I had been working
Future perfect	I will have worked
Future perfect continuous	I will have been working

Use

English tenses contain two kinds of meaning: time (past, present or future) and aspect (the speaker's viewpoint). There are two aspects: the perfect aspect and the continuous aspect (for the continuous aspect see Unit 2).

The perfect aspect always looks back from one point in time to an earlier time. The exact time of the action or situation is not specified.

Present perfect simple

The present perfect looks back from now to actions or situations in the past that are in some way connected to the present. We use the present perfect simple:
• to talk about completed actions that are connected to the present.
The film has started. (the film is on now)
I've pumped up the car tyres. (the car's safe to drive now)
• with time expressions that mean up to now, e.g. *today, this week.*
Have you spoken to Max this week?

We also use the present perfect simple with *be, have, know* and other stative verbs to talk about unfinished actions and situations that continue until now.
We've known about the problem for a while.

Present perfect continuous

We use the present perfect continuous:
*   to talk about something that started in the past and is continuing now.
    He's been talking on the phone for over an hour.
*   to talk about how we've been spending time recently.
    Sorry, I haven't called. I've been working really hard.

Remember that some verbs aren't used in the continuous form.
I've had this bike for six years. (Not ~~I've been having this bike for six years~~.)

Past perfect simple

The past perfect looks back from a point in the past to an earlier event.

We use the past perfect simple to talk about:
*   single, completed events.
    Somebody stole her car because she had left it unlocked.
*   repeated actions, when we give the number of times the action is repeated.
    I'd looked at five guitars before I decided which one to buy.

Past perfect continuous

We use the past perfect continuous to talk about how long an action, or series of actions, was in progress.
He was exhausted because he'd been travelling for 24 hours.

We don't usually use stative verbs (*be, have, like, love, hate, want*) in the past perfect continuous.
I'd known him for years. (Not ~~I'd been knowing him for years~~.)

Future perfect

We use the future perfect to look back from a point in the future to a finished or unfinished action. We often use the future perfect with expressions with *by*.

Future perfect simple

We use the future perfect simple to talk about an action that is going to be completed at or before a given time in the future.
They'll have finished repairing the bridge by next week.

Future perfect continuous

We use the future perfect continuous to talk about how long an action will have been in progress before a given time. It emphasises the fact that the action will take place over an extended period of time.
By the end of this year, I'll have been working here for 25 years.

Practice

3 Complete the sentences. Use the correct present perfect, past perfect or future perfect tense of these verbs.

be	double	forget	~~have~~	miss	not do
study	work				

1   He ___*'d had*___ several relationships before he decided to settle down.

2   It is predicted that the world's population _____ by the end of the century.
3   The business _____ very well lately.
4   It's my grandparents' diamond wedding anniversary next spring. They _____ married for 60 years!
5   Your essay is good on the whole, but you _____ out some important points.
6   I sent off the contract and then I realised I _____ to sign it.
7   By the end of this year, I _____ English for six years.
8   She got ill because she _____ too hard.

UNIT 2

The continuous aspect

Form

Continuous verbs are made with *be* + *-ing*.

Name	Example
Present continuous	I'm **coming** now.
Past continuous	She called while I **was having** a meeting.
Present perfect continuous	We've **been** driving for hours.
Past perfect continuous	They **had been waiting** for ages when I arrived.
Future continuous	I'll **be seeing** Ian later.

Use

Verbs in the continuous aspect describe incomplete actions that are in progress at a specific time. The actions are temporary and of limited duration.
I'm having a meeting at the moment.
This time tomorrow we'll be relaxing by the pool.
Last year I was living in Madrid.

We also use the continuous aspect to describe repeated actions. Compare:
She knocked on the door. and *She was knocking on the door.*
He hasn't eaten much. and *He hasn't been eating much recently.*

We can use the continuous to make questions, requests and statements less direct.
I was wondering if you could help me.
Will you be going anywhere near a post office?

Stative verbs such as *believe, know, realise, suppose, understand, agree, remember, wish*, etc. are rarely used in the continuous form. However, they can be used in the continuous forms if a dynamic use is intended. Compare:
I think that's ridiculous. and *I'm thinking about resigning from my job.*

Special uses of the continuous aspect

We use the present continuous to talk about trends and changing situations.
The business is expanding.
Pollution is getting worse.

We use the future continuous to talk about what we expect people to be doing now.
I won't ring her now. She'll be having her supper.

We use *always* and words with a similar meaning with the continuous to make complaints and criticisms.
She's always texting while I'm talking to her.
He's forever mislaying his keys.

Practice

1 Complete the sentences with the simple or continuous form of the verb in brackets.

1 I didn't have a break at the weekend because I _was preparing_ (prepare) my presentation.
2 I've got a colleague who _____ (sing) while she's working. It drives me mad.
3 I cut myself this morning while I _____ (shave).
4 Pete sounded stressed when I spoke to him earlier. He said he _____ (try) to resolve a computer issue for the past two hours.
5 We shouldn't postpone the meeting again. We _____ (put) it back twice already.
6 Do you think you _____ (still / work) here in a year's time?
7 I _____ (finish) this report then I'll go home.
8 I _____ (have) to pump up this tyre a lot recently. I think it may have a slow puncture.

Present and perfect participles
Form

Present participles are formed with verb + *-ing*.
Turning the handle slowly, he opened the door.
Not being a strong swimmer, I wore a life jacket while I was on the boat.

Perfect participles are formed with *having* + past participle.
Having graduated from university, he started work at a law firm.
Not having heard from his sister for several weeks, he decided to call her.

Use

We can use participial clauses to describe actions that happen simultaneously or consecutively.
Holding the knife firmly in his hand, the chef chopped the vegetables finely.
Backing slowly away from the bear, we turned and fled.

The main clause describes the most important event and the participial clause a secondary event. If we want to emphasise that the first action finished before the second, we use the perfect participle.
Having weighed up the pros and cons, he decided against resigning.

We can use a participial clause to express the idea of *because*.
Being a perfectionist, she sets herself very high standards. (Because she is a perfectionist, …)

We can also use a participial clause to express a result.
The vase blew over in the wind, damaging the newly tiled floor. (and as a result, it damaged the newly tiled floor)

Remember that the subject of a participial clause is the same as the subject of the main clause.

Practice

2 Choose the correct option.

1 *Having /* (*Having had*) a shower, I went downstairs for breakfast.
2 *Spending / Having spent* three years in Argentina, she now speaks Spanish fluently.
3 The woman slipped on the wet floor, *twisting / having twisted* her ankle.
4 *Not flying before, / Not having flown before,* I found the experience quite terrifying.
5 *Considering / Having considered* your application carefully, we would like to offer you the job.
6 *Being / Having been* the daughter of two doctors, I consider myself quite knowledgeable about medical matters.
7 I didn't understand the joke but *not wanting / not having wanted* to appear foolish I laughed.
8 I was very nervous giving a speech at my brother's wedding, *not speaking / not having spoken* in public before.

UNIT 3
Intensifying adverbs
Form and use

Intensifying adverb + gradable adjective	Intensifying adverb + ungradable/limit adjective
extremely, incredibly, pretty, quite, really, so, very	absolutely, completely, entirely, quite, really, so, totally, utterly
Intensifying adverb + gradable verb	**Intensifying adverb + ungradable/limit verb**
completely, entirely, really, totally	absolutely, completely, really, utterly

We use intensifying adverbs to make a verb, adjective or another adverb stronger. With adjectives and adverbs, they go directly in front of the word they intensify.
*The views are **absolutely** stunning.*
*The design was **totally** impractical.*
*The house **quite** literally shakes when a train goes by.*

Intensifying adverbs sometimes go before and sometimes after the verb they intensify.
*I agree with you **entirely**.*
*I **totally** understand.*

We use different adverbs with gradable adjectives and with ungradable adjectives.

Gradable adjectives can be measured on a scale,

e.g. *small*: a room can be a more or less small. Ungradable or limit adjectives, on the other hand, are not measured on a scale. They express only extreme qualities, e.g. *empty, wonderful*.

As with adjectives, verbs can be gradable or ungradable. For example, *agree* and *like* are gradable. You can agree with or like something to a small or large extent.

When used with an ungradable adjective or verb, *quite* means 'extremely'.
*The views were **quite** incredible!*

Practice

1 Choose the correct option. In one sentence, both options are correct.

1. The heating bills must be *very /(absolutely)*huge.
2. You'd be utterly *sensible / foolish* to buy that house.
3. I don't agree *entirely / extremely* with his views.
4. If you could help me to set up the meeting room, I'd be *absolutely / extremely* grateful.
5. You were *quite / incredibly* right to complain about the service.
6. I've had a totally *tiring / exhausting* day at work.
7. Why is this carpet so *dirty / filthy*?
8. I'm *quite / incredibly* certain that picture wasn't on the wall last time I was here.
9. I *really / totally* don't want to have this discussion right now.
10. Watching the way the birds built their nest was *extremely / absolutely* fascinating.

Emphatic structures
Form and use

There are several ways of adding emphasis to a sentence.

Cleft sentences (*what / it's / the thing*)
We can use *it's/it was* to highlight the part of the sentence we want to emphasise. We put the rest of the sentence into a *that*-clause.
I don't like the layout of the house. (no emphasis)
*It's the layout of the house **that** I don't like.* (with emphasis)

We can use *What* or *The thing … is/was* to put the words we want to emphasise at the end of a sentence.
I don't like the layout of the house. (no emphasis)
What *I don't like **is** the layout of the house.* (with emphasis)
The thing *I don't like **is** the layout of the house.* (with emphasis)

Negative inversion
Some negative adverbs can be used at the beginning of the sentence to add emphasis. In these cases we put the auxiliary verb before the subject. If there is no auxiliary verb, we use *do, does* or *did*. These structures are often quite formal and literary.

You rarely see houses built in this style. (no emphasis)
Rarely *do you see houses built in this style.* (with emphasis)

I've never seen such an untidy house before. (no emphasis)
Never before *have I seen such an untidy house.* (with emphasis)

The same pattern is used with *seldom, hardly (… when), little, no sooner (… than), not once, not only, only* + time expression, *under no circumstances*.

do, does, did
We can use the auxiliary verb *do* to add emphasis to the main verb.
I like that decorated ceiling. (no emphasis)
*I **do** like that decorated ceiling.* (with emphasis)

Practice

2 Rewrite the sentences adding more emphasis.

1. This city needs more low-cost housing.
   What ___*this city needs is more low-cost housing.*___
2. I hadn't witnessed such a violent thunderstorm before.
   Never ___
3. We could really do with more storage space.
   What ___
4. I'm particularly concerned about the lack of facilities in the area.
   It's ___
5. Houses rarely come up for sale in this village.
   Rarely ___
6. He didn't complain once about the poor living conditions.
   Not once ___
7. I won't believe a word he says ever again.
   Never again ___
8. I didn't buy any trousers but I bought a belt.
   I didn't ___
9. I'll really miss this wonderful view.
   It's ___
10. She had just arrived home when the doorbell rang.
    No sooner ___

UNIT 4
Past modals
Form and use

Obligation
We use *had to* to express obligation in the past. It is the past of *must* (for obligation) and *have to*.
*I **had to** work hard to persuade people to buy the product.*

Necessity
We use *needed to* + infinitive to say that it was necessary to do something.
*I **needed to** come up with a new idea.*

We use *needn't have* + past participle to say that a past action turned out not to be necessary.
We **needn't have brought** *our bikes. We haven't used them once.*

We use *didn't need to* or *didn't have to* to say that something wasn't necessary whether we did it or not.
*I **didn't need to use** my laptop so I left it at home.*

Speculation

We use *must/might/may/could/can't* + *have* + past participle to speculate about past events.
must have → you feel certain that something happened or was true
*They **must have got** held up in the traffic.*

may, might, could → you think it's possible something happened or was true
*Their car **might have broken** down.*

may not / might not have → you think it's possible something didn't happen/wasn't true
*He **may not have taken** a different route.*

can't have / couldn't have → you feel certain that something didn't happen
*He **can't have seen** the one-way sign.*

Notice that the opposite of *must have done* for speculation is *can't / couldn't have done* (not ~~mustn't have done~~.)
We use *must have* and *can't have* when we know or believe something by logical deductions.
*Her bag's still here so she **can't have left**.*
*Her bag isn't here so she **must have gone**.*

Advisability

We use *should have* or *ought to have* + past participle to talk about the correct, advisable or morally right thing to do in a past situation. It is often used to express regret about our own actions or criticism of other people's.
*I **should have brought** my camera with me.* (but I didn't)
*The company **ought to have provided** us with more training on the new software.* (but they didn't)

Other uses of past modals

We use *might have* and *could have* + past participle to criticise people for not doing things. *Might*, used in this way, is more formal than *could*.
*You **could have cleared** up the mess you made!*
*You **might have told** me he was vegetarian. I wouldn't have made chilli con carne!*

We can also use *should have* + past participle to talk about something that we expect to have happened.
*They left an hour ago. They **should have arrived** by now.*

Practice

1 Rewrite the sentences in italics using past modals.

1 'I went to a technology exhibition at the weekend.'
   '*I bet that was interesting.*'
   That must have been interesting.

2 'The microwave seems to be working again.'
   '*Perhaps Andy fixed it.*'

3 'Luke's given that watch away to a friend.'
   '*Clearly he didn't like it then.*'

4 'The electricity's gone off.'
   '*Maybe there's been a power cut.*'

5 'Our Internet at work was down for most of yesterday.'
   '*I'm sure that was frustrating.*'

6 'I got lost on my way here.'
   '*It would have been sensible to use your sat nav.*'

7 'Look! The cinema's completely empty.'
   '*So pre-booking our tickets was a waste of time.*'

8 'James wasn't at the meeting.'
   '*It's possible he didn't realise it was happening.*'

Probability
Form and use

We can express probability in a number of ways.

Modal verbs: *may, might, could, should*

We use *may, might* and *could* to talk about the probability that something is true now or will happen in the future. Their meaning is essentially the same.
*It **may / could / might snow** later.*

We use *may well, might well, could well* to say that something is quite probable.
*If sales continue to fall, the company **may well** be forced to close.*

Might not and *may not* express future possibility but we don't use *could not* in this way.
*The rumours **could be** true, but they **might not be**.*

We use *should* to describe a situation that you expect to happen.
*The roads are clear so we **should arrive** in good time.*
*They've fixed the printer so we **shouldn't have** any more problems with it.*

We only use *should* to talk about the probability of something good happening.
We don't say ~~The traffic's bad so we should be a bit late~~.

Adverbs: *perhaps, maybe, probably, almost certainly, almost definitely*

Perhaps and *maybe* go at the beginning of a sentence.
***Maybe** one day they'll invent fully automated cars.*

Other adverbs of certainty go before a main verb and after the auxiliary in affirmative sentences and before the auxiliary verb in negative sentences.
*The batteries **will probably need** to be replaced soon.*
*He **definitely won't** pass the exam.*

The adjective (un)likely

Likely and *unlikely* are adjectives (not adverbs). We can use subject + *be* + *likely/unlikely* or *it is likely/unlikely* + *that* + clause.
*The new tablet **is (un)likely to** be launched this year.*
***It's (un)likely that** the new tablet will be launched this year.*

Be likely to and *will probably* have the same meaning but *be likely to* is more formal.

Other common adjectives of probability are *bound* and *sure*. We use *be bound + to* + infinitive and *be sure + to* + infinitive to say that you think something is certain to happen or to be true.
*The truth is **bound to come** out sooner or later.*
*She's **sure to be** on time.*

Noun phrases

Noun phrases such as *The likelihood is*, *The chances are*, *There's a good chance* and *There's no doubt* are followed by *that* + a clause.
*The **likelihood is that** this software will become very popular.*

Practice

2 Rewrite the sentences using the words in brackets.

1 I don't think you'll get a phone signal here. It's too remote. (probably)
You _probably won't get a phone signal_ here. It's too remote.

2 The company probably won't upgrade its computers for another year. (unlikely)
It's _____ for another year.

3 We might be living abroad next year. (chances)
The _____ next year.

4 There's a good chance that the president will be re-elected. (might well)
The president _____ .

5 If we don't insure the washing machine, I bet it'll break down. (bound)
If we don't insure the washing machine, _____ down.

6 Are you sure the DVD player isn't working? (definitely)
_____ working?

7 I'm not sure that we need to buy a new printer. (may)
We _____ a new printer.

8 I'll be surprised if you don't receive a call from him shortly. (should)
You _____ from him shortly.

9 There's no doubt that she'll find an excuse for her behaviour. (likelihood)
The _____ for her behaviour.

UNIT 5

Substitution

Form and use

In English, there are a number of ways to avoid repeating words or phrases. Two of these are **substitution** (replacing one word or phrase with another) and **ellipsis** (omitting something completely).

Substituting lexis

We can use synonyms to avoid repetition of lexis, both in our own speech and when responding to others.
*I thought he was rather **blunt**. I'm not used to people being that **direct**.*
*'I thought she looked quite **stressed**.' 'Yes, she did seem a little **tense**, didn't she?'*

Substituting nouns

We can use pronouns to refer back to previous nouns.
*It was a simple **solution**, but an effective **one**.*

If two nouns are mentioned, we use *the former* to refer back to the first one and *the latter* to refer to the second.
*We could take the motorway or the scenic route: **the former** would get us there more quickly than **the latter**.*

Substituting verbs and verb phrases

We often use just the auxiliary of a verb phrase to avoid repeating verbs or verb phrases.
*I love **going trekking** in the mountains, but my girlfriend **doesn't**.*
*I didn't **go scuba diving** last year, but I **did** this year.*

We can use the expression *do so* to replace a verb phrase.
*I'd love to **go on a round-the-world trip**, but to **do so** would be extremely expensive.*

When we respond to another person's comment, we can use a different auxiliary.
*'I'd like to take a boat trip around the glaciers in Southern Argentina.' 'Yes, you **should**.'*
*'You should have taken the train.' 'Well, we **didn't**.'*

When there is more than one auxiliary, we can use one or more auxiliary when we respond.
'It would have been better to come here out of season.' 'Yes, it would / would have / would have been.'

Substituting clauses

We can substitute an entire clause with *that*, *so* or *not*.
'Do you think it'll be sunny for the rest of the week?' 'I hope so.'
'It'll be hard to find a hotel because there's a conference that week.' 'Ah, I wasn't aware of that.'

Ellipsis

Ellipsis means omitting words completely. We can use *to* instead of repeating a complete infinitive phrase.
'Will you see the Pyramids when you're in Egypt?' 'We hope to.' (= we hope to see them)

Practice

1 Delete the unnecessary words in the sentences and make substitutions where appropriate.

1 We took some insect repellent, but we didn't have to use ~~the insect repellent~~. _it_
2 This queue is for e-passport holders only. You haven't got an e-passport so you need to join the longer queue. _____
3 If I can take time off work next month, I will take time off work next month. _____
4 The hotel rooms were very expensive, but ours was one of the cheaper rooms. _____
5 You could hire a car when you go abroad, but to hire a car when you go abroad you need to have held a licence for a year. _____
6 'Did you book the flights?' 'I meant to book the flights but I didn't get a moment.' _____
7 Hindi and English are both spoken in New Delhi. Hindi is the principal spoken language and English is the principal written language. _____
8 This train goes to the airport but that one doesn't go to the airport. _____
9 'Did you remember to bring the map?' 'I'm afraid I didn't remember to bring the map.' _____

Nominalisation
Form and use

We can form nouns from other parts of speech, especially from verbs and adjectives. We call this process 'nominalisation'. We often use nominalisation in more formal situations (e.g. in formal emails or reports).

Verb → noun nominalisation
We complained about our accommodation.
→ *We made **a complaint** about our accommodation.*
Please acknowledge that you have received this email.
→ *Please acknowledge **receipt** of this email.*

We sometimes form nouns from a different verb with a similar meaning, for example with phrasal verbs.
The cost of flights has gone up in the last few years.
→ *There has been an **increase** in the cost of flights in the last few years.*

Adjective → noun nominalisation
I'm grateful to you for supporting me.
→ *I would like to express **my gratitude** for all your support.*
Thank you for being so generous.
→ *Thank you for **your generosity**.*

Nominalisations are often followed by a preposition, e.g. *in recognition of, on arrival at* and *on receipt of*.

Other types of nominalisation

We can use nouns to replace relative pronouns such as *who, when, why, what, where*.
I don't know why they went on strike.
→ *I don't know the reason for the strike.*
Can you show me where it is on the map?
→ *Can you show me the location on the map?*
I can't remember when it was.
→ *I can't remember the occasion.*
Do the police know who the culprit was?
→ *Do the police know the identity of the culprit?*
I couldn't tell you how it was done.
→ *I couldn't tell you the method that was used.*
I don't know what the lecture will be about.
→ *I don't know the subject of the lecture.*

Practice

2 Rewrite the sentences using a noun in place of the words in italics.

1 Why do you think Hergé's books are *successful*? What do you think is the reason _for the success of Hergé's books?_
2 I don't know *where the* hotel *is* exactly. I don't know _____
3 We said *we would prefer* an earlier start date. We expressed _____
4 She was impressed by *how much I knew* about the region. She was impressed _____
5 I *tried* to contact you several times, but was told you were unavailable. I made _____
6 The weather conditions have *improved*. There has _____
7 We were surprised that we *recovered* so quickly from jetlag. We were surprised _____
8 We will confirm your booking *when we receive* your deposit. Your booking will be confirmed _____
9 Thank you for *assisting* me in this matter. Thank you for _____
10 Everyone was relieved *when he arrived* early. Everyone was relieved by _____

UNIT 6

Phrasal verbs
Form and use

A phrasal verb is a verb + particle (preposition or adverb). The same verb may be used with a number of different particles and the meaning of the verb changes each time. The meaning of the phrasal verb is sometimes idiomatic: i.e. the meaning is different from the meanings of the verb and particle.

There are four kinds of phrasal verb:

1 Intransitive phrasal verbs: verb + adverb (no object)

Intransitive phrasal verbs don't have objects.
Sit down!   *This situation can't go on.*

2 Separable phrasal verbs: verb + adverb + object

Many phrasal verbs are transitive and need an object. Transitive verbs can be separable or inseparable. With separable phrasal verbs, the object can come before or after the particle.
Can you turn down the volume?
Can you turn the volume down?

If the object is a pronoun, it must go between the verb and the particle.
Can you turn it down? (Not *Can you ~~turn down it~~?*)

If the object is a long noun phrase, the particle comes immediately after the verb.
She gave up going to the gym. (Not *She gave ~~going to the gym up~~.*)

3 Inseparable phrasal verbs: verb + preposition + object

With inseparable phrasal verbs, the object must go after the particle. It cannot go between the verb and the particle.
It took him a long time to get over his leg injury.

4 Three-part phrasal verbs: verb + adverb + preposition + object(s)

Some phrasal verbs have three parts: a verb and two particles. The object must come after the particles.
We're looking forward to seeing the play.

Most three-part verbs have one object.
It's hard to get down to work in this heat.
He always comes up with innovative ideas.

A few three-part phrasal verbs have two objects. The first object comes after the verb and the second object comes after the two particles.
I'll take you up on your offer to make dinner tonight.

Practice

1 Rewrite the sentences substituting a pronoun for the words in italics.

1 I need to print off *some copies of this report.*
   I *need to print them off.*
2 Who will be looking after *your cats* while you're away?
   Who _____ while you're away?
3 Let me run though *the rules of the game* again.
   Let me _____ .
4 He admitted that he'd made up *the whole story.*
   He admitted _____ .
5 I'm sorry. I take back *what I said.*
   I'm sorry. I _____ .
6 Tennis players often put off *their opponents* by making grunting noises.
   Tennis players often _____ by making grunting noises.

2 Write the words in italics in the correct order.

1 I won't be coming to the yoga class tonight because I've *down / come / flu / with.*
   come down with flu
2 I think it's too late to *talk / out / of / her* resigning.
3 Many people think we should *with / do / the monarchy / away.*
4 Black football players shouldn't have to *put / racial abuse / with / up* from the crowds.
5 Could I *take / up / your offer / on / you* of a lift to the meeting?
6 The restaurant didn't quite *live / our expectations / up / to.*

Verb patterns
Form and use

After certain verbs, we use *to* + infinitive.
*The player **pretended to be** injured.*

Common verbs which are followed by *to* + infinitive include: *afford, expect, fail, seem, tend, want.*

Some verbs are followed by an object + *to* + infinitive.
*The doctor **advised her to rest** her ankle.*

Common verbs which are followed by an object + *to* + infinitive include: *force, encourage, require, want, warn.*

Some verbs are followed by an object + infinitive (without *to*).
*My manager **made me stay** late yesterday.*
*I **saw him pass out**.*

Common verbs which are followed by an object + infinitive (without *to*) include: *help, let see, hear.*

Some verbs are followed by the *-ing* form.
*I **suggest leaving** before the rush hour begins.*

Common verbs which are followed by the *-ing* form include: *avoid, dislike, mention, miss, recommend, risk.*

Some verbs are followed by both an infinitive or an *-ing* form with little or no change in their meaning, e.g. *begin, continue, like, love, hate, prefer, start.*
*It **started to pour** with rain.*
*It **started pouring** with rain.*

Some verbs are followed by both an infinitive or an *-ing* form with a change in their meaning, e.g. *forget, regret, remember, stop, try.*
*Winning this point would **mean winning** the match.*
*I **meant to call** her but I forgot.*

Some verbs are followed by a preposition + *-ing* form.
*He finally **succeeded in giving** up smoking.*

Other verbs which are followed by a preposition + *-ing* include: *complain about, insist on, rely on, think about, worry about.*

Some verbs are followed by an object + preposition + -ing form.
*The press **criticised the referee for making** poor decisions.*

Other verbs which are followed by an object + preposition + -ing include: *accuse (someone) of, blame (someone) for, discourage (someone) from, prevent (someone) from.*

Verbs + *that* + clause
Sometimes a *that*-clause can be used instead of the infinitive or -ing form. *That* can be omitted.
*The player **pretended to be injured**.*
*= The player **pretended (that) he was injured**.*

However, it is not always possible, e.g.:
He wanted me to come. (Not He wanted ~~that I come~~.)

Perfect and passive forms
The gerund and -ing forms also have perfect and passive forms.
*I wanted **to be given** another chance.*
*I didn't like **being made** to queue.*
*I regret **having lost** my temper.*

Practice
3 Complete the sentences with the verbs in brackets in the correct form. You need to use a preposition in some of the sentences.

1 If you fail _to arrive_ (arrive) on time, you won't be let in.
2 The high cost of parking discourages people .... (bring) cars into the city centre.
3 Police warned the public .... (not / approach) the escaped prisoner.
4 The government was criticised .... (violate) human rights.
5 Anyone who doesn't abide by the rules risks .... (be) disqualified.
6 He put antiseptic on the wound to prevent it .... (become) infected.

UNIT 7
Linking words
Form and use

Additional point

and + clause		The Aztecs arrived in Mexico in 1325 **and** founded the city of Tenochtitlán.
as well as in addition to not to mention	+ noun or gerund	She studied ancient history **as well as** Latin at university. **In addition to** writing an essay, we have to give a presentation.
moreover furthermore in addition	+ new sentence	Julius Caesar was a general and a historian. **Moreover**, he was a talented mathematician.

Reason

because since as	+ clause	He repeated the instructions **since** nobody heard them the first time.
because of on account of owing to due to as a result of	+ noun	The Greeks expected to lose the battle **owing to** the size of the Persian army.

Contrast

although but even though	+ clause	**Although** the Romans didn't invent the arch, they were the first to use them in bridges.
despite in spite of notwithstanding	+ noun or gerund	**Despite** living to the age of only 33, Alexander the Great built a huge empire.
however nevertheless	+ new sentence	It is often believed that Columbus discovered America. **However**, this is disputed by some.

Time

after, as, before, when, since, as soon as, until, while	+ clause	The Middle Ages began **after** the Roman Empire collapsed.
after since	+ noun or gerund	**After** visiting the Valley of the Kings, we went on a cruise on the River Nile.
following	+ noun	The Great Fire of London broke out **following** a fire in a bakery in 1666.
Subsequently	+ new sentence	The remains of the palace were uncovered in 2001. **Subsequently**, archaeologists discovered many more artefacts.

There are a number of different kinds of linkers.

Conjunctions, e.g. *when, although, because*
Conjunctions are followed by a clause.
Although I had slept for several hours, I felt exhausted.

Some conjunctions can be followed by a noun or gerund.
Since discovering this restaurant, we rarely eat anywhere else.

Adverbs, e.g. *however, moreover, nevertheless*
It rained throughout the concert. However, it didn't spoil it for us.

Adverbs usually go at the beginning of the sentence. They can, however, go in the middle.
He doesn't usually give press interviews. Today, however, he is making an exception.

Prepositional words or phrases, e.g. *in spite of, owing to*

These are followed by a noun (or pronoun), a gerund or *the fact that* + clause.

She accepted the job in spite of the low salary.
She accepted the job in spite of the fact that it was very poorly paid.

Practice

1 Combine the sentences using the linking words in brackets.

1 Her father died in 1952. Queen Elizabeth II came to the throne. (following)
   Queen Elizabeth II came to the throne following the death of her father in 1952.

2 History is an enjoyable subject to study. It can help us understand the present. (in addition to)

3 The event was cancelled. There was not enough funding for it. (owing to)

4 We hadn't heard from you. We assumed you weren't coming. (since)

5 The Pharaohs of ancient Egypt were seen as kings and gods. (as well as)

6 Herodotus was a very famous historian. Little is known about the man himself. (although)

7 I've lived in this flat since July 2010. I moved to Madrid in July 2010. (since)

8 The new law was passed. Some people objected to it. (despite)

Subordinate clauses
Form and use

Sentences are made up of one or two clauses. Sometimes these are two main clauses, joined by a conjunction such as *and, but* or *or*.
*The lecture finished **and** the students went home.*

The two clauses are called main clauses because they can both make sense on their own:
The lecture finished.
The students went home.

Other sentences are made up of a main clause and a subordinate clause, joined by a conjunction such as *when, if, although, because*.
***When you get a moment**, have a look at this website.*

The main clause makes sense on its own if the subordinate clause (in bold) is removed, but the subordinate clause does not make sense without the main clause.

The subject of the subordinate clause can be different from the subject of the main clause.

Subordinate clauses add meaning to the main clause by giving more information about, for example, cause, comparison or time.

cause/reason	*as, because, considering (that), given (that), in view of the fact that, since*
condition	*as long as, assuming (that), if, provided that, supposing (that), unless*
contrast	*although, even though, having said that, in spite of the fact that, regardless of the fact that*
time	*as, before, when, while*
precaution	*in case, in the event of*
comparison	*compared to, contrary to, relative to*
other	*as far as … is concerned, thinking about it, insofar as*

Practice

2 Choose the correct option.

1 I've brought a jacket *unless /* (*in case*) */ if* it gets colder later.

2 *Contrary to / Compared to / Thinking about* modern eating habits, the Romans used to recline whilst having dinner.

3 *In spite of the fact that / Given that / Supposing that* we're trying to save money, I don't think we should go abroad this summer.

4 He was offered the job *given / in view of / regardless of* the fact that he had no experience.

5 You are allowed to organise a dig *provided that / in case / even though* you have a licence.

6 In the Middle Ages, most children didn't know their grandparents *although / since / in case* they had died before they were born.

7 Let's take some cash with us *if / considering / in case* the shop doesn't accept credit cards.

8 The meeting was scheduled to begin at 2 p.m. *in spite of / in view of / assuming* the fact that people had a long way to travel.

9 Temperatures, *insofar as / while / provided that* weather forecasters can tell at this stage, are expected to be above average next month.

UNIT 8

Passive reporting verbs
Form

We can report actions and events using the passive in two different ways:
A: It + passive verb + *that* clause
***It is believed that** the company **was sold** for $20 million.*
B: subject + passive verb + *to* + infinitive
*The company **is believed to have been sold** for $20 million.*

A: *It* + passive verb + *that* clause
Reporting verbs that commonly follow this pattern are: *agree, allege, announce, assume, believe, claim, consider, decide, estimate, expect, fear, hope, know, presume, report, say, suggest, think, understand.*

Present

It is thought that the eyespots on butterfly wings **startle** *their enemies.*
It is believed that the minister **is considering** *resignation following the scandal.*

Past

It is estimated that ten thousand people **took part** *in the demonstration.*
It was alleged that the boy **hacked** *into his school's computer.*
It wasn't thought that permanent damage **had been caused**.

Future

It is expected that the new stadium **will open** *in January.*

B: Subject + passive verb + *to* + infinitive

Reporting verbs that commonly follow this pattern are: *allege, assume, believe, consider, estimate, expect, know, report, say, think, understand.*

Present

The eyespots on butterfly wings **are thought to startle** *their enemies.*
The minister **is believed to be considering** *resignation following the scandal.*

Past

Ten thousand people **are estimated to have taken** *part.*
The boy **was alleged to have hacked** *into his school's computer.*
No permanent damage **was thought to have been caused**.

Future

The new stadium **is expected to open** *in January.*

Infinitives		
	affirmative	**negative**
active		
simple	to sell	not to sell
continuous	to be selling	not to be selling
perfect	to have sold	not to have sold
perfect continuous	to have been selling	not to have been selling
passive		
simple	to be sold	not to be sold
perfect	to have been sold	not to have been sold

Notice how we use passive reporting verbs with *there*.
It is known that there are small traces of mercury in fish.
There is known to be small traces of mercury in fish.

Use

We use reporting verbs in the passive when:
- we cannot verify the source of the information.
- we assume that the reader or listener is not interested in who the agent or source is.
- the agent or source is obvious from the context.

This structure is very common in formal writing e.g. newspaper articles, academic essays and business documents, as well as in formal speaking contexts, e.g. academic discussions and business meetings or presentations.

Practice

1 Rewrite the sentences using passive reporting verbs.

1 Conservationists fear that polar bears may soon become extinct.
It *is feared that polar bears may soon become extinct.*
2 Journalists reported that an oil spill has occurred off the coast of Mexico.
An oil spill _____
3 Detectives know the robbery took place in the early hours of this morning.
The robbery _____
4 Insider sources say that the player has not been selected for the Olympic team.
The player _____
5 Scientists think that dinosaurs were wiped out when an asteroid hit Earth.
Dinosaurs _____
6 Doctors say a climber who fell 100 metres down a steep ridge is recovering well.
A climber who _____
7 The finance minister is expected to announce a tax increase tomorrow.
It _____
8 The police believe there weren't any witnesses present.
No witnesses _____

Expressions with *no*
Form and use

Only certain nouns are used in these expressions. Here are some of the most common.

no + noun + *-ing*
There's no point (in) worrying.
I had no difficulty (in) finding the venue.
There's no harm (in) trying.
There's no sense (in) waiting.
It's no use arguing.
It's no good complaining.

no + noun + *of* + *-ing*
There's no way of finding out.
He had no intention of leaving.
There was no mention of having to pay.
She made no suggestion of changing it.
We had no means of getting there.
I've got no chance of winning.
There's no hope of finishing the project on time.

no + noun + *that*
There's no question that it'll work.
There's no doubt that she's right.
There was no suggestion that we would have to attend.
There was no expectation that he would pay.

no ... except/but to + infinitive
I had no choice but to resign.
We have no alternative except to sell the house.
He had no option but to report the matter to the police.

no matter + relative pronoun
No matter what I say, he won't believe me.
No matter how hard I try, I can't forget what happened.

Practice

2 Rewrite the sentences using an expression with **no** and the word in brackets.

1 You've got nothing to lose by applying for the job. (harm)
   There's _____

2 The advertising campaign has definitely been effective. (doubt)
   There's _____

3 Why pay for an expensive laptop if you don't really need one? (point)
   There's _____

4 The reality is, however many possessions we have, we always want more. (matter)
   The reality is, _____

5 Calling him is a waste of time as he never answers his phone. (use)
   It's _____

6 Pilots say that they will be forced to go on strike if an agreement isn't reached. (alternative)
   Pilots say _____

7 You can't access the data without a password. (way)
   There's _____

8 I assure you I don't intend to leave before this matter is resolved. (intention)
   I assure you _____

UNIT 9

The adverb *just*
Form and use

The adverb *just* can appear in several positions within a sentence. It is placed before the word it emphasises.
- before the main verb: *They've **just** released a new album.*
- before a preposition: *The band split up **just** over a year ago.*
- before a noun: *It's **just** a suggestion.*
- before an adjective: *Her voice is **just** amazing.*
- before a conjunction: *I'll be with you **just** as soon as I've finished this call.*

Just is often used in spoken English and has a number of different meanings.

very recently	*She's just left the office.*
simply	*It's just a matter of luck.*
only	*He just sings – he doesn't write the music.*
exactly	*It's just the kind of music I love.*
a little	*They were on stage for just over two hours.*

In some cases *just* has no particular meaning but is used for emphasis.
*I **just** love this track!*   *That's **just** not acceptable!*
*It's **just** amazing!*   ***Just** taste this pizza!*

Other uses of *just*
We use *just* when something almost doesn't happen.
*I can **just** hear you.* (with difficulty)
*We **just** made it to the station on time.* (but we nearly didn't)

Just about means *almost*.
*I've **just about** had enough of this.*
*The programme's **just about** over.*

Just as is used to emphasise that something is equal to something else.
*The view is **just as** good from here.*

Practice

1 Put the words in the correct order.

1 to / I / for / can't / just / wait / come out / the new album
   I *just can't wait for the new album to come out.*

2 just / we / stood / of / the stage / in front
   We _____

3 the new single / raving / about / were / the reviews / just
   The reviews _____

4 bought / came out / after / just / I / it / the CD
   I _____

5 just / one day / sell out / tickets / for / often / in / the music festival
   Tickets _____

6 an hour / been / just / for / over / we've / waiting
   We've _____

7 I / you / were / wondering / just / where / was
   I _____

8 my essay / about / finished / I've / just
   I've _____

9 as / just / her / sister / talented / she's / as
   She's _____

10 misunderstanding / was / it / unfortunate / just / an
   It _____

Expressing purpose
Form and use

We can use several structures to express the reason why we do something.

Infinitive of purpose
We can use *to* + infinitive on its own.
*I went to the post office **to collect** a parcel.*
***To get** the best deal, we'll need to book well in advance.*

Or we can use *in order to* or *so as to* + infinitive. *In order to* is more formal than *so as to*.
*We need to increase sales **in order to make** a profit.*
*We moved forward **so as to get** a better view.*

It is common to use *in order not to* or *so as not to* before a negative
Handle the CD carefully **so as not to / in order not to** *damage it.*
(Not *Handle the CD carefully* ~~not to damage it~~.)

for + noun
I'm learning English **for pleasure**, *not for work.*

avoid + *-ing* or *avoid* + noun + *-ing*
I keep my guitar in a case to avoid scratching it.
I keep my guitar in a case to avoid it getting scratched.

so that / *in order that* + clause
So that and *in order that* are conjunctions and are followed by clauses. The subject of the clause may be different from the subject of the main clause. When we talk about the present or the future, *so that / in order that* are often followed by *can* or *will*.
I've learnt the songs by heart **so that I won't need** *to bring any sheet music with me.*
I've kept the receipt **so that she can return** *the CD if she wants to.*

We sometimes use the present tense to talk about the future.
I'm going to take some sun cream **so that we don't / won't** *get sunburn.*

In sentences about the past we usually use *would, could* or *should* after *so that / in order that*.
The concert tickets were free **in order that everyone could have an opportunity to go**.

So that is more common than *in order that*, especially in informal English. In informal English, we can omit *that* after *so*.
I'll send you the playlist **so (that) you can use it** *for your party.*

Practice

2 Rewrite the words in italics using the word in brackets.

1 The band went on tour *because they wanted to promote their new album.* (to)
   to promote their new album.

2 I often wear headphones while working *because I like to block out the surrounding noise.* (order)

3 I took some painkillers *because I wanted to get rid of my headache.* (to)

4 He didn't complain to the noisy neighbours *because he didn't want to cause a scene.* (avoid)

5 I went to bed early *because I wanted to feel fresh on the day of my exam.* (so that)

6 The burglar wore gloves *because he didn't want to leave fingerprints.* (so as)

7 He took his laptop with him *because he wanted to be able to work on the train.* (in order that)

8 I'll send him the concert tickets *because I want him to get them by Friday.* (so that)

UNIT 10
Tag questions
Form

To form tag questions, we use the auxiliary of the verb in the main sentence. When the main verb in the sentence is affirmative, the tag question is negative. When the main verb in the sentence is negative (including sentences with words with a negative meaning like *no one, never, hardly*), the tag question is affirmative.
You're Evie, aren't you?
He didn't stay late, did he?

Note that when the subject is a noun, we use an appropriate pronoun in the tag question.
Mike *travels to South Africa every year, doesn't* **he?**

Verb or verb form (+ auxiliary)	Examples
to be (*is, are, was, were*)	*It's interesting, isn't it?* *I'm right, aren't I?* (With *I am …*, we don't say *I'm right, am not I?*) *You were at the festival, weren't you?* *There was a problem, wasn't there?*
Present simple (*do, does*)	*You live in Melbourne, don't you?* *She doesn't work here, does she?*
Past simple (*did*)	*He worked for HBC, didn't he?* *She didn't explain it clearly, did she?*
Perfect and continuous (the same auxiliary verb)	*They haven't voted before, have they?* *You aren't paying attention, are you?*
Modal verbs (the same modal auxiliary verb)	*It should have arrived by now, shouldn't it?* *I couldn't borrow some change, could I?*
Imperative (*will, won't*)	*Send me some photos, won't you?* *Don't forget to reply, will you?*
Let's (*shall*)	*Let's have a break, shall we?* *Let's not stay too late tonight, shall we?*

Use

We use tag questions in speech or in informal writing to check that something is true or to request agreement.

The meaning is shown by the intonation we use. If the tag is a real question to check something is true, we use rising intonation.
We're meeting at three, aren't we?

If we are just requesting agreement, we use falling intonation.

That was a very productive meeting, wasn't it?

We can also request agreement with the word *surely*. *Surely he's made a mistake?* means the same as *He's made a mistake, hasn't he?*

It is possible to have an affirmative question tag after an affirmative sentence. We use this structure to express interest, surprise or concern.

*So your mother's from Guatemala, **is she**?*

If the subject of the sentence is *no one, someone* or *anyone*, the pronoun in the question tag is *they*.

*Someone will meet us at the airport, **won't they**?*

Practice

1 Add question tags to these sentences.

1 It's been a long day, _____ ?
2 There hasn't been a phone call for me, _____ ?
3 Hardly anyone turned up to the meeting, _____ ?
4 He never takes responsibility for his actions, _____ ?
5 I'm going to be late, _____ ?
6 Give me have a hand, _____ ?
7 She should ask for help if she needs it, _____ ?
8 We had great fun at the carnival, _____ ?
9 Let's meet up again next week, _____ ?
10 Don't tell anybody what I said, _____ ?

Adverbs
Form and use

Adverb + verb

Adverbs of manner describe how something is done. They often, but not always, end in *-ly*, e.g. *quickly, carefully, quietly, well*.
*Ants depend **primarily** on pheromones.*

Adverbs of manner usually come after the verb they describe. If the verb has an object, the adverb goes after the object.
*Ants behave **fearlessly**.*
*The ants attacked their prey **fearlessly**.*

They can also come in the middle of the sentence, between the subject and the main verb. When there is an auxiliary verb, the adverb comes after the auxiliary and before the main verb.
*The ants **carefully** carried the crumbs back to their nest.*
*The ants were **busily** searching for food.*

They can also come at the beginning of the sentence.
***Carefully**, the ants carried the crumbs back to their nest.*

We don't usually use adverbs of manner between the subject and verb or at the beginning of the sentence, when no other additional information is given after the verb, e.g. an object, a prepositional phrase.
*They behave **fearlessly**. (Not ~~Fearlessly, they behave~~.)*

Adverb + adjective

We can use adverbs of manner to add information or comment on an adjective or another adverb.
*Ants are **remarkably** strong.*
*They adapt to new situations **surprisingly** quickly.*

Adverbs with the same form as the adjective

Some adverbs have the same form as the adjective.
*Ants work **hard**.   This is **hard** work.*
*He's a **fast** runner.   He can run **fast**.*

Other words which behave in this way include: *direct, easy, fine, free, high, late, long, pretty, straight, tight, well, wide*.

Adverbs meaning *almost … not*

The adverbs *hardly, barely* and *scarcely* mean 'almost not'. They are often used with words like *any* or *anyone* and with adjectives and verbs.
*There was **barely/scarcely/hardly** anywhere to sit.*
*It was so dark we could **barely/scarcely/hardly** see.*
*Some ants are so tiny that they are **barely/scarcely/hardly** visible.*

These words have a negative meaning and aren't used with *not* or other negatives: ~~I couldn't hardly see~~.

Adverbs not formed with the *-ly* suffix.

When an adjective ends in *-ly*, e.g. *friendly, lively*, it is not possible to make them into adverbs with an *-ly* suffix. They need to be expressed in a different way, e.g. with an adverbial phrase such as *In a … manner / way / fashion*.
They spoke to me in a friendly way. Not ~~He spoke to me friendly~~. or ~~He spoke to me friendlily~~.

Other adjectives ending in *-ly* include: *cowardly, daily, deadly, early, likely, lively, lonely, lovely, orderly, ugly, worldly*.

Some adjectives ending in *-ed* cannot be made into adverbs by adding the *-ly* suffix.
They communicate in a civilised way. Not ~~They communicate civilisedly~~.

Practice

2 Rewrite the sentences, adding an adverb or adverbial phrase formed from the adjective in brackets. It may be necessary to make other changes to the sentence.

1 He explained what we had to do. (complicated)
He explained what we had to do in a complicated way.

2 I was speechless when I heard the news. (complete)
_____

3 It was so airless in the room that I couldn't breathe. (bare)
_____

4 The best way to get rid of ants is to go to the source: the nest. (straight)
_____

5 He devoured everything that was on his plate. (hungry)

6 She pushed him aside. (unfriendly)

7 It solved the problem. (instant)

8 He agreed to let me pay for the taxi. (reluctant)

UNIT 11

Unreal past

Form and use

There are a number of structures in English that are followed by past tenses which have a present or future meaning. We use these structures to express unreal or hypothetical situations.

would rather / would just as soon

We use *would rather* or *would just as soon* + subject + past tense to express a preference.
I'd rather they didn't visit us this weekend.
I'd just as soon you didn't mention this to anyone else.

It is also possible to use *I'd rather* and *I'd just as soon* + infinitive without *to* when there is no change of subject: *I'd rather not see him.* However, if the subject changes, we use the past tense. *I'd rather he didn't see me.* (Not *I'd rather he not see me.*)

I wish / if only

We use *I wish* and *if only* to express regrets and wishes for things that are unlikely to happen. *If only* has a more emphatic meaning than *I wish*.
I wish / If only you didn't live so far away.

We use the past perfect to express regrets about the past.
I wish I'd spent more time preparing for this presentation. (but I didn't)
If only I had trusted my instincts. (but I hadn't)

We use *wish* + *would* to express a wish for action: for someone to do something about a situation or for the situation/action to stop.
I wish you would stop making that noise.

We also use *would* + *wish* to talk about another person's annoying habits or unwillingness to do/not do something.
I wish / If only she would listen to my advice.
I wish he wouldn't interrupt me while I'm speaking.

Notice that we don't use *would* if the subjects in both clauses are the same.
I wish I didn't live here. (Not *I wish I wouldn't live here.*)

what if / supposing / suppose

We can use *what if*, *supposing* and *suppose* at the beginning of a question to ask about the consequences of something.
What if I wasn't here to help you – what would you do?

We can also use these structures to make suggestions.
Supposing we were to offer you a salary increase – would you stay?

What if is more informal than *suppose* and *supposing*.

it's (high) time

We use *it's time* + subject + past tense to say that something needs to be done very soon. We can use *high* before *time* to add emphasis.
It's (high) time I had a holiday.

Note that we can use *were* instead of *was* with these structures, especially in a formal style.
I wish I was/were somewhere else.
Supposing I was/were to be made redundant – what would we do?

It is occasionally possible when we talk about a hypothetical situation to use the present instead of the past tense.
What if nobody comes/came?

Practice

1 Rewrite the sentences using the words in brackets.

1 He ought to take a break. (time)
   It's time he took a break.

2 I'd prefer it if you would break the news to her. (rather)

3 She might leave him. Then he'd be devastated. (what)

4 Why does he have to be so critical about everything? (wish)

5 The government urgently needs to change the laws on gun ownership. (high)

6 Would it help if we employed someone to clean the flat? (supposing)

7 It would be so good to have more free time. (only)

8 I'd be as happy for you to drive as for James. (soon)

Inversion in conditionals

Form and use

In more formal speech and writing we can make conditional sentences by putting an auxiliary verb before a subject instead of using *if*. This structure is most common after *should*, *were* and *had*.
Had we known there were tickets left, we'd have bought some. (= If we had known there were tickets left, we'd have bought some.)

should

Should you have any questions, please don't hesitate to contact me. (= If you have any questions, please don't hesitate to contact me.)
Should you ever need a place to stay in London, you'll always be welcome here. (= If you ever need a place to stay in London, you'll always be welcome here.)

Second conditional

Were we in a stronger financial position, we'd offer to lend you the money. (= If we were in a stronger financial position, we'd offer to lend you money.)

We can use *were + subject + to* to talk about future possibilities, but not about unreal situations.
Were my parents to lend me some money, I'd be able to buy the flat. (= If my parents lent me some money, I'd be able to buy the flat.)

We can use the structure *were it not for (the fact that)* to say that without this situation or person things would be different. We use this structure in more formal speech.
If she hadn't encouraged me, I wouldn't be a professional athlete. → Were it not for her encouragement, I wouldn't be a professional athlete.
If my friends didn't live here, I would move to a different town. → Were it not for the fact that my friends live here, I would move to a different town.

Third and mixed conditional

If I'd read the reviews, I wouldn't have bought the book. → Had I read the reviews, I wouldn't have bought the book.
If I hadn't had the operation, I'd still be in a lot of pain. → Had I not had the operation, I'd still be in a lot of pain.

We can use the structure *had it not been for (the fact that)* to say that without this person or situation things would have been different.
If she hadn't been so persistent, she wouldn't have found such a good job. → Had it not been for her persistence, she wouldn't have found such a good job.

Note that negative auxiliaries are not contracted in inversion sentences.
Had you not given clear directions, I would never have found this place. (Not ~~Hadn't you given …~~)

Practice

2 Put the words in the correct order to make conditional sentences with inversion.

1 the police / acting / you / should / please / suspiciously / notice / contact / anyone
    Should you notice anyone acting suspiciously, please contact the police.

2 not / into / cold / so / town / were / we / could / it / walk
    ....

3 you / should / know / our plans / I'll / change / let
    ....
    ....

4 you / the helpline / any / experience / technical problems / please / call / should
    ....

5 offered / I / to be / a promotion / were / stay / the company / I / would / at
    ....

6 would / have / the weather / had / better / been / we / longer / stayed
    ....

7 your help / I / known / wouldn't / what / have / it / not / for / to / do / were
    ....

8 be asleep / my alarm / I / had / would / still / not gone off
    ....

UNIT 12

Approximation
Form and use

It is common in spoken English and informal written English to use approximate language when it is not important to give exact details or when exact details aren't known.

Numbers

*30-**odd** people; two hundred **or so** trees*
***some** fifty books*
***around, about, roughly, approximately, in the region of, something like** ten properties*
*500 dollars, **more or less***
dozens of** jobs, **hundreds of** birds, **loads of** time, **in a** month **or two
***(well) under, above, below** zero*

-odd can mean 'approximately' or 'a little more than the number mentioned'. *Some* before a number suggests a large number.

Adjectives

We use *kind of* when we can't think of a better adjective to describe something.
It's kind of rubbery.
I felt kind of foolish.

We can add the suffix *-ish* to an adjective to make it less exact. It is usually added to words describing physical features: size, colour, etc. and time.
It's reddish, it's brownish, it's longish, it's roundish.
'What time are we meeting?' 'One-ish.'

some

We use *some* plus a singular noun to refer to a person, thing or time that is unknown to us.
*We'll arrive **some** time in the afternoon.*
*I read about it in **some** newspaper article.*
***Some** idiot reversed into my car.*

Vague words

We use vague words like *stuff* and *things* to refer to a substance, material or group of objects when we don't know the name, when the name is not important, or when it's obvious what we're talking about. *Stuff* is more colloquial than *things*.

*What's that green **stuff** in the water?*
*Leave your **things** in the locker.*

Practice

1 Complete the sentences with these words.

around	-ish	kind of	or so	~~some~~	stuff
things	well				

1 I hope to see you ___*some*___ time soon.
2 Life has been _____ tough recently
3 The leaves had turned a yellow _____ colour.
4 There was a lot of urgent _____ to deal with this morning at the office.
5 It takes an hour _____ to get there.
6 My swimming _____ are in this bag.
7 The National Park spans _____ over 1,500 square kilometres.
8 The village stands at _____ 1,500 metres above sea level.

Qualifiers
Form and use

A qualifier is a word or phrase that modifies the meaning of the words that follow it. It can either intensify or soften the meaning of the words.

quite, *pretty* and *fairly*

We use *fairly* to modify the meaning of adjectives and adverbs. It means 'to a limited degree'.
*It was **fairly** easy to understand.* (it was quite, but not very easy)
*'Are you certain that it'll work?' 'I'm **fairly** certain, but I wouldn't bet on it.'*

Quite often suggests a higher degree than *fairly*.
*His explanation was **quite** confusing. I didn't really understand what he meant.*

Quite can also qualify nouns and verbs.
*I **quite** like reading poetry.*
*It was **quite** a difficult assignment.*

When modifying an adjective + noun, *quite* comes before *a/an*.
*The story had **quite** an unexpected ending.*

Pretty can only modify adjectives and adverbs. It suggests a higher degree than *fairly* and *quite*. It can also suggest 'more than usual' and 'more than expected'. *Pretty* is slightly more informal than *quite* or *fairly*.
*It's **pretty** unlikely that things will change.*
*The tickets were **pretty** expensive.*

rather

Rather is stronger than *quite*. It can modify adjectives, adverbs, nouns or verbs. It can express disappointment, criticism or surprise.
*It's **rather** spicy.*   *It was **rather** a disaster.*
*He speaks **rather** slowly.*   *I **rather** hoped he'd come.*

When qualifying an adjective and a noun, *rather* can come before or after *a/an*.
*It was **rather** a small portion. OR It was a **rather** small portion.*

slightly, *a little*, *a bit*

Slightly, *a little* and *a bit* soften the meaning of the words they qualify. They can qualify adjectives, adverbs and verbs. We often use these words to make a criticism sound less direct.
*It seems **slightly** / **a little** / **a bit** unnecessary.*
*She drives **slightly** / **a little** / **a bit** fast.*
*His attitude surprised me **slightly**. / His attitude **slightly** surprised me.*

A bit is more informal than *slightly* and *a little*.

Slightly, *a little* and *a bit* can be used before comparative adjectives whereas *quite*, *fairly* and *pretty* cannot.
*The view is **slightly** better from this window.* (Not ~~The view is quite better from this window.~~)

When we use *a bit* or *a little* before a non-comparative adjective, the meaning is usually negative.
*He's **a bit** spoilt.* (Not ~~He's a bit intelligent.~~)

We can use *a bit of a/an* before a noun.
*He can be **a bit of a** pain.*
*I've got **a bit of a** headache.*

Practice

2 Cross out the qualifier or qualifiers which do not fit in each sentence.

1 It was *rather* / ~~a bit~~ / ~~fairly~~ a steep drop.
2 He told a *rather* / *quite* / *bit* long-winded story.
3 The meadows feel *slightly* / *quite* / *a little* more lush than last time I was here.
4 It was *rather* / *quite* / *fairly* an uncomfortable journey.
5 The mountain views are *pretty* / *a bit* / *rather* stunning.
6 My legs were beginning to ache *rather* / *slightly* / *quite*.
7 The landscape was a *bit of* / *bit* / *bit of a* bleak for my liking.
8 It's *a bit of* / *pretty* / *quite* an unspoilt beach.

Unit 1

💿 1.1

Speaker 1

I think the most valuable lesson anyone has ever taught me was when I was about 25. I was getting really frustrated with a guy I was working with. We'd set up our own web design business and Giles – that was the name of my business partner – would always get lost in little details and take ages making a first design to show the customer. And my dad said, 'Look, you can't change other people; you can only change the way you behave towards them.' So I accepted that was just Giles's way – that he loved the little details – and I tried to think of it as a positive thing, and we've got on so much better ever since and worked much more effectively. So that's become a sort of guiding principle for me in life – not to try to change others – and I have to say, it's stood me in very good stead.

Speaker 2

Here's a good rule of thumb: 'Don't come to blows over small things.' But it's a lot easier said than done. The number of times I've sent off an angry email without thinking about the consequences, or got upset because something wasn't done the way I wanted it to be done, you'd think I'd have learned my lesson. The other day my friend, John, asked for my help writing a job application, and I told him the letter he had written was much too informal. He didn't agree and I ended up getting really frustrated and shouting at him. He didn't talk to me for days afterwards. I feel really ashamed when I think about it. Now I always make a point of not reacting too quickly to things I disagree with.

💿 1.2

So let's start by considering these descriptions of people.

'Oh, John – he's a family man'; 'Sarah's an anthropologist – she's spent most of her life studying apes in Africa'; 'Frank's a keen coin collector – he's been collecting coins since he was a boy'; 'Jack is one of life's drifters – he will have been just about everywhere by the time he's 60'; 'Anne's a committed animal rights campaigner – that came as a shock to her friends because she had never even owned a pet before she joined the Animal Defence League!'

We define each person by a different criterion: their interests; their profession; their outlook on life; or by their values – like the importance of family for John – and their beliefs. So which of these things is it that really defines a person?

What if we asked the same question about a six-year-old child? Well, you'd actually say that what defined them first and foremost are the common factors that make them a child – being curious about the world, often playful, a bit vulnerable maybe. In ten years, that child will have become a teenager and teenagers, of course, share certain defining characteristics too. They tend to be quite self-centred and moody. Often they're angry at the world. And because they're not sure of what their identity is, they define themselves by what they are not and by the things they dislike. 'But Mum, I don't want to go to technical college. I hate maths.'

Now let's look again at the adults we described at first. John, our family man, has a job as a carpet salesman, which is OK. It's a job and it keeps him and his family comfortable. He had had an opportunity to run his own business at one point, but he decided job security was more important.

His real passion is his family and spending time with his two boys. Sarah, the anthropologist, on the other hand, lives for her work. She's visited Central Africa many times to study Bonobo apes and is fascinated by their social behaviour. Jack – 'the drifter' – has been doing bits and pieces of carpentry and building work. He loves travelling and experiencing different environments, so he picks up work as and when he can. He fell in love when he was 25, but the relationship ended and he hasn't committed to anyone else since.

So, we can see that what defines each of these people in the end is their life experiences. It could be within their job or interests or relationships that these occurred, but it's the experiences themselves that shape each of us as individuals. So when someone asks you, 'What do you do?', they are …

💿 1.3

1 odds and ends, by and large
2 law and order, peace and quiet
3 ifs and buts, in this day and age
4 rough and ready, heart and soul

💿 1.4

1 Oscar's a dreamer. Each evening he spends hours reading astronomy magazines, hoping to become an astronaut one day.
2 Kate's a worrier. When I first met her, she had just left her job and was wondering what to do with her life.
3 Ben's a free spirit. I imagine he will settle down one day. But he will have done a lot more than the rest of us by then.
4 I like to think of myself as a doer. I have written eight books so far and now I am working on my ninth.
5 Harry's a joker. For a long time he'd been joking about joining the army, so his friends were shocked to hear he actually had.

💿 1.5

M = Manager, K = Katy

M: OK, Katy, so tell me about yourself.

K: OK, so I'm Katy. I'm 24 years old and I'm a very active person. I don't just mean that I play a lot of sports – although I do run and go to the gym several times a week. What I mean is that, um I'm a person who likes to get involved in things. I've organised a lot of social events in my life and I've been part of a lot of campaigns, um … A recent one was campaigning against the building of a new car park in the centre of my home town. And that was successful actually, we got it stopped or at least delayed so, um … Excuse me, I'll just take a sip of water … Yes, so, as I was saying, I'm a firm believer in taking action. I don't think it's enough to want to change things and to say the right things, I think you have to act – to get out of your chair and do something that makes a difference.

M: And your current situation?

K: Well, I graduated from university two years ago with a degree in journalism, but I haven't been able to find a job that really suited me. To be honest, newspapers aren't an easy world to break into, unless you have the right contacts. So instead, I decided on a fresh approach, which was to seek out companies I admire; basically any company or organisation that's working for some positive good in society. And that's how I found you. And my hope is that when I find the right company, they'll

see that I have the right attitude and the right skills, so that we can both benefit from working together, um, yeah …

💿 1.6

K: OK, so I'm Katy. I'm 24 years old and I'm a very active person. I don't just mean that I play a lot of sports – although I do run and go to the gym several times a week. What I mean is that, um I'm a person who likes to get involved in things.

Unit 2

💿 1.7

The animal herders of western Mongolia have been called the last nomads. The horses, goats and cattle that they move from pasture to pasture on horseback are their livelihood. From them, they get their food, clothing and money to buy other goods.

Among these nomadic peoples are Kazakhs. Increasingly, many of these are trying to make a better living by seeking jobs in the city, but there are others who try to maintain the traditional nomadic way of life, living in tents by summer and in small houses during the cold winters. Among their customs, the most unusual, perhaps, is hunting with eagles, an art practised since the days of Genghis Khan.

For many hunters these days, eagle hunting is less a job and more a sophisticated sport. An eagle hunter spends ten years with each bird, training it – a task which requires great skill and patience – and sharing the meat of the animals which it kills, usually fox. At the end of the ten years, the hunter must part company with the eagle, because at this age, eagles are ready to start having chicks.

In the past, the skins of the foxes and other animals were traditionally sold to clothes makers. Winters are cold in Mongolia, and wearing fur is the best way to keep warm. These skins still provide some extra income to Kazakh nomads, but it isn't only for the money that they hunt with eagles: they want to keep alive this ancient tradition.

💿 1.8

P = Presenter, K = Kerry

P: We'd all like to jump into a fire, right? Er … I don't think so, but that was how smokejumper Kerry Franklin explained her career choice to me earlier when I interviewed her for GBC. For those of you who don't know, smokejumpers are firefighters who are dropped into remote and inaccessible areas to combat forest fires. Here's what Kerry told me.

K: Women firefighters are well suited to this kind of work. Weighing on average around 70–80 kilos, we're the right weight for it. If you're a lot heavier than that, you descend too fast and hit the ground hard, risking serious injury. And if you're a lot lighter and there's a strong wind, it can take your parachute and leave you a long way from your intended landing point.

P: You mean like in the centre of the fire itself?

K: Yeah, that's been known to happen. But we wear a lot of protective gear. Of course we're aware of our personal safety, but it's not the first thing on our minds – in this kind of job you can't wrap people in cotton wool.

P: No, I imagine not. So, having landed near the fire, what do you do then? I mean, not having a fire engine or a fire hydrant nearby, you can't exactly start fighting the fire in the conventional way, can you?

K: You see, we're like the initial line of attack. We get dropped in with tools – chainsaws, axes, chemicals for fighting fires – we get water pumps too, portable ones. But first we need to assess how bad the fire is, how we think it's going to develop and get that news back to base. If it's cooking pretty good, we've got to look for a way to try and contain it. Usually that means finding a natural firebreak.

P: What's that?

K: It's something like a road, or an area of rock, or thinner vegetation that the fire's going to have to cross before it continues on its path of destruction. So having located a firebreak, we do our best to make sure it's going to be effective, getting anything that could burn easily out of the way, sometimes using controlled burning to burn back to the main fire as it approaches the break.

P: And what's it like being a woman in this world, because firefighting is traditionally a male-dominated domain?

K: Fire doesn't distinguish between men and women, nor do the trainers at smokejumping school for that matter – you either make the grade or you don't. Having faced the same challenges together in training, those who make it have a natural respect for each other. Sure, doing my training I met a few guys who had a different attitude, but I haven't met any who didn't just end up thinking a smokejumper is a smokejumper.

🔊 1.9

The aim of today's session is to raise awareness of health and safety issues and to ensure they become second nature to you all, so that everyone who works here learns to always be on the safe side. As I'm sure you'll appreciate, food preparation on this scale is fraught with danger. There's no safety net here – mistakes can seriously endanger people's health. So we take every precaution to ensure that there's no risk to health. Everything has to be done by the book – there's no room for improvisation or for cutting corners.

🔊 1.10

Hello, everyone. I hope you're enjoying your first day. I imagine you're feeling pretty overwhelmed by everything you've had to take in, and I don't want to keep you long. I've been brought back as someone who's been through the system and come out the other side, and so the university asked me to talk to you as one of you and to give you a student's side of the story.

So with that in mind, I'd just like to say one thing really, which is: get involved in something other than your course as soon as you can. You'll be amazed by how quickly time goes here. Before you know it, you'll be in your third year and you'll be thinking, 'What now?' How many of you actually know what you're going to do when you leave? I'm sure there will be some people who know what career they'd like to embark on, but there will be an awful lot of you – and I was definitely one of those – who don't.

That's where university clubs, societies and volunteer groups come in. I remember when I first came here to study history, I had no idea of what job I'd end up doing. But in my first year, I joined the university broadcasting society. I was interested in reporting, so I used to go out and find interesting stories about university life, and then come back and present them – when they were interesting enough to everyone else, that is. I did that once a week. Then in my second year, I got a holiday job, helping out as a researcher at the local BBC radio station, and really it all led

on from there, because first of all I was clear about what I wanted to do – which was to work in broadcasting – and secondly, I had some contacts I could call on, which in this line of work is a key thing.

So that's really my message to you today. Don't delay, get out there, join some clubs and societies and start developing your interests. This university has so many fantastic opportunities to do that and you won't get another chance in life like it. So, thanks for your time. Oh, and do come and chat afterwards if you'd like to … I'll be in the bar.

🔊 1.11

Hello, everyone. I hope you're enjoying your first day. I imagine you're feeling pretty overwhelmed by everything you've had to take in, and I don't want to keep you long. I've been brought back as someone who's been through the system and come out the other side, and so the university asked me to talk to you as one of you and to give you a student's side of the story.

🔊 1.12

Hello, everyone. First of all, can I extend a warm welcome from me and all the staff. My name's Sarah Curtain, and I'm the principal here at King's College. I'm very happy to see, once again, such a large and diverse range of nationalities at the college. This year we have over 60 different nationalities, speaking 33 different languages. It's that diversity and international perspective that makes King's College a unique place to study.

I'm afraid I have to mention a few administrative matters first, but then I'll give you some more general advice about how to make the most of your time here.

So, immediately after this session, there will be coffee in the student's union where you can meet and chat to staff and other students. That's from 11 to 12.30 p.m.

Course registration takes place on Monday morning. That is compulsory for everyone to attend and it'll be in the main university hall – this room – between 10 a.m. and 2 p.m. You must attend to officially register for the courses you are going to do this year.

Also during the next week, I'd ask those of you who haven't done so already, to bring copies of all your documents to the Admissions office – Room 301 – so that we can keep them on file. So that's all official documents – secondary education certificates, student visas, bank account details – to Room 301 by the end of next week. This applies to all overseas students, that is everyone except those from the UK and the European Union. Even if you don't think you have all of these, please come and see us anyway – that's very important.

Now, as for your orientation here at King's College, …

🔊 1.13

OK, everyone, I'd just like to say a few words about reading – something you're going to be doing a lot of here. At the end of this session, I'll give you your reading list for this particular course. Your other tutors will do the same. There'll be 30 or so books on each list, but please don't think that means you have to read every page of every book. There are three or four key books highlighted at the top of each list, which we do recommend that you read in full, but the others will mainly be for reference – that's to say, there'll be one or two chapters in them that are relevant to a particular essay or piece of work.

So, most importantly, when I give you the list, please don't go out to the nearest bookshop and buy them all. If you do that, you'll leave yourself no money for food or anything else. All these books are, in principle, available in the library – some may be out on loan of course when you want them. You'll probably want to buy some of the more important ones. My advice to you is first to look at one of the internet booksellers and see if you can pick up any second-hand or at least cheaper copies there. There's also a second-hand section in the main university bookshop, where you might find what you're looking for.

What about strategies for reading? As I said at the beginning, you'll have a big volume of reading to do, so it's important that you get faster at it. Is there a secret to that? Well, I'm afraid the answer is not really. What I would say though is that the more you read, the faster you will get. So don't worry too much if it seems like it's taking ages at first – everyone feels that …

Unit 3

🔊 1.14

A: I love this picture. The mountain behind and the colours of the rock are absolutely wonderful, but there's something about the simplicity of the building that sets it all off. A plain, wooden, Old-West-style shop – nothing fancy about it. It blends in very naturally with its surroundings.

B: It looks like something from the set of a western film – like those buildings you see cowboys tying up their horses in front of.

A: Funny you should say that. This one's near a place called Kanab in Utah, also known as Little Hollywood because of all the westerns that get filmed around there. This one's been well preserved, so visitors can get an idea of what buildings were like in those days. It's also used by film-makers. What's interesting too is the false front on the building. A lot of buildings had those in the Old West, although this one's not particularly spectacular. They were usually bigger and more ornate – and every building along the main street would have one, disguising a more modest structure behind it. So as you walked down the street, you got the impression that the town was much grander than it actually was – which was the intention of course.

🔊 1.15

P = Presenter, J = Jonas Wilfstrand

P: Welcome to *Grand Architecture*. We're changing focus completely today and looking at small homes. I'm very pleased to welcome Swedish architect Jonas Wilfstrand, who specialises in the design of compact living spaces. I've been looking at some of these on your website, and I must say some of them are absolutely stunning. I really liked the timber and glass vacation house with the built-in sauna. Is this a trend we're seeing, Jonas, for smaller homes?

J: I don't think it's really a trend in the sense that lots of people are wanting smaller homes, but I think there *is* definitely more interest in them. In a lot of places, dwellings are small from necessity – people are either incredibly short of space or they simply can't afford a bigger house.

P: And where have you taken your inspiration from? Where did you look for ideas?

J: Well, there were two homes in particular that got me interested in this. One was the houses of the Dolgan people in central north Russia, who live a lot of the year in freezing temperatures, as low as minus 40 degrees. Their houses are shaped a bit like a sugar cube and extremely basic – just a single room with two or three beds, a table and a stove. They're constructed from wooden frames and reindeer skins, which is a great insulator. The Dolgan are nomadic people who tend reindeer, and when it's time to find new feeding grounds, they move house, quite literally. Their houses are on sled runners and they get pulled along by the reindeer to the next stop.

P: Why did these Dolgan houses impress you so much?

J: Well, several reasons: their mobility, the way the Dolgan use only readily available materials, and the fact that they're just so simple. They were what got me thinking about the whole concept of more compact living.

P: And you mentioned another home that inspired you.

J: Ah yes, that's not at all simple. It's the apartment of an architect in Hong Kong. As you probably know, space is at a premium in Hong Kong. It's a really overcrowded city. Gary Chang lives in a tall apartment block in a flat that's only 32 square metres. And he used sliding walls – partitions – within the flat to be able to transform it into a living room, a kitchen, a library, a bedroom; in fact, he claims he can have 24 different rooms in all. He entirely rethought the way we arrange living space – I thought it was wonderfully innovative. There are some great photos of it on his website. Here's one …

P: It looks distinctly cramped to me, but very stylish.

1.16

1 You're absolutely right.
2 That's really kind of you.
3 I'd be very grateful.
4 It's completely out of the question.
5 Yes, I'm quite certain.
6 That's so typical.

1.17

I have to say, I really like this piece. It has several things to recommend it. First of all, as a work of art, it seems very accessible. What I mean is it's not too intellectual or difficult to understand, like a lot of modern art pieces. So in that way, I think everyone – children and adults – should be able to relate to it. Also, the fact that it's in the shape of an open book will give it popular appeal. It reflects the long tradition of our city as a place of learning very well. It's a clever touch, I think.

Thirdly, and I don't think we should underestimate this, it's just good fun. The quotes and jokes that appear on the pages will attract a lot of attention. People will be able to sit on benches and watch as the different messages roll across the screen. So it becomes an interactive work of art, and I think this is important, given its central location in the city. And the idea that it could become a tourist destination also really appeals to me.

Well, that more or less sums up my position. What does everyone else think?

1.18

1 'What I mean is it's not too intellectual …'
2 'The idea that it could be a tourist destination …'
3 'The water and the area in front of the fountain …'

Unit 4

1.19

In the late nineteenth century, someone had the bright idea of mounting a bicycle-like contraption on rails. The idea was to give a smoother ride than could be achieved on conventional bicycles. At the time, no one recognised that a breakthrough had been made but, more recently, the idea of a pedal-powered monorail has been revived and updated at an amusement park in New Zealand by a company named Shweeb.

Google, always good at spotting a trend, has invested $1 million to support further development of the system for an urban environment. Like the original bicycle railway, the Shweeb system is meant to reduce friction between the wheel and the surface it makes contact with 'by running hard wheels on hard rail', just like a train. But the Shweeb concept also takes the idea one stage further. Drivers lie back in bullet-shaped hanging 'pods' and pedal with their feet forward, as on a reclining bicycle. The pods hang from 20-centimetre-wide rails constructed above street-level pedestrians and traffic.

There's no need to worry about overtaking because two Shweebs travelling in a line are more efficient owing to reduced air resistance.

And is there a real demand for this? Well, both Google and Shweeb are convinced that it fills an important need for transport which is green, convenient, cost-competitive and fun. You could say they've reinvented the wheel!

1.20

P = Presenter, M = Martha Kay

P: It's difficult to imagine what life must have been like before the invention of certain things. If you're in your teens or twenties, you might never have wondered how people searched for information before the Internet existed. The electric light is another thing that we all take for granted. But how do such inventions come about? Is it necessity that drives innovation? Or commercial profit? Or something else? Here to discuss these questions is business historian Martha Kay. Martha, there are a lot of things around us that we clearly could live without, so the necessity argument is not the whole answer, is it?

M: Hello, Evan. No, of course it isn't. History is littered with inventions that people thought they didn't need at the time. In 1878, a British parliamentary committee, which had to comment on the usefulness of Alexander Graham Bell's telephone, said, '… it is good enough for our transatlantic friends, but unworthy of the attention of practical men.'

P: Yes, well, perhaps they should have been more open-minded. But in 1878 people didn't need to have phones, did they? You could conduct your daily business and daily life perfectly well without one. But now it's become a necessity, a need has been created, if you like.

M: Well, people in the nineteenth century needed a way to communicate at a distance more effectively; they just hadn't envisaged the telephone. Of course, there are some inventions which fill an urgent need – vaccines against particular diseases come to mind. But most innovations aren't like that. Entrepreneurs have often come up with ideas to make our lives a little more convenient or comfortable and then, over time, we come to rely on them. Television is a case in point. Remote shopping – that's to say mail-order, or

these days internet shopping – is another. It was dismissed by *Time* magazine in the 1960s because they said, 'women like to get out of the house and like to be able to change their minds.'

P: I'm sure they did – like to get out of the house, that is. That certainly was a different era …

M: Another form of innovation is to take something that's at first expensive to produce and therefore exclusive to rich people, and make it available to many. There are quite a few things that we now see as everyday necessities that have come to us in this way – where an entrepreneur has found a way to produce something more cheaply, like the mobile phone or the computer. Another example, in the 1890s, the motor car was thought to be a luxury for the wealthy. *Literary Digest* predicted that it would never 'of course, come into common use'.

P: I see, so in that sense what it comes down to is wants rather than needs. But what about all those things that we don't really need? How do you explain …?

1.21

1 You should have told me.
2 Did you have to wait?
3 He must have forgotten.
4 You needn't have worried.
5 She may have left already.
6 I didn't need to be there.

1.22

1 a You might have told me.
  b You might have told me.
2 a You shouldn't have waited.
  b Flowers? Oh, you shouldn't have.

1.23

We have an idea to encourage volunteering. It's a new phone app called 'Volunteer Planner'. What is it? It's an interactive diary that links volunteers to organisations looking for voluntary help. Why is it necessary? Because there are a lot of people out there who'd like to give their time to help others in the community – helping the disabled or the elderly. But they never come forward because their time's limited and it's too complicated to organise. So what does Volunteer Planner do exactly? The app allows organisations to show when they need voluntary help; it allows the volunteer to communicate their availability; and it allows both parties to make changes to the schedule in real time. What's our ambition for Volunteer Planner? Ultimately, it means more people giving a little of their time rather than a few people giving a lot. So it encourages and spreads the practice of volunteering.

1.24

What is it?

How does it work?

Why is it necessary?

What does it do exactly?

'So what?' I hear you say.

Isn't it going to be expensive?

So, how do we achieve this?

What's our ambition for …?

Unit 5

1.25

Three people visit the same place and each one leaves with a different story. One remembers a romantic evening in a cosy restaurant and a long walk through a beautifully lit city by night; another remembers an argument with an officious museum curator about the closing time of an art gallery; another remembers sitting and watching the world go by on a lazy, hot afternoon in an elegant park.

Our travel experiences are influenced by so many different factors: the circumstances and state of mind in which we arrive; the people we happen to meet – an affable fellow traveller or a wary local; the preconceptions that we bring to each place we visit. The gift of a good travel writer is to capture the essence of a place in a way that we can all identify with, so that it's instantly recognisable, not just superficially – in its grand architecture or lively cafés – but in the way that a particular place feels and thinks. Because the best travel writers aren't really writing about travel, they're writing about how people have shaped places and how places have shaped people.

1.26

P = Presenter, S = Sophie

P: … to places you and I would probably never think of visiting. And Sophie, what's your book?

S: My choice is *Where the Indus is young* by the Irish writer Dervla Murphy. It's about a trip that she took with her daughter up the Indus River valley – a region called Baltistan – into the heart of the Himalayas when the girl was only six years old. This was in the 1970s.

P: And why have you chosen this one particularly?

S: Well, travelling in this region is dangerous enough at the best of times, but to do so with a six-year-old girl is just incredible. They encounter raging rivers, falling rocks, steep rocky ascents. Murphy herself says in the book that the extremeness of the landscape in this region cannot be exaggerated. In fact, Rachel – that's her daughter's name – became the hero for me, because where many kids would be complaining constantly, she never does. Her mother takes advantage of this, and so keeps pressing on, along narrow paths next to deep ravines. I'd like to read a short extract if I may, where they're coming down a track on horseback next to the side of a mountain:

We found ourselves looking into a ravine so profound that one's first reaction was incredulity. The shadowy chasm was very narrow and perhaps half a mile long. It lay between the brown mountain we now stood on and the white mountain ahead, and at a conservative estimate it was 1,500 feet deep, with absolutely sheer sides. This scene was the very quintessence of Himalayan drama – vast, beautiful, cruel – belonging to a landscape that has no time for the paltry endeavours of men.

P: I've heard critics say that Murphy can be political. Would you agree with that?

S: Well, perhaps. She does mention a few times in this book and in others, how unspoiled places like this are being ruined by 'technological progress' and western ideas. An example of the former is when she talks about modern transport bringing diseases to areas that hadn't suffered these before. Other writers of course have said the same thing, and I'm always a bit suspicious of people who want to enjoy unspoilt parts of the world and then return home to the comforts of their own western lives. But you can't say that the point of this book is to put across a political message. It's not. It's just a

wonderful description of an amazing journey, and the ability of a young child to overcome fear and a completely different environment. I found it absolutely gripping.

1.27

1 **A:** You have to be careful not to get ripped off in the local markets.
   B: Yes, I know that.
2 **A:** Would you like to drive?
   B: No, I'd rather you did.
3 **A:** Did he take warm clothes with him?
   B: I hope so.
4 **A:** Do you mind travelling alone?
   B: No, I actually prefer it.
5 **A:** Are there many good guidebooks about this region?
   B: Well, there are some.
6 **A:** Have you got an up-to-date map of Russia?
   B: No, but I've got an old one.

1.28

I'd like to read an extract from *The Third Man*, a thriller by Graham Greene. The context for this story is post-Second World War Vienna, around 1948. A writer, Rolly Martins, has come to Vienna to find his old friend, Harry Lime, but he discovers that Harry has died in suspicious circumstances. At this point in the story Martins is walking back through the deserted streets of Vienna at night. It's a great example of how to build suspense.

'Passing by the end of the street he happened to turn and there just around the corner, pressed against a wall to escape notice, was a thick, stocky figure. Martins stopped and stared. There was something familiar about that figure: perhaps, he thought, I have grown unconsciously used to him during these last twenty-four hours: perhaps he is one of those who have so assiduously checked my movements. Martins stood there, twenty yards away, staring at the silent motionless figure in the dark side-street who stared back at him. A police spy, perhaps, or an agent of those other men, those men who had corrupted Harry first and then killed him: even possibly the third man? It was not the face that was familiar, for he could not make out so much as the angle of the jaw: nor a movement, for the body was so still that he began to believe that the whole thing was an illusion caused by shadow. He called sharply. "Do you want anything?" and there was no reply. He called again. "Answer, can't you?" and an answer came, for a window curtain was drawn petulantly back by some sleeper he had awakened and the light fell straight across the narrow street and lit up the features … of Harry Lime.'

1.29

He began to believe that the whole thing was an illusion caused by shadow. He called sharply. "Do you want anything?" and there was no reply. He called again. "Answer, can't you?" and an answer came, for a window curtain was drawn petulantly back by some sleeper he had awakened and the light fell straight across the narrow street and lit up the features … of Harry Lime.'

1.30

'Passing by the end of the street he happened to turn and there just around the corner, pressed against a wall to escape notice, was a thick, stocky figure.'

Unit 6

1.31

W = Woman, R = Rashmi

W: How do you advise people to stay fit and healthy, Rashmi?

R: You know, there's so much contradictory information out there about how to keep in shape: whether you should watch your weight by controlling what you eat or by exercising; what kind of exercise regime is best, and so on. I was reading a scientific journal just this morning saying that working out at the gym is actually less effective than going for a walk regularly in the park.

W: Really? Why did it say that?

R: I think the idea is that if you do really intensive exercise, then your body demands calorie compensation afterwards – in other words, you're more likely to reward yourself with a bigger snack at the end of the session. Whereas if you just stretch your legs often or take regular gentle exercise, it doesn't have the same effect.

W: So what do you do? You're in pretty good shape.

R: Well, mainly I try not to obsess too much about my weight. I don't go on diets and I don't weigh myself every day. I just do active things that I enjoy. I've never been a fan of the gym, I have to say, and I never go for a run – I find it boring. The kids keep me pretty active anyway. But recently I've got into road cycling. You've got to try it. Every couple of weeks a few of us go out for a ride in the countryside – 40 or 50 kilometres. We often go up in the woods and hills around Springvale. The scenery's beautiful and it's a great way to enjoy nature and stay fit at the same time.

1.32

P = Presenter, B = Ben

P: … thanks for those comments, Sarah. I'd like to turn now to someone who should know more about sports injuries than most and that's ultrarunner Ben Newborn. Ben, before we get into the questions of injuries, can you just explain for our listeners what ultrarunning is?

B: Sure, basically ultrarunning is running distances beyond a usual marathon distance. So, it could mean running 100 kilometres in a single day, or it could involve running several marathons on consecutive days.

P: And how did you get into it?

B: I was a runner anyway and I just wanted to take it to another level – to really test myself physically and mentally. So in 2008, I registered for the Ultra-Trail race in the Alps which requires runners to run 161 kilometres around Mont Blanc.

P: Didn't you worry about doing yourself real damage?

B: Actually, I wasn't so concerned about regular running injuries. I was more worried about failure. And I knew that to succeed in overcoming exhaustion and the things that make you feel nauseous, I had to get my diet and nutrition right. That's ultimately what would let me run in relative comfort.

P: Comfort's not a word I'd automatically associate with a 160-kilometre run, but anyway … What about injuries? This must put intense strain on your body.

B: I think the most important thing in any sport is to recognise when your body's in pain. A lot of sportspeople try to go through the pain. I'm not talking about when they're in a really bad way, but if they have a small muscle strain or a twinge in a joint – an ankle, for example – they tend to take some painkillers or put on some kind of support and just carry on. Because they feel they can't afford to rest. But that of course is completely wrong. Pain is your body warning you to be careful – to stop often – because minor problems will inevitably develop into more severe injuries. So that's the first thing: to listen to your body.

P: Yes, but we all get aches and pains. Surely that shouldn't discourage us from doing exercise?

B: Well, my point actually is that if you do the right kind of preparation, you can avoid getting injuries in the first place. I follow a method developed by a sports physiologist, which is a series of stretches and gentle exercises that strengthen the key muscles and ligaments. It's definitely prevented me from getting ankle sprains and helped with other things I used to suffer from: lower back pain, runner's knee and so on …

💿 1.33

1 A: I heard Sarah came off her bicycle. Is she in a bad way?
   B: Luckily she didn't break anything; she was pretty shaken up though.

2 A: Is it true that Jack nearly cut his finger off?
   B: Yes, he practically passed out when he saw what he'd done. It was quite a deep cut, but he's on the mend now, I think.

3 A: You look a bit off colour. Are you feeling under the weather?
   B: No, I'm not ill. I'm just run down from working too much.

💿 1.34

A: So, everyone, this is an initial brainstorming session, to come up with some concrete ideas for promoting health and fitness among employees. As you're probably aware, health is an issue that's very topical at the moment and our own chairman and CEO are very keen that we, as a company, take the lead on it. Of course, there's also an obvious benefit to us in terms of productivity and days not lost through sickness. So, I'd like to hear any ideas you have, really. Yes, Michelle …

B: Well, as I see it, there are two routes we could go down: one is just promoting the idea of health and fitness at work by encouraging people to do simple things like walking to work, not spending long periods sitting at their computers, that kind of thing. Or we could spend some serious money on the problem and do something like install a gym or fitness centre on site that people can use in their breaks or after work. But I realise that there may not be a budget for that.

A: Hmm, OK. Yes, Ben …

C: I don't know what others think, but for me the key is getting people to enjoy exercise. If you offer activities that employees think are fun, you'll get much better participation.

A: Such as …?

C: Such as team sports – football, basketball and so on – and we can arrange competitions. Also dance classes. Admittedly, a lot of people may do these things anyway in their free time, but I bet there are a lot more who'd like to and never get round to it.

A: Thanks, Ben. And what about the idea of group exercises in the mornings? The kind of collective warm-up routine you used to

see in companies fifty years ago. It's not a particularly original idea, I'll grant you, but it might be fun and also build team spirit.

B: I think you have to be careful there. People may think that you're trying to coerce them into some kind of forced exercise regime. I know that isn't the intention, but it could look that way. I think it'd be much better to give people incentives to do things on their own. So, for example, if we had a 'bike to work' scheme where we offered to pay part of the cost – of a new bicycle to encourage people to cycle to work – I haven't thought through exactly what proportion of the cost, but I think that that kind of individual incentive probably works much better.

A: Mmm, I like that …

B: Of course, it wouldn't be so easy to monitor whether they used the bike to commute to work or for leisure, but you'd probably just have to accept that risk.

C: Yeah, I definitely think that idea could work and it wouldn't really matter if …

💿 1.35

1 It's not a particularly original idea.
2 It wouldn't be so easy to monitor …

💿 1.36

1 I know it's not a very practical solution.
2 It wouldn't be that simple to convince people.
3 I'm not actually sure of the exact figures.

Unit 7

💿 2.1

What do we really know about the Mongolian leader Genghis Khan? It's a fact that he built a great empire across Asia in the thirteenth century. But was he a great general that brought peace to these lands, or a cruel warrior? Well, of course there are two sides to every story. In his homeland of Mongolia, his achievements are viewed with great pride and the stories about him focus on the great Mongolian traditions of archery and skill with horses. Khan's cavalry could shoot with a bow and arrow forwards or backwards while riding at full speed – or so the story goes.

However, in other countries, among the people he conquered, Khan is known as a ruthless warlord, who crushed city after city as his armies swept across Asia. It is often said that it's the victor who writes history, but in the case of Genghis Khan, it is the accounts of those he defeated that seem to have prevailed. These accounts say that the evidence tells its own story, quoting Genghis Khan himself: 'the greatest happiness is to scatter your enemy, to drive him before you; to see his cities reduced to ashes'.

But now some western historians are suggesting that Genghis Khan also had his good points. According to them, he did many positive things: opening up trade and cultural links between East and West, abolishing the slave trade, and giving greater legal rights to his citizens, both men and women. So perhaps it's true to say that …

💿 2.2

P = Presenter, J = James

P: A recent archaeological dig on the banks of the River Thames in London has uncovered evidence about the lives of children in the Middle Ages. Archaeologist James Newman is here to tell us a bit more about it. James, correct me if I'm wrong, but compared to children today, I imagine children in medieval times didn't have much of a childhood!

J: Well, as far as historians are concerned, that is – or certainly *was* – the accepted view of it. In the 1960s, a French social historian, Philippe Ariès, claimed that parents in the Middle Ages didn't really form emotional attachments with their children, but rather sent them off to work as soon as they could to be economic providers for the household. According to Ariès, the idea of a childhood didn't really appear until the sixteenth or seventeenth century. Up until then, children were just little adults, expected to do what adults did. If you look at paintings of children in medieval and renaissance times, in fact they do appear as small versions of grown-ups.

P: But considering people had much shorter working lives, you can understand why they'd want to get their children working earlier. Having said that, it does seem a pretty harsh view of human nature: to assume that people in the Middle Ages had no emotional bond with their children. But you think you've found some evidence to show this wasn't actually the case.

J: Yes. I was working on a dig, retrieving objects from mud banks by the River Thames. We found various items dating back to the thirteenth century: little cannons and guns, metal figurines, and miniature household objects such as chairs, jugs, and even frying pans complete with little fish. And insofar as the objects have great historical value, you could say we struck gold! Also, assuming that these *are* all medieval toys – and they look just like doll's house furniture – they paint a different picture of childhood in the Middle Ages.

P: You mean that perhaps children *were* allowed to be children, more than people thought anyway.

J: Yes, exactly. Someone clearly went to the trouble of making toys for them so they could play. The other interesting thing is that, regardless of what they tell us about children at the time, some of these objects are things we didn't know existed in medieval households, like a birdcage and a three-legged stool.

P: Mmm, sounds fascinating. Now, in case any listeners want to see these items, the collection will be going on tour around the country and a list of …

💿 2.3

1 Insofar as the objects have great historical value, you could say we struck gold!
2 Assuming that these *are* all medieval toys, they paint a different picture of childhood in the Middle Ages.
3 Regardless of what they tell us about children at the time, some of these objects are things we didn't know existed in medieval households.
4 In case any listeners want to see these items, the collection will be going on tour around the country.

💿 2.4

L = Lecturer, A = Student 1, B = Student 2, C = Student 3, D = Student 4

L: Yes, you in the third row.

A: Yes, hello. Thanks for a very interesting talk. Er, I'd just like to make sure I understood what you said about the plague that affected the Roman Empire so badly. Am I right in thinking that the drought in Africa caused an increase in the number of rats?

L: Well not exactly. The drought actually caused a lot of animals to die – rats and mice and also those animals that *hunted* rats and mice. But when the rains returned, the numbers of mice and rats grew much more quickly than the number of the animals that hunted them so they quickly spread everywhere and so did the plague. Yes …?

B: I always understood that there were a lot of different reasons for the decline of the Roman Empire, but the logical conclusion of your argument is that it just wouldn't have happened without the drought. No drought, no decline. Is that what you're saying?

L: Well, I don't know – and I don't think anyone knows precisely, but climate change certainly set off a chain of events: the plague was caused by changes in the weather, and in turn a lot of people within the Roman Empire died in the plague, and so the world order was changed. And, girl at the back …

C: Yes, I have a question. You mentioned the 'Little Ice Age'. Can you explain what you meant by that? Was it really that bad?

L: No, the term 'little' really describes both the fact that it was quite short and that it wasn't as intense as a proper Ice Age, but it certainly had an effect – on northern countries in particular. Crops failed and animals died. When people don't have enough food, of course, this has political and social consequences. You can see that throughout history. Yes, you in the blue shirt …

D: Yes, sorry, perhaps I missed something, but how do punishments fit in with the Little Ice Age?

L: Ah, people always look for someone to blame when things go wrong, even if it's something out of our control like cold weather. So they found people that they thought were troublemakers anyway and punished them.

2.5

1 Am I right in thinking that the drought was the cause?
2 Would you go along with that?
3 Can you explain what you meant by that?
4 How do punishments fit in with the Little Ice Age?
5 And what's your own opinion?

Unit 8

2.6

Do the different types of digital media available today change the way people experience the world? Perhaps. They certainly change the way we record and share those experiences with others. Never before has so much been written for such a large audience; nor have so many photos been taken and distributed so widely. Digital media – that is blogs, social networking sites, internet forums, online photo albums, downloadable music, viral marketing – have increased accessibility to others' experiences enormously.

But do digital media change the experience itself? That's a more difficult question to answer. In a way they do. If you go to a concert or a festival, or even a conference these days, everyone's busy recording and sharing the experience as it happens: taking photos, sending texts or tweeting. In fact, people seem to spend almost as much time recording the experience as they do actually watching or listening to what's going on. Does this detract from the experience itself? Some would argue that it does. I'm inclined to think that it's a question of moderation – as with any tool. It's a good thing as long as you don't let it take over your life.

2.7

P = Presenter, S = Sarah Palmer

P: OK, we hear about companies being customer-focused all the time these days, but there's no point being focused on your customer if *they* aren't focused on *you*. Sarah Palmer from the e-marketing consultancy firm Excite is here to tell us how organisations can generate that kind of interest. Sarah …

S: Thanks, Greg. The key to good marketing is being able to turn your customers into fans, in other words people who want to share a passion for what you do with others. These days, a company has no hope of doing that unless they use social media: not just to sell their products and services, but to really involve people in what they're doing. Basically, customers want to know your story, and they want to learn something. And *you*, the company, want to get them to buy into your story. There's no doubt that a straight sell can work occasionally, for example, if a customer happens to be looking for a particular thing at a particular time and an ad pops up on their screen. Companies are getting much better at engineering that kind of event, but creating a loyal following is far more effective.

P: So, can you give us some examples of organisations that use social media effectively, in the way that you're describing?

S: Yes, we've been looking at examples of best practice in social media marketing and a good one is *National Geographic*. They actively encourage fan interaction: inviting users to share travel stories, or to do surveys on how ecologically they live, and then compare their scores with their friends. You can enter competitions, and there are also links to different causes you can support – like helping to protect an endangered species.

P: OK. That all sounds great, but is there no mention of selling at all?

S: Yes, there is … there are offers of discounts for magazine subscribers, coupons you can use for *National Geographic* products. It's a business too.

P: And I see how this fan-building works for an organisation with a worthy mission. But what about a company that's just trying to sell a regular product, like bathroom cleaner? They have no alternative but to present the product in an ordinary way.

S: No, it's really no different – the same principles apply. Try to tell a story or engage customers in a way that's fun. No matter what you're selling, if you can involve people, you'll find an audience. I was recently looking at a company that sells tea, and their website had this great widget that gave you an interactive tour of the teas of China. It was really fun, and you wouldn't believe the number of varieties and how much some of them cost. It's a whole other world out there.

2.8

P = Presenter, M = Martin Roddick

P: Hello and welcome to the *Nature Today* podcast. Today we're going to look at some new evidence about what is arguably one of the most spectacular sights in nature: the phenomenon where waves glow at night and mirror the stars with lots of tiny, blue lights. It's been known for some time that the source of this light is organisms called phytoplankton. But how they produce the strange blue light has been a mystery – until now. Here's Martin Roddick of the Oceanographic Institute.

M: Hello. There are a number of different sea creatures that are bioluminescent, in other words, that are able to glow in the dark. The creatures which have this ability tend to spend most of their lives in deep ocean waters, which suggests that being able to light yourself up, as it were, is useful for finding food or scaring away predators, or perhaps just lighting your way as you move around. But the most common bioluminescent organisms – phytoplankton – live near the surface. And it's these that create this strange, blue light that people see on beaches and in waves.

P: And how do they do it?

M: It seems that electrical signals in the phytoplankton cause a chemical reaction to take place, producing a blue light. The light is usually emitted in waves, so it's reasonable to assume that the electrical signal is generated by motion in the water.

P: Thank you, Martin. And if you'd like to know more about this research, you can read details of the study on the OI website …

2.9

Today we're going to look at some new evidence about what is arguably one of the most spectacular sights in nature: the phenomenon where waves glow at night and mirror the stars with lots of tiny, blue lights.

Unit 9

2.10

Like a lot of buskers, I started busking because I wanted to get more confidence as a performer; it wasn't really about the money. I'm a singer-songwriter – I don't have my own band, and it's not easy to get gigs as a solo artist. Also I'd always been drawn to buskers. You know, I don't think there's anything better than coming across a really good live performance on the street when you're not expecting it.

So, I went out busking when I was seventeen – just me and my acoustic guitar – not in my home town, because I didn't want people to recognise me, but in a nearby town. It was pretty nerve-racking at first and I think that came across in my performance because I didn't get much attention, nor a lot of money. I think the first time I got about $15 and a cheese sandwich that someone threw into my guitar case.

But I got better at it, no doubt, and it had the desired effect of building my confidence. And then one time around Christmas, another musician approached me, a saxophonist who worked on and off as a session musician, and he asked if I'd like to team up with him. And I did. And I guess that's how my career got started. We play R&B mainly, some soulful ballads, some instrumentals … we prefer music that's soothing and melodic. We've now made our first single together and I'm pretty hopeful it'll get picked up by a record company.

2.11

1 Just a minute.
2 Phew! Just in time.
3 I just don't get it, I'm afraid.
4 Thanks, I just had one.
5 Thanks, I'm just looking.
6 Hello. You just tried to call, I think.
7 We're just friends.
8 I just wondered.

2.12

The study of the effects of music on the brain is still a work in progress, but exciting things are coming to light all the time. We know that music activates many different parts of the brain – there's no one music centre. We also know that music has the power to release endorphins. As you're probably aware, endorphins are chemicals that are vital to our well-being, released at times of stress to help us deal with pain, but also used by the body to produce feelings of happiness, elation even. So when we listen to music, we're rewarded with this boost of feel-good chemicals. Hospitals now make use of music to calm people before surgery or for pain relief after an operation.

But what I'm particularly interested in is another recent finding: that of the close relationship between music and language. If you're someone who has to strain so as to hear what people are saying in a noisy room, the chances are that you're not musically trained. That's because we use the same parts of the brain to process both music and language. So those people with musical training have improved their brain's ability to distinguish specific sounds, whether musical or simply spoken.

What are the implications of this? Well I'm not saying you should take up the violin so that you can hear people better at parties, or in order to be a better linguist – though that's not a bad idea. There are some important medical applications here. This relationship between music and language means we could use music to help people overcome conditions like dyslexia, or other learning disorders. At Harvard, a neuroscientist called Dr Gottfried Schlaug has had amazing results using music therapy with people who had suffered strokes. He conducted experiments with people where the stroke had affected the left side of their brain – the side that principally deals with language. Before the music therapy, these patients responded to questions with incoherent sounds and phrases, but when taught to sing phrases or to speak in time to the rhythm of the music, within minutes they were able to recite their addresses, say their names, and even sing extracts of songs. The results were really remarkable.

Similar positive results have been recorded with patients with dementia and memory loss. This news should be music to our ears, if you'll forgive the pun. Degenerative memory function is going to become more of a problem for all of us as we live longer, and we clearly need to find a way to lessen the impact of this on people's lives. Music may just hold the key.

2.13

P = Presenter, F = Frank Steel

P: Today's castaway is a disc jockey who's been hosting his own radio show for over 30 years. Where most disc jockeys come and go with the changing of fashions in music, he has managed to maintain a loyal following of listeners over the last 35 years, and to attract new ones from each new generation. He is Frank Steel. Frank, what's the secret of your continuing success?

F: That's a good question, but it isn't something I've often thought about. I don't think it's a secret really. I take an interest in what's happening now in the music world, and I look out for new trends. People do that in other fields, like science or art. It's just that with pop music, you're not supposed to stay trendy after you're 30. But I don't agree with that.

P: So you still get excited by new music. What, for you, makes a good record?

F: I honestly don't know. What makes a particular piece of music move you is something that can't really be described or identified. I'd rather not think too much about why I like a particular song or record.

P: And what's your first record?

F: This is a song by John Etheridge, a blues and jazz guitarist. I think it was the first blues record I ever heard and it opened up a whole new world to me. I also associate it with the summer of 1976, which was a really hot summer. I was supposed to be revising for exams, but I spent most of my time lazing around in the park. It was too hot to work.

P: *Crossroad Blues* by John Etheridge. Your taste in music is very wide – eclectic some would say. How did that come about?

F: That's difficult to say. It wasn't planned, if that's what you mean. I just keep my ears open for anything interesting, and I don't confine myself to any particular source for that. It's a question of staying curious, I suppose.

2.14

That's a good question.

That's an interesting question.

I've never really thought about it.

It's not something I've often thought about.

I don't really look at it like that.

I honestly don't know.

I couldn't tell you really.

That's difficult to say.

Frankly, I've no idea.

2.15

1	perhaps	3	I'm not sure
2	maybe	4	I can't say

Unit 10

2.16

P = Presenter, A = Alejandra Sanchez

P: Did you know that Melbourne, Australia, has the third biggest Greek population of any city after Athens and Thessaloniki? Or that London, England, is now France's sixth biggest city? In Denver, Colorado, over a third of the population are Hispanic, mostly from Mexico. The majority of these ethnic groups – with the possible exception of the French in London – aren't made up of first-generation migrants, but second, third, fourth, even fifth generation. So what's it like to belong to a long-standing immigrant community? What are the implications for the individual and the community as a whole? I put this question to a resident of Denver, Alejandra Sanchez.

A: My grandparents came here from Mexico 40 years ago as migrant workers, but I'm an American citizen and I participate fully in American life. I'm also Mexican-Hispanic and with that comes certain values, whether you are first or fourth generation. The most important thing for us is not the individual, it's the family. We grow up surrounded by our extended family: our brothers, our sisters, our cousins, our aunts and uncles. They're also our friends and without them, we're nothing. I think more than anything else, these deep-rooted values make us a very close-knit community. When we Hispanics come together at social gatherings, we celebrate this part of our heritage and treat each other as family. You can see this spirit of harmony at the Cinco de Mayo festivities, which is a wonderful celebration of our rich heritage.

2.17

P = Presenter, L = Louis James

P: Citizenship education is a hot topic at the moment and we're seeing more countries introduce it into the curriculum in schools. But many people wonder if the approach of teaching children about the country's laws and political institutions and so on actually helps them to be better citizens. Here to discuss this is sociologist Louis James. Louis, surely any training is better than none, isn't it?

L: Well, I'd like to say yes and I know the intentions are good, but I'm afraid this kind of citizenship education is missing the point.

P: And what *is* the point?

L: Of course, teaching people about the way institutions function is important, but what's far more important is to get people to think about what their duties and responsibilities to society are.

P: And in your view, young people don't know what those are.

L: Well, I don't think there are any clear-cut answers. That's why I said 'get them to *think* about' these things. It's a question of taking notice of others in your community. There was an interesting survey done, some years ago now, by the ISSP – that's the International Social Survey Programme – which asked people from all around the world what they thought the duties of a good citizen were. People were asked to rate the importance of various duties, for example: 'to be active in social organisations'; or 'always to obey laws and regulations'. But there were some duties on a more human level, like 'to try to help people who are worse off than you'; and 'to try to understand the reasoning of people with other opinions'.

P: And you think that sort of duty is closer to the spirit of good citizenship, do you?

L: Yes, I don't think the starting point should be how we relate to state institutions, but how we relate to each other, at a more basic level.

P: And how did people rate these duties? I imagine there wasn't that much difference in the way different nationalities responded, was there?

L: Actually, there was – huge variation. For example, 60 per cent of Filipinos thought it was very important to be involved in social organisations, whereas only 15 per cent of Japanese did. There were also some unexpected findings. In Switzerland, only half the people surveyed thought always obeying laws and regulations was very important.

P: That *is* surprising, isn't it?

L: It is. And there were great differences too when it came to feelings of duty to one another. 80 per cent of Mexicans thought it was very important to help people worse off than you. In some other countries, it was as low as 30 per cent.

P: So you'd like to see more discussion in schools about our duties to each other then?

L: Yes, I think we need to get children thinking about the basic things they can do to help a community function better: taking care of their environment, helping poorer people in the community, being open-minded and tolerant of differences. If you get those things right, the other elements will naturally follow.

2.18

1 Surely any training is better than none, isn't it?
2 And what is the point?
3 And you think that sort of duty is closer to the spirit of good citizenship, do you?
4 And how did people rate these duties?
5 I imagine there wasn't that much difference in the way different nationalities responded, was there?
6 That is surprising, isn't it?

2.19

1 I'm disturbing you, aren't I?
2 Nothing bad happened, did it?
3 Let's go, shall we?
4 Don't be late, will you?

2.20

1 You couldn't give me a hand, could you?
2 He would say that, wouldn't he?
3 You think I'm overreacting, do you?
4 Surely the answer is four, isn't it?
5 She didn't give a great performance, did she?
6 Let's go, shall we?
7 Nobody noticed I wasn't there, did they?

2.21

A: Hi, Justin! Have you got time for a game of tennis this afternoon?
B: Oh hi, Rebecca! 'Fraid not – I'm too busy.
A: Why? What are you doing?
B: Working. I have to get that sociology essay in by tomorrow afternoon.
A: Oh, yes. I've done mine already. What have you chosen to write about?
B: Er … I've been researching a model society set up in the 1880s in Chicago by George Pullman, the guy who made the restaurant carriages and sleeping cars for trains.
A: Have you? Sounds interesting.
B: It *is* actually. What's odd is that he based his society on capitalist principles, thinking that capitalism was the best way for a society to fulfil its material and spiritual needs.
A: Unusual idea.
B: Yes, isn't it? 'Cos usually utopian societies are based on some kind of communal living ideal – principles of sharing and equality and being unmaterialistic and that kind of thing. As you probably found out yourself.
A: So how did Pullman's society work?
B: Well, I'm still reading about it, but as far as I can see it was basically a purpose-built town with his factory at the centre. It had a very rigid class structure with everyone knowing their place – manual workers, skilled workers, managers – with Pullman at the top of course living in a grand house while his workers lived in small tenements. He owned all the buildings and rented them to the workers.
A: Doesn't sound very utopian.
B: No, it doesn't, does it? And I think the workers weren't very happy. They weren't allowed unions; there was only one bar in the town and that was for visitors.
A: So, it probably failed in the end then, I suppose.
B: I expect so – these things often do. But I haven't got to that bit yet. I'll let you know.
A: Yeah, do. No, seriously, I'd be very interested to know because it's a really unusual story. The one I chose was a farming community in Oklahoma. Anyway, good luck and let me know if you want a break from it. I'd love a game of tennis some time.

B: Yeah, me too. See you soon, anyway.
A: Yeah, hope so.

2.22

1 Really?
2 Are you?
3 Yes, wasn't it?
4 No, it doesn't, does it?
5 He didn't, did he?
6 Yes, do.

2.23

1 I'm afraid not.
2 I suppose so.
3 I expect so.
4 I hope so.
5 I doubt it.

Unit 11

2.24

I've spent the last ten years documenting – through photos – how people express their emotions. The thing is that wherever you go in the world, emotions are expressed in more or less the same way. People used to think facial expressions were something culturally specific, like language or certain gestures, but that isn't actually the case. Expressions are universal; everyone can identify with a picture showing a look of surprise on a person's face, like someone who's taken aback when you take their photo; or showing someone looking despondent because things aren't going well. There are endless shades of emotion too: a look of contentment or sheer unadulterated happiness; someone who's absolutely livid or just feeling mildly irritated.

Children are great to photograph, because they tend not to hide their emotions as much as adults do. I love this one. These two are obviously having a great time, but the boy looking at the camera is also feeling quite proud and pleased with himself. He's smiling in a rather mischievous way as if to say, 'Look at me. I know it looks a bit risky and I oughtn't to be doing this, but I'm having fun and you can't stop me now.'

2.25

I = Interviewer, N = Naomi Myers
I: Now, does modern life stress you out? Do you wish that you felt more in control of things? If so, perhaps it's time you looked into 'emotional intelligence training', a fast-growing area in the field of practical psychology. Our guest today is Naomi Myers, from the EIQ Institute: EIQ being Emotional Intelligence Quotient. Naomi, can you tell us a little more about how this works?
N: Sure. Simply put, emotional intelligence is about two things. One is understanding your own feelings so that you can recognise which are constructive and which are harmful emotions; when to follow your gut feeling and when to follow your head. The other's about understanding how others around you are feeling, and that can be particularly useful in work relationships.
I: And why do people need this training? We've got along without it up to now.
N: Well, as you said, modern life is stressful and confusing. And it's led to an increase in anxiety disorders across the world. In Japan right now there are nearly one million hikikomori: young people who have withdrawn totally from society and stay shut up in their bedrooms at home. We're able to help people understand their fears and overcome them. Suppose you were someone who felt very on edge when speaking in public – we have techniques for helping you deal with that.
I: Such as?

N: Well, I'd rather your listeners took one of our courses than got advice free over the radio! But, for example, we help people to eliminate negative predictions about how they're going to perform.
I: Mmm … And what about reading other people's emotions? How do you help people do that?
N: OK, well one thing we do is train people to read micro-expressions.
I: And what are they?
N: Well, most facial expressions remain on the face for several seconds, but micro-expressions – and we all make them – appear for only a fraction of a second. They're so short because they're a glimpse of a concealed emotion or an emotion that's been very rapidly processed. What if I were to tell you that you'd already made one of these during our discussion?
I: I'd be a bit alarmed.
N: No need to be – it was just a momentary look of shock when I said I wasn't going to tell you about our training techniques. The point is that an ability to read these micro-expressions is very useful – in a business negotiation, for example, or when deciding whether to trust someone. A doctor came to me recently and said, 'If only I was better at building rapport with my patients, I'd be so much better at my job,' and we were able to help by training him to read people's emotions better.

2.26

1 I wish he would listen to me.
2 I wish you were coming with me.
3 If only it were true.
4 If only you would relax a bit.

2.27

1 a Was that a deliberate mistake?
  b Don't deliberate for too long.
2 a We need to separate my books from yours.
  b That's a separate issue.
3 a He's very articulate.
  b He couldn't articulate what he meant.
4 a Let's not duplicate the work.
  b I have a duplicate copy.

2.28

Conversation 1
A: Hi there, Phil, good to see you. How are you? Do we have time for a coffee before we go into the meeting?
B: Actually, we're late already – we really need to go in straightaway. Do you have the report and other papers with you?
A: Yes, I have all that. You look a little troubled, though. Is everything OK?
B: Do you know, Fernando, it's just that perhaps you had a different attitude to time-keeping in your previous company. Punctuality is very important here, particularly for people like Jeff Kravitz, who we're about to see, and I'm very anxious to start this meeting on the right note.
B: Oh, sorry, Phil. Honestly, I didn't realise. You're right, it wasn't such a big deal in my last company – the attitude to time was much more laid-back. I'll definitely try to be more punctual in future. And don't worry – I'm very well prepared for this meeting. It's going to be good.

Conversation 2
C: Becky, have you got a minute to talk about your design for the new advertisement? I don't think it's quite there yet and we need to send it over to the web designer tomorrow.

D: Oh, I'm surprised. I included all your suggestions from our last meeting. I thought it was looking OK. Mmm, perhaps you should get another person in to look at it.

C: Sorry, I didn't mean to offend you. These things are always subjective, but please don't take it personally.

D: No, *I'm* sorry, Alicia, that came out wrong. I'm not offended. I genuinely meant it would be a good idea to get a third opinion. But whatever you want. I'm very happy to work with you to get it looking right.

C: Thanks. I appreciate that. I'll call Stacey and see if we can arrange a meeting with all three of us to look at it this afternoon.

Conversation 3

F: Hi Megumi. I haven't seen you for ages. How are you? Jen said you'd got a new job with an American company in Tokyo.

E: That's right. With Disney. I'm going to be in charge of all the merchandise for classic storybook characters, like Winnie the Pooh, Alice in Wonderland, Pinocchio. I'm very excited. Why are you smiling? Did I say something funny?

F: Oh, sorry, please don't think me rude – I wasn't laughing at *you*. It was just the idea of being in charge of all those characters, like a playgroup leader or something. It conjured up a funny mental picture. But it sounds great fun. When do you start?

 2.29

alarmed   concerned   distressed   embarrassed insulted   offended   shocked   surprised worried

Unit 12

 2.30

Speaker 1

People think of the desert as a bleak environment – sparse vegetation and a monotonous, flat landscape. But actually, it's those things that make it so beautiful for me. A vast expanse of sand and rock under a cloudless sky – it just feels very pure. I think what appeals to me is a place which is completely untouched by people. You don't find that so often these days. I'm not saying I'd want to live there, mind you, but as a place to be alone with nature, you can't beat it.

Speaker 2

I prefer an urban landscape myself. I don't really go in for the chocolate-box vista, I have to say – snow-capped mountains or a pretty rustic scene with a farmer ploughing the fields. That's most people's idea of a landscape; they don't seem to count urban features like buildings and factories because they think of those as blots on the landscape. But my favourite views are those you see from rooftops looking out over a big city, particularly a night-time skyline, because I love to imagine what all the people there are doing.

Speaker 3

I love this landscape with its old farmhouses, rolling hills and lush meadows because it feels as if nothing's changed for hundreds of years. I guess that's because it's very rich farmland – they grow olives and grapes and cereal crops and raise animals, so its use hasn't had to change. It hasn't been artificially preserved, like some scenery can be. We used to come here on holiday when I was young. We'd drive through some dramatic changes of scenery to get here: across the open plains of northern Italy, through medieval towns in the mountains and then we'd arrive here, in this idyllic, gentle countryside.

 2.31

Around five years ago, I took a trip to Madagascar to photograph the landscape. An amateur photographer I had met at some party told me it had the most wonderful scenery. Normally I spend two months or so researching a place before I go there. But in this case, I had only a shortish amount of time before I had to be back. So, I packed my stuff and left the next day. During the course of the assignment, I took some 2,000 pictures. The photographer that recommended Madagascar said the landscape was kind of varied. That was a huge understatement. There's desert, marshes, rainforest, sandy beaches and rocky coves; and all of this is home to well over 200,000 different species of plants and animals.

 2.32

I = Interviewer, B = Biographer

I: Sophie Huxter, you're best known for writing travel guides, but recently you've been writing about the Japanese poet Matsuo Basho. Can you tell us what attracted you to him?

B: Yes, it was the subject of observing nature, especially its little details – the brilliant colour of a particular flower or the way light catches the spray from a waterfall and makes a rainbow. When I started to look into it, it really struck me how much I took the natural world for granted. And I think that's probably true for most of us: that observing nature is either a bit of a luxury, or just something that gets forgotten, because we all get rather caught up in our own busy lives.

I: And how does that relate to Basho?

B: Yeah, well, that's quite interesting, because as a poet one of his preoccupations was observing nature and writing down his thoughts. But fairly late in life, he decided he needed to get away from it all and get closer to nature. You see, Basho was already quite a well-known poet in his lifetime and he wanted to escape his celebrity and live a more simple life. So at the age of 46, he set off on a journey across the island of Honshu. That journey was the background to his masterpiece in poetry, *Narrow Road to a Far Province.*

I: Ah, yes, I know it … at least parts of it.

B: So, he travelled on foot through Japan's backcountry – a distance of slightly less than 1,200 miles – and he kept a kind of diary of the things he saw in poem form as he went. So he would stop along the way to observe nature's modest dramas: a leaf floating through reflections in a crystal clear stream, the splash of a frog as it hopped from a leaf into the water, the sunlight on an avenue of trees on an autumn evening.

I: That's a lovely way of putting it – nature's modest dramas.

B: Well, what I love about the poems is that the language he uses is rather plain and simple, but the overall effect is very profound. Each haiku is like a polished stone; it captures the beauty and simplicity of nature in just a few words. I'll read you an example of one which pretty much sums this up. At one point he came across an old ruined military fort, overgrown with grass, and it upset him rather. He wrote: 'Mound of summer grass / Are soldiers' heroic deeds / Only dreams that pass?'

 2.33

1 It's quite a long way.
2 I feel pretty confident.
3 The water's quite cold.
4 It's fairly important.
5 He's a pretty well-known writer.
6 It's quite a big lake.

 2.34

A: OK, so we'd like to hear your views about two possible ways of relieving traffic congestion in the city centre. Craig is just going to summarise the two main proposals before we open up the discussion. Craig …

B: Thank you. The first proposal is a congestion charging scheme, that's to say creating a zone in the centre of the city which vehicles have to pay a fixed charge to enter. The exact limits of the zone haven't been defined yet, nor has the exact amount of the charge. The second proposal involves simply banning all private cars from the centre and providing a park and ride bus service from various points on the outskirts of the city into the centre.

A: Thanks, Craig. So now we'll open the discussion to the floor. Please try and keep your comments reasonably short so that everyone gets a chance to have their say.

C: Well, I don't see how we can really comment on the first proposal without knowing what the scope of the zone is and how much it's going to cost: those really are key issues. I mean, if it's going to mean that local residents have to pay to get into the centre then that's not really fair, is it? I live in Charles Street, which is …

D: Sorry, can I just say something in answer to that? We had a similar scheme where I used to live and people who lived within the zone were exempted from paying the charge.

B: Yes, I think that's absolutely right, and you can also give a discount to people who need to come into the centre for their work so that it doesn't discriminate against them either. Otherwise you find that a lot of people who really need their cars …

D: No, hang on a minute. If you keep making exceptions for different groups of people, you're going to end up with a system that costs a lot of money and doesn't bring much benefit. I think you have to be strict about this …

C: Yes, but how much is the charge going to be? No one's given us any …

D: Sorry, can I just finish what I was saying? The point is that unless you're strict about it, the scheme won't bring in enough revenue to pay for itself, and so those who do pay will question the whole scheme.

 2.35

Sorry, can I just interrupt you there?

Can I just say something in answer to that?

No, hang on a minute …

No, I'm sorry I have to stop you there …

Yes, but …

Sorry, can I just finish what I was saying?

Just a moment, please …

OK, you can make your point in a moment.

NATIONAL GEOGRAPHIC
L E A R N I N G

Life Advanced Student's Book
Paul Dummett, John Hughes and Helen Stephenson

Publisher: Gavin McLean

Publishing Consultant: Karen Spiller

Editorial Project Manager: Karen Spiller

Development Editor: Jess Rackham

Development Editor (DVD): Jennifer Nunan

Development Editor (Video): Jennifer Nunan

Strategic Marketing Manager:
    Charlotte Ellis

Project Editor: Amy Borthwick

Manufacturing Buyer: Elaine Willis

Art Director: Natasa Arsenidou

Cover Designers: Sofia Fourtouni
    and Vasiliki Christoforidou

Text Designer: Keith Shaw

Compositor: emc design ltd

National Geographic Liaison:
    Wesley Della Volla

Audio: Prolingua Productions

DVD: Tom, Dick and Debbie Ltd

Contributing Writer: Caroline Krantz
    (grammar summary)

Contributing Editor: Katy Wright

The publishers would like to thank the following for their advisory roles in preparation of the material: Lobat Asadi (Middle East), Jennie Cadd (Teacher, language school, Spain) and Sharon Bromwich (Teacher, language school, Australia)

For product information and technology assistance, contact us at
Cengage Learning Customer & Sales Support, cengage.com/contact
For permission to use material from this text or product,
submit all requests online at **cengage.com/permissions**
Further permissions questions can be emailed to
permissionrequest@cengage.com

ISBN: 978-1-133-31573-5

National Geographic Learning
Cheriton House, North Way, Andover, Hampshire, SP10 5BE
United Kingdom

National Geographic Learning, a Cengage Learning Company, has a mission to bring the world to the classroom and the classroom to life. With our English language programs, students learn about their world by experiencing it. Through our partnerships with National Geographic and TED Talks, they develop the language and skills they need to be successful global citizens and leaders.

Locate your local office at **international.cengage.com/region**

Visit National Geographic Learning online at **NGL.Cengage.com/ELT**
Visit our corporate website at **www.cengage.com**

CREDITS
Although every effort has been made to contact copyright holders before publication, this has not always been possible. If notified, the publisher will undertake to rectify any errors or omissions at the earliest opportunity.

The publisher would like to thank the following sources for permission to reproduce their copyright protected images and videos:
Cover photo: Bruce Dale/National Geographic Image Collection
Inside photos: pp 6 ml (Jimmy Chin/National Geographic Image Collection), 6 bl (Michael Melford/National Geographic Image Collection), 6 br (Mike Goldwater/Alamy), 7 tl (imagebroker/Alamy), 7 tr (Lynn Johnson/National Geographic Image Collection), 7 ml (Micael Martel/National Geographic Image Collection), 8 tl (Bobby Model/National Geographic Image Collection), 8 tm (Viacheslav Smilyk/National Geographic My Shot/National Geographic Image Collection), 8 tr (Diane Cook & Len Jenshel/National Geographic Image Collection), 8 um (Fred Derwal/Getty Images), 8 ur (PCN Photography/Alamy), 8 ll (James L. Stanfield/National Geographic Image Collection), 8 lm (Raul Touzon/National Geographic Image Collection), 8 lr (Greg Dale/National Geographic Image Collection), 8 bl (John McEvoy/National Geographic Image Collection), 8 bm (Jhulan Mahanta), 8 br (Gianluca Colla/National Geographic Image Collection), 9 (Bobby Model/National Geographic Image Collection), 10 tm (Wildlife GmbH/Alamy), 10 tr (Chris Johns/National Geographic Image Collection), 12 (Bruno Schlumberger/Ottawa Citizen), 15 (Damir Spanic/Vetta/Getty Images), 16 (Justin Guariglia/National Geographic Image Collection), 18 (Norbert Rosing/National Geographic Image Collection), 20 (Brent Stirton/Getty Images/National Geographic Image Collection), 21 (Viacheslav Smilyk/National Geographic My Shot/National Geographic Image Collection), 22 (Pierre Perrin/Zoko/Sygma/Corbis), 24 (Bates Littlehales/National Geographic Image Collection), 25 (Barrett & MacKay/All Canada Photos/Corbis), 27 (Jimmy Chin/National Geographic Image Collection), 28 mr (Richard Levine/Alamy), 28 br (Claudia Wiens/Alamy), 30 (Jimmy Chin/National Geographic Image Collection), 32 (Pete McBride/National Geographic Image Collection), 33 (Diane Cook & Len Jenshel/National Geographic Image Collection), 34 ml (Borge Ousland/National Geographic Image Collection), 34 bl (Mike Clarke/AFP/Getty Images), 36 ml (Catherine Karnow/National Geographic Image Collection), 36 bl (China Photos/Stringer/Getty Images), 39 mr (Jeff J Mitchell/Getty Images), 39 b (Marka/Alamy), 40 (Melissa Farlow/National Geographic Image Collection), 41 (JLImages/

Printed in China by RR Donnelley
Print Number: 08   Print Year: 2018

Alamy), 42 (imagebroker/Alamy), 44 (View Pictures Ltd/Alamy), 45 (Shweeb), 46 (Bettmann/Corbis), 48 (Rebecca Hale/National Geographic Image Collection), 51 (Noel Vasquez/Getty Images), 52 (ZUMA Wire Service/Alamy), 54 (Chad Hamre), 56 (Stephen Barnes/Energy/Alamy), 57 (Fred Derwal/Getty Images), 58 (Alex Treadway/National Geographic Image Collection), 59 (Eland Publishing/Jane Sweeney/Robert Harding World Imagery/Corbis), 60 (Tony French/Alamy), 63 (Beth Wald/National Geographic Image Collection), 64 (Jeff Morgan 07/Alamy), 65 (GlowImages/Alamy), 66 (Mauricio Abreu/JAI/Corbis), 68 (Mark Cosslett/National Geographic Image Collection), 69 (PCN Photography/Alamy), 70 tl (Marcus Spedding/Alamy), 70 ml (Christopher Furlong/Getty Images), 70 bl (Emanuele Ciccomartino/Robert Harding World Imagery/Corbis), 72 (Fry Vanessa/Alamy), 74 tfl (Catchlight Visual Services/Alamy), 74 tl (Fancy/Alamy), 74 tml (O. Louis Mazzatenta/National Geographic Image Collection), 74 tmr (Bill Bachmann/Alamy), 74 tr (Photo Japan/Alamy), 74 tfr (LJSphotography/Alamy), 75 (Frans Lemmens/Getty Images), 76 (Werli Francois/Alamy), 78 (Micael Martel/National Geographic Image Collection), 80 (Lynn Johnson/National Geographic Image Collection), 81 (James L. Stanfield/National Geographic Image Collection), 82 (James L. Stanfield/National Geographic Image Collection), 83 (Chris Fragassi/Alamy), 84 (Cooperphoto/Corbis), 85 (James A. Sugar/National Geographic Image Collection), 86 (Osomedia/age fotostock), 87 m (Amy Toensing/National Geographic Image Collection), 87 b (Amy Toensing/National Geographic Image Collection), 88 (Angela Bousman/National Geographic Image Collection), 89 (Lawrence Smith/National Geographic Image Collection), 90 (O. Louis Mazzatenta/National Geographic Image Collection), 92 (B. Anthony Stewart/National Geographic Image Collection), 93 (Raul Touzon/National Geographic Image Collection), 94 (Reuters/Handout), 95 (Emmanuel Lattes/Alamy), 96 (Jon Feingersh/Blend Images/Corbis), 97 (Joshua Hee/Alamy), 99 (Lou Lesko), 100 (Doug Perrine/Alamy), 101 (AP/Press Association Images), 102 (Lynn Johnson/National Geographic Image Collection), 104 (EPA European Pressphoto Agency b.v./Alamy), 105 (Greg Dale/National Geographic Image Collection), 106 (AlamyCelebrity/Alamy), 108 (Nisian Hughes/Taxi Japan/Getty Images), 110 (Trinity Mirror/Mirrorpix/Alamy), 111 (Tino Soriano/National Geographic Image Collection), 112 (Mayday/Alamy), 113 (Mark Eveleigh/Alamy), 114 (Michael Melford/National Geographic Image Collection), 116 (NY Daily News via Getty Images), 117 (John McEvoy/National Geographic Image Collection), 118 (Howard Barlow/Alamy), 120 (Jason Edwards/National Geographic Image Collection), 121 ml (Anton Luhr/Imagebroker/FLPA), 121 bl (John Hinkle/National Geographic My Shot), 123 (PhotoStock-Israel/Alamy), 124 (Bettmann/Corbis), 125 (Alex Treadway/National Geographic Image Collection), 126 (Mike Goldwater/Alamy), 128 (James Forte/National Geographic Image Collection), 129 (Jhulan Mahanta), 130 bl (Joel Sartore/National Geographic Image Collection), 130 bm (Joel Sartore/National Geographic Image Collection), 130 br (Joel Sartore/National Geographic Image Collection), 131 (photomall/Xinhua Press/Corbis), 132 (Daisy-Daisy/Alamy), 134 tm (Simon Belcher/Alamy), 134 tr (AF archive/Alamy), 134 fr (JJM Stock Photography/Alamy), 135 (AFP/Getty Images), 136 (Joel Sartore/National Geographic Image Collection), 138 (AFP/Getty Images), 140 (Ice Tea Media/Alamy), 141 (Gianluca Colla/National Geographic Image Collection), 142 (William Albert Allard/National Geographic Image Collection), 143 (Hemis/Alamy), 144 (amana images inc./Alamy), 145 (Cameron Lawson/National Geographic Image Collection), 146 (Greg Dale/National Geographic Image Collection), 147 (Abelardo Morell), 148 (Randy Olson/National Geographic Image Collection), 149 (Unlisted Images/Corbis), 150 (Shutterstock), 152 (Frans Lanting/Corbis)

DVD photos: Alamy (unit 5: Pep Roig , unit 9: Pictorial Press Ltd, Ron Chapple Stock); Corbis (unit 9: Esther Anderson); Ethican Ocean (unit 4); Getty Images (unit 9: Frederic Nebinger/WireImage); National Geographic Image Collection (unit 9: Michael Melford, unit 5: Karen Smith, Lynn Johnson)

DVD videos: National Geographic Video Collection (units 2, 3, 5, 10 and 12); Explore.org (unit 1); Getty Images (units 6, 7, 8, 9 and 11)

Illustrations by Alex Hedworth (Eye Candy Illustration) p 156; Bob Lea p 45 (inset); David Russell pp 18, 32, 76, 82, 122; Laszlo Veres (Beehive Illustration) pp 153, 155

Text

We are grateful to the following for permission to reproduce copyright material:

National Geographic for extracts on pages 22, 27, 48, 75, 87, 99, 120, 123, 135, 142, 147 adapted from 'Sea Gypsies of Myanmar' by Jacques Ivanoff, April 2005 http://ngm.nationalgeographic.com; 'Yosemite Climbing: Daring. Defiant. Free' by Mark Jenkins, May 2011, http://ngm.nationalgeographic.com; 'Jimmy Chin' by Bill Hatcher, http://photography.nationalgeographic.com; 'The Big Idea', 15 September 2009, http://ngm.nationalgeographic.com; 'The Enigma of Beauty' by Cathy Newman, January 2000, http://ngm.nationalgeographic.com; 'Diamond shipwreck' by Roff Smith, October 2009, http://ngm.nationalgeographic.com; 'The hackers life – my weekend at Defcon' by Lou Lesko, 6 August 2010, http://nationalgeographicassignmentblog.com; 'Army Ants: Inside the Ranks' by Mark W. Moffett, August 2006, http://ngm.nationalgeographic.com; 'The Hadza' by Michael Finkel, December 2009, http://ngm.nationalgeographic.com; 'Us. And them' by Chris Carroll and Max Aguilera-Hellweg, August 2011, http://ngm.nationalgeographic.com; 'Under the big sky' by William Albert Allard, October 2010, http://ngm.nationalgeographic.com; 'Rooms with a view' by Tom O'Neill, May 2011, http://ngm.nationalgeographic.com; copyright © National Geographic. Reproduced with permission; The Random House Group Limited and Rogers, Coleridge & White Ltd for an extract on page 63 from In Patagonia by Bruce Chatwin, published by Jonathan Cape, copyright © Bruce Chatwin, 1977. Reproduced with permission from The Random House Group Limited and the author c/o Rogers, Coleridge & White Ltd., 20 Powis Mews, London W11 1JN; David Higham Associates Limited for an extract from The Third Man by Graham Greene, Vintage 2005. Reproduced by permission of David Higham Associates Limited; The Random House Group Limited and Bill Bryson for extracts on pages 153, 156 from Neither Here Nor There: Travels in Europe by Bill Bryson, published by Secker & Warburg. Reproduced with permission from The Random House Group Limited and the author Bill Bryson; Lou Lesko for material on page 99 from his blog 'The hackers life – my weekend at Defcon', 6 August 2010, http://nationalgeographicassignmentblog.com/2010/08/06/the-hackers-life-my-weekend-at-defcon/. Reproduced with kind permission; and ISSP International Social Survey Programme for material on page 118 from ISSP Research Group (2012): International Social Survey Programme 2004: Citizenship (ISSP 2004). GESIS Data Archive, Cologne. ZA3950 Data file Version 1.3.0, doi:10.4232/1.11372. Reproduced with permission.

In some instances we have been unable to trace the owners of copyright material and we would appreciate any information that would enable us to do so.